Outlaws
of the Atlantic

Also by Marcus Rediker

The Amistad Rebellion:
An Atlantic Odyssey of Slavery and Freedom

The Slave Ship: A Human History

Villains of All Nations:
Atlantic Pirates in the Golden Age

The Many-Headed Hydra:
Sailors, Slaves, Commoners, and the Hidden History
of the Revolutionary Atlantic
(with Peter Linebaugh)

Between the Devil and the Deep Blue Sea:
Merchant Seamen, Pirates, and the Anglo-American
Maritime World, 1700–1750

Outlaws
of the Atlantic

*Sailors, Pirates, and Motley Crews
in the Age of Sail*

✦

MARCUS REDIKER

Beacon Press, Boston

Beacon Press
Boston, Massachusetts
www.beacon.org

Beacon Press books
are published under the auspices of
the Unitarian Universalist Association of Congregations.

17 16 15 14   8 7 6 5 4 3 2 1

This book is printed on acid-free paper that meets the uncoated paper
ANSI/NISO specifications for permanence as revised in 1992.

Text design and composition by Wilsted & Taylor Publishing Services

Library of Congress Cataloging-in-Publication Data

Rediker, Marcus.
Outlaws of the Atlantic : sailors, pirates, and motley crews in the Age of Sail /
Marcus Rediker.
page cm
Includes bibliographical references and index.
ISBN 978-0-8070-3309-8 (hardcover : alk. paper)
ISBN 978-0-8070-3310-4 (ebook)
1. Merchant mariners—United States—History. 2. Merchant mariners—
Great Britain—History. 3. Sailors—Atlantic Ocean Region—History.
4. Pirates—Atlantic Ocean Region—History. 5. Slave ships—
History. 6. Merchant marine—United States—History. 7. Merchant
marine—Great Britain—History. 8. Seafaring life—Atlantic Ocean—
History. 9. Atlantic Ocean—Navigation—History. I. Title. II. Title:
Sailors, pirates, and motley crews in the Age of Sail.
HD8039.S42U6644 2014
387.509163'0903—dc23   2014000486

✦

To Staughton Lynd, Jesse Lemisch, and Gary Nash

and to the memory of
Alfred F. Young and Edward Thompson

my teachers in history from below

✦

Contents

Preface

I begin this book about Atlantic outlaws with a story about my late mother, Lucille Fadell Robertson, who was born in a little town called Dunmor in the utterly landlocked state of Kentucky. As far as I could tell as a child, Dunmor was made up entirely of poor people. My mother's father, my grandfather, was a coal miner. Her mother died when she was two years old, no uncommon thing among people of her class. Like many poor rural people, my mother had a dense network of kin, including double first cousins. One of them was a factory worker of artistic bent. Over the years he sent us an endless series of sentimental paintings. One day my mother pointed proudly to a recent arrival and proclaimed, "It's a painting of the bank in Russell-ville, Kentucky."

"It's what?" I was puzzled. "Why would anyone want to paint the bank of Russellville, Kentucky?" I asked innocently. "Ooooh," came the retort, "Mr. Hotshot Professional Historian doesn't know the historical significance of the bank of Russellville, Kentucky." I hung my head. "No, Mother, I don't. Tell me." She smiled as she answered with a history lesson: "The Russellville bank was the first bank the James boys robbed."

She referred, of course, to Jesse and Frank James, the notorious

James boys, who robbed banks all over the Upper South and Midwest and became two of the greatest outlaws in all of American history. My embarrassment faded as I sensed an opportunity. I asked, "What did all of the people around Dunmor think of the James boys?" She paused a second, pensively, and answered in her lilting Southern Kentucky accent: "They's good boys. Jus' got in a lil' trouble, is all."

A little trouble? They committed dozens of bank and train robberies and many murders. Local, state, and federal authorities engaged them in an all-out manhunt, which resulted in torrid shoot-outs and more deaths. Jesse himself was eventually killed in 1882 by a bounty hunter, who later committed suicide in trembling fear that Frank James would track him down and kill him. By the standards of small, quiet Dunmor (current population 317), this seemed to me to be something rather more than "a little trouble." I was amused, and not a little excited, to discover these outlaws kicking around in our family history. I ventured another question: The people around Dunmor didn't care that the James boys robbed the bank in Russellville? My mother did not need to pause and think this one over. She replied sharply: "People in Dunmor didn't have any money in that bank. They were too poor."[1]

Thanks to my cousin's painting, I learned that the people of Dunmor, including my mother, did not consider the James boys to be criminals or even bad people. They were good boys who just got into a little trouble. That's all. They were outlaws who commanded some degree of popular support and even pride in what they had done. Or to put the point a different way, the law does not a criminal make. The James boys were classic "social bandits" as described by historian Eric Hobsbawm.[2]

✦ ✦ ✦

I have been writing about outlaws my entire career as a historian, so it is a special pleasure to gather my thoughts and writings on the subject and to present this volume, *Outlaws of the Atlantic*. I first wrote about sailors, mutineers, and pirates, the quintessential outlaws, in *Between the Devil and the Deep Blue Sea* (1987) and followed up on the topic on a grander scale in *Villains of All Nations* (2004). *The Many-Headed Hydra* (2000), written with Peter Linebaugh, concerned the role of outlaws in the making of Atlantic capitalism: the sailors, slaves, indentured servants, and others who were, many of them, launched into oceanic orbits by convictions for crime and who once upon the great Atlantic became new kinds of outlaws such as pirates and smugglers, rebels and revolutionaries of various sorts. Then came *The Slave Ship* and *The Amistad Rebellion*, both of which emphasized uprisings from below decks by enslaved Africans whose determined actions deeply shaped the histories of slavery and abolition.[3]

This book explores the sea as a setting for human activity and historical change against the backdrop of the Atlantic and global rise of capitalism. The Prologue sets the scene of the Atlantic in the "age of sail." Chapter 1 treats the sailor as yarn spinner and global vector of communication, showing how Jack Tar, as he was called, because of his tarred breeches, influenced the lofty histories of philosophy, political thought, drama, poetry, and literature. The sea appears as a place of profound, although seldom understood, communication. The next six essays offer a roughly chronological survey of resistance by sea that covers sailors, indentured servants, and enslaved Africans as mutineers, runaways, and pirates—maritime rebels of all kinds—from the late seventeenth to the early nineteenth century, the age of wooden ships and iron men. Chapter 2 studies the life of seaman Edward Barlow and the sea as a place of work. Chapter 3 offers another "biography from below," following Henry Pitman, who after Monmouth's Rebellion in England in 1685 was sold as the commodity called "indentured servant." He used the sea as a place of escape. Chapter 4 takes as its subject the pirates of the 1710s through the 1720s and analyzes the sea as a place for the construction of an alternative social order. Chapter 5 discusses the Atlantic sailor, the enslaved African, and the interracial mob as revolutionary agents in the coming of the American Revolution—the sea as a site for the generation of radical ideas. Chapter 6 studies eighteenth-century West Africans as both the commodity called "slave" and as agents who profoundly resisted that conceptualization and practice. They made

Prologue

The European deep-sea sailing ship—and the seamen who made it go—transformed the world. On the *Santa Maria*, on which Columbus crossed the Atlantic, on the *Victoria*, on which Magellan circled the globe, and on the ever-growing fleets of merchant and naval vessels that linked the seven seas, their continents, and their peoples, the motley crews who worked aboard the most sophisticated machines of their day made history. By moving commodities such as silver, spices, and sugar over long distances they built the world market and the international economy. By carrying traders, settlers, and empire builders to Africa, Asia, and the Americas, they changed the global political order. Deep-sea sailors thus made possible a profound transformation: the rise of colonialism, capitalism, and our own vexed modernity.

Yet sailors have never gotten their due in the history books. Bertolt Brecht asked, "Who built the seven gates of Thebes?" He answered, "The books are filled with the names of kings," but then he wondered, "Was it kings who hauled the craggy blocks of stone?" Explorers like Columbus and Magellan, and admirals like Horatio Nelson, have long dominated our view of the history of the sea, but that at last has begun to change. Histories of "great men" and national glory by sea have, over the past generation, been challenged by chronicles

1

of common sailors and their many struggles. Maritime history has grown to include indentured servants and enslaved Africans, whose transatlantic lives were mediated by a gruesome yet formative Middle Passage across the sea. The rise of social history since the 1970s has of course transformed our view of many historical subjects, but few have witnessed as dramatic a reorientation as maritime history.[1]

Within the more recent rise of transnational and world history the sailor has begun to move from the margins—his customary position in national histories—to a more central position as one whose labors not only connected, but made possible, a new world. It is increasingly obvious that crucial historical processes unfolded at sea and that seafaring people were history makers of the first importance. This collection of my work over the past thirty years focuses on both transformations, bringing together the Atlantic and global histories of seafaring and slavery, the rise of capitalism and the many challenges to it from below—often literally, from below decks.[2]

In writing maritime history from below, I have encountered not only the elitism of the old maritime history but an obstacle more subtle and less understood: the uninspected assumption that only the landed spaces on the earth's surface are real. Perhaps it is not quite right to call this assumption a matter of thought; it is more an instinct, a mental reflex, and perhaps all the more powerful and pervasive for being unconsidered. One suspects that it is a matter of mentalité, a deep structure of Western thought that has an ancient history. Yet it must also be noted that this way of looking at the world—I call it *terracentric*—was surely strengthened by the rise of the modern nation-state in the late eighteenth century, after which power and sovereignty would be linked to specific ethnic, civic, and national definitions of "the people" and their land, their soil. At the same time the Romantic generation simultaneously "evacuated" the sea of real ships and sailors—"dirty bilge water and people at work," writes literary scholar Margaret Cohen—substituting a sea wild and sublime, populated with imaginary figures, fit for aesthetic contemplation.[3]

The other side of terracentrism is the unspoken proposition that the seas of the world are unreal spaces, voids between the real places, which are landed and national. This logic—the bias of landed society—is evident in the work of thinkers as radically different as novelist Joseph Conrad and philosopher Michel Foucault. Conrad, who spent considerable time at sea, called the oceangoing ship "a fragment detached from the earth." The statement suggests that the ship is disconnected not only from the land, but somehow from the planet, existing in a realm apart. Foucault called the ship "a floating piece of space, a place without a place, that exists by itself, that is closed in on itself, and at the same given over to the infinity of the sea." The ocean, in this formulation, is not only a place apart, it is "no place"—the original meaning of utopia. In both cases there is a refusal to consider the ocean as a real, material place of human work and habitation, a place where identities have been formed, where history has been made.[4]

The West Indian poet Derek Walcott exposed and attacked Western terracentric bias in his poem "The Sea Is History," which reflects on the experience of the peoples of the African diaspora:

Where are your monuments, your battles, your martyrs?
Where is your tribal memory? Sirs,
in that gray vault. The Sea. The sea
has locked them up. The sea is History.[5]

Walcott challenges us to overcome a deeply inculcated, often unconscious terracentrism, which would have us believe that the oceans are empty places, without history. It is our job to unlock the gray vault and make it give up its deep, hidden secrets.

✦ ✦ ✦

This book tries to unlock these secrets by examining the Atlantic Ocean as a historical space within which the formation of empires and rise of capitalism depended on a specific maritime technology: the Northern European deep-sea sailing ship. During the "age of sail," roughly 1500 to 1850, this was the world's most sophisticated and important machine. The novelist Barry Unsworth called it an "engine of wood and canvas and hemp." This global instrument of European power made possible extraordinary things—plunder,

"A Ship of War, of the Third Rate, with Rigging, &c., at Anchor"

conquest, and finally a political and economic dominance that has lasted to this day.[6]

This image of a third-rate man-of-war demonstrates the architecture of the deep-sea sailing ship: the three decks; the numerous compartments; the storage of supplies in casks and hogsheads; the small arms, gunpowder, and cannon; and the extraordinary complexity of rigging. The "gunned warship" combined mobility, speed, and great destructive power. When it showed up in parts of the world that had never before witnessed such a machine, it caused wonder. It was called a "floating island" and indeed it was: some men-of-war had crews of a thousand men, as many as a small town. The firing of the guns turned astonishment to terror. One observer noted that it was enough to make non-Europeans "worship Jesus Christ."[7]

The armed European deep-sea sailing ship was the means by which a vast oceanic commons was made safe for private property. It projected European imperial sovereignty onto the seas around the world. It made possible the circulation of commodities and the resulting global accumulation of capital from the late fifteenth century onward, unleashing a profound set of interrelated changes. Perhaps the greatest of these was the creation of the world market, whose existence can be summed up simply: no ships, no world market, because water links the continents of the globe. And of course the ship moved only because of the collective labor of the sailor, who slowly and fitfully knit together the world economy, integrating the various regions (Africa, the Americas, Asia) at different moments into an expanding whole.[8]

Historian Eric Hobsbawm wrote, "the creation of a large and expanding market for goods and a large and available free labor force go together, two aspects of the same process." So it was that the deep-sea sailing ships of Europe were operated by an ever-growing mass of free wage laborers. Global shipping required a maritime proletariat, whose members, aboard ship, were called "hands." Sailors usually had no means of production (no land, skill, or craft tools) and were thereby reduced to the labor of their hands to get a living. In organizing the sailing ships of the world, the ruling classes of Europe learned to think about labor as a commodity, buying and selling the labor power of seamen in an international market, for money. As the father of modern economics, Sir William Petty, wrote in 1690, "the Labour of Seamen, and Freight of Ships, is always of the nature of an Exported Commodity, the overplus whereof, above what is Imported, brings home mony, &c."[9]

The European rulers of the terraqueous globe also saw that there

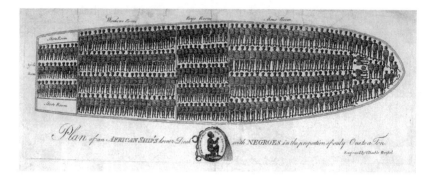

"Plan of an African Ship's Lower Deck" (Bristol Record Office)

were other important ways to think about labor power as a commodity. Tall ships were once again central to the process. The slave ship *Brooks* sailed out of Liverpool between 1782 and 1804 and carried more than five thousand Africans across the Atlantic to the burgeoning slave societies of the Americas. This familiar image (*Plan of an African Ship's Lower Deck*), drawn by abolitionists, was designed to make real to contemporary readers the human horrors of the slave trade—the tight packing of bodies in cramped spaces below decks. No small part of the horror lay in the systematic annihilation of individual identity built into the process. The slave ship appeared as a factory, mass-producing African bodies for the plantations of the Americas. Labor power was brutally rendered for what it was: a commodity. The sinister industrial quality of the image drove the point home.[10]

This image bears useful comparison to another, less familiar one, of a naval vessel from the same era, HMS *Bedford*. Here labor power is represented, not by actual bodies, but more discreetly as individually drawn hammocks in which sailors slept below decks, with not much more room than enslaved Africans had on slave ships. If the representation of the *Brooks* was meant to shock and horrify, the image of the *Bedford* had a more prosaic purpose: to show how hundreds of sailors (originally shown in blue) and marines (in red) might physically in-

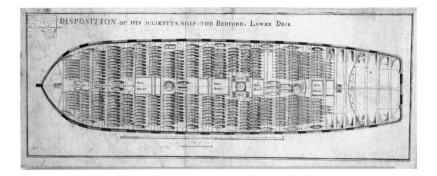

Lower deck of HMS Bedford *(National Maritime Museum)*

habit the lower deck of a warship. In both cases the depiction of labor power as a commodity was the order of the day. The fundamental class relationships of modern capitalism, involving both slave and free labor, were thus mediated by the ship.

As European rulers organized a transoceanic capitalist economy, they necessarily created new relationships among workers, in their own nations and around the world. To put the same point a different way, the organization of production for greater profits *required* a new cooperative division of labor worldwide. As the great West Indian scholar/activist C. L. R. James wrote: "The more capital succeeds in organizing itself, the more it is forced to organize the working class." The dynamics of transoceanic accumulation depended on collective working relationships among ever larger and more diverse bodies of workers, to produce and transport the commodities of the world. Agricultural laborers had to be linked to craft workers, who in turn had to be linked to dockworkers and sailors. As these linkages multiplied with the expansion of the capitalist economy, something new began to happen: these groups of people brought together by the productive power of capital began to conceive projects of their own. In short they transmuted their cooperation for capital into something else. For example, the sailors who cooperated to sail the ships of London discovered their common interests in 1768, when after a wage cut they went from vessel to vessel, striking (taking down) the sails and immobilizing the world's greatest shipping fleet. The "strike" was born and would circulate rapidly among working people around the world. Other forms of resistance, from running away, to mutiny, piracy, slave revolt, urban riots and insurrections, and even revolution—all examined in this book—emerged from new forms of cooperation. Atlantic commercial networks of accumulation became Atlantic networks of self-activity and subversion. The organization of capitalism and empire from above created resistance to capitalism and empire from below, as we shall see in the following chapters.[11]

ONE

✦

The Sailor's Yarn

In 1724 Captain Charles Johnson, a man who knew about things maritime, made an important observation about the global circulation of knowledge. He wrote that mathematicians and geographers, "Men of the greatest Learning," seldom travel farther than their private studies for their knowledge and were therefore not qualified to give accurate descriptions of peoples and places around the globe. Such knowledge was beyond their experience. These learned gentlemen were "obliged to take their Accounts from the Reports of illiterate Men"—that is to say, from sailors. "It is for this Reason," Johnson solemnly concluded, "that all our Maps and Atlasses are so monstrously faulty."[1]

Captain Johnson was wrong, in my view, to blame faulty mapping on sailors; he was also wrong in saying that sailors were illiterate. (About two-thirds of the common seamen of his day could sign their names.) But in another, more profound respect he knew exactly whereof he spoke. Learned gentlemen—not only mathematicians and geographers but philosophers and statesmen and writers, among others— had long gone down to the docks to talk to, and learn from, sailors, who occupied a strategic position in the worldwide division of labor. In the age of sail, the workers of the wooden world were themselves, in their minds and bodies, vectors of global communication. This is one of the great discoveries made by maritime historians over the last generation and one that is highly relevant to our understanding of the history of the planet. If we are to comprehend human community in the age of sail, we must understand another concept with the same root: communication.

If the port city was the world's most cosmopolitan place in the eighteenth century, the waterfront was the port city's most cosmopolitan place. The several blocks by the ocean, sea, or river were where the commodities of the world market were shipped and transshipped, loaded and unloaded by as motley (that is, multiethnic) a collection of humanity as could be found anywhere on the planet at the time. From the decks of the ships to the wharves and the streets, to the warehouses, the grog shops, the taverns and public houses, the waterfront was a "cultural contact zone" of the first and most formative order. These places constituted the material setting of a "proletarian public sphere," the importance of which has rarely been recognized. It had its own means of communication and sailors were central to them.[2]

That sphere, that zone, those places, and those cosmopolitan maritime workers are the subjects of this chapter. The sailor's "reports" in the broadest sense—his stories, more specifically his yarns—helped to create cosmopolitan community in the age of sail. It is a big subject and in some ways an impossible one, even for someone who has been studying sailors for more than thirty-five years as I have. I therefore begin this volume by offering an essay in the original meaning of the term: "a first tentative effort in learning or practice." The sailor's yarn is a key to understanding how the world worked when men on tall ships connected the oceans and continents.

The Storyteller

On my voyage to understand the genesis and meaning of this elusive thing, the sailor's yarn, I have found a good shipmate in the German-Jewish writer and critic Walter Benjamin. In a famous essay entitled "The Storyteller" Benjamin explains that historically there have been two essential types of tale tellers: those who traveled, who have "come from afar" with stories to tell, epitomized by the roving sailor; and those who "stayed at home" and worked the soil, those who know the local tales and traditions, epitomized by the peasant. Late in the essay he adds a third type, which combines aspects of the previous two and is based on yet another kind of labor: the artisan, whose workshop (the storytelling venue) contained within it both the sedentary master craftsman and the mobile journeyman. Benjamin thus creates a storytelling typology, and something of a circuit, among workers in the countryside, in the city, and on the ocean. These types combined "the lore of faraway places, such as the much-traveled man brings home, with the lore of the past, as it best reveals itself to natives of a place." Benjamin anchors communication in workplace experience.[3]

Within this brilliant formulation Benjamin makes several points about stories and their tellers that help to illuminate the sailor's yarn. First, stories are social, indeed communal. They are fundamentally about the exchange of experience within a group, about the relationship between a speaker and a group of listeners. (This defining characteristic Benjamin contrasts to the novel, in which both the narration and the reading are largely individual and private.) Storytellers may be nameless, but they are always "rooted in the people" and their oral, often poetic traditions.

Second, stories often have a class dimension. Many reflect "the traditional sympathy which storytellers have for rascals and crooks." This truth was captured by Friedrich Engels, who noted that many workers in Manchester, England, in the late 1830s and early 1840s "had never heard the name of the Queen, nor other names such as Nelson, Wellington, Bonaparte; but it was noteworthy that those who had never heard even of St. Paul, Moses, or Solomon were very well informed as to life, deeds, and character of Dick Turpin, the street-robber, and especially of Jack Sheppard, the thief and gaol-breaker." The people knew, and endlessly repeated over more than a century, the stories of heroic proletarian lawbreakers, fashioning their own "history from below" against the official histories of great men, secular or religious.[4]

Third and crucially, according to Benjamin, stories are linked to work cultures: storytelling thrives "in the milieu of work—the rural, the maritime, and the urban." Because storytelling is always the art of manufacturing and repeating stories, it requires the "weaving and spinning to go on while they are being listened to." What Benjamin calls "the rhythm of work" is therefore built into the story, "an artisan form of communication." The relationship of the storyteller to human life is that of a craftsman, who fashions "the raw material of experience, his own and that of others, in a solid, useful, and unique way." Note the word *useful:* no matter how fantastic a story may be in certain respects, it always contains something useful, whether a moral, a piece of advice, a maxim, or simply practical information, often about the treacherous arts of survival so necessary to workers trapped in precarious conditions of life. The sailor/yarn spinner weaves what Benjamin calls "the multicolored fabric of a worldly view."

Fourth and finally, storytelling derives much of its authority from the unusual experience of the teller. This was especially true for the sailor, who had to be "at home in distant places," which gave him a worldly wisdom and a knowledge of social and economic conditions around the world. He had come from afar, traveled the globe in a small, brittle wooden vessel, and returned to tell a story enhanced by the authority of movement. (The same principle lies behind the picaresque novel, as we shall see below.) And to take the matter one step further, the maritime storyteller takes additional authority from his proximity to death. Benjamin writes, "Death is the sanction of everything that the storyteller can tell. He has borrowed his authority from death. In other words, it is natural history to which his stories refer back." Or to put the same point another way, as Herman Melville did through the character of Ishmael the storyteller in the epilogue of the great maritime novel *Moby-Dick,* "And I only am escaped alone to tell thee."[5]

The Genesis of the Yarn

Building on Benjamin, let us explore briefly the genesis of the sailor's yarn, which grows from four related worlds of work: textile manufacture, fishing, rope making, and seafaring. The term "yarn" in its original definition refers to spun fiber—cotton, wool, silk, or flax—

prepared for use in weaving or knitting. On the eighteenth-century waterfront the meaning shifted to cord and rope: a fisherman's net is made of yarn, as are the strands (eighteen-, twenty-, and twenty-five-thread yarns) in rope making. We are getting closer to the ship.

"Yarn" soon takes on a meaning in nautical slang: to spin a yarn is to tell a story or tale, usually one of maritime adventure, about dramatic shipwrecks, bloody battles, tyrannical officers, or determined resistance. These were often long, complex, and colorful narratives, incorporating humorous, marvelous, and fantastic elements as well as communal lore, practical knowledge of class and work, and death-defying experience. The yarn is perpetually invented and reinvented in each and every maritime setting, whether at sea or ashore, as individual storytellers add their own talents and fashion their tales for an ever-changing audience.

The maritime story is called a yarn because of a specific labor process on the ship, where work was collective, lonely, and noncontinuous. Ships were isolated for long periods, and the crew lived in close, forced proximity. Many times there was nothing to do. This could happen in the doldrums, when there was little or no wind, and it could happen when the ship was clipping along at a good pace in high winds. Captains therefore created "make-work" of various kinds to fill the porous workday, holy-stoning the deck (scrubbing and whitening it with sandstone) being one of the most dreaded and infamous among sailors.[6]

Another was "picking oakum." The running rigging on a deep-sea vessel was made of hemp rope covered with tar. When the tar wore out (and the rope went slack when wet), the rigging had to be replaced. The old hemp rope would be cut into short strands, a couple of feet long, and sailors would gather on deck to pick it apart—picking oakum. This was dull and tedious work, hard on the fingers, even though the hands of sailors were rough to begin with from hauling rope. The sailors sat together and untwisted the hemp rope to individual fibers, then they rolled and twisted the hemp fibers back together. The oakum would then be used on the ship for caulking: mixed with tar, it would be forced by the ship's carpenter, using spe-

cial tools—a caulking iron and a mallet—between the seams, or in-
tervals, of the hull planking, to stanch leaks. (Picking oakum always
had low and slavish associations. It was often part of "hard labor" in
a workhouse or a prison. It was historically linked to coerced, unfree
work, as sailors well understood.)[7]

As sailors sat together picking apart the yarn of their ropes, someone would spin a yarn for a bored, unhappy, unwilling, ready-made
audience of common labor. The yarn, then, was in several ways a
spoken-word equivalent of the work song. One of its purposes was to
entertain, to help to overcome drudgery, to make the time pass, to
transport both speaker and listener to a different, better place. It was,
in short, born of alienation at work aboard the ship, which proved to
be a nursery of narrative talent.

Forms and Functions of the Yarn

Sailors' yarns took many forms and served many functions in the
wooden world of the deep-sea sailing vessel. They helped to recruit
and socialize new sailors into the shipboard order. They taught fundamental knowledge about the ship and its social relations, not least
about survival in a deadly line of work. As part of that survival they
imparted the history and practices of resistance, which shaped the
politics of the ship and the larger Atlantic society. They engaged and
inflamed the imagination; they fueled fantasy. In doing all of these
useful and important things and more, they entertained.

Saturday Night at Sea represents a yarn-spinning occasion on the
lower deck. Seventeen sailors gather on the gun deck of a man-of-
war, around a bearded storyteller who holds a tankard of grog in one
hand as he gestures expansively with the other. His fellow tars relax,
taking in the tale while seated on overturned buckets, boxes, cannon,
and the deck itself. The sailors have made the workplace their own.
Heads are cocked in rapt attention to the spoken word; faces beam
with smiles. This is a significant moment in the social life of the ship.

A major purpose of the yarn was to reproduce maritime culture,
that is, to emphasize the adventurous, sometimes heroic aspects of
the work so as to lure young men to go to sea and join the fraternity

SATURDAY NIGHT AT SEA.

Saturday Night at Sea (National Maritime Museum)

of deep-sea sailors. Many went precisely because they had heard a good yarn, as explained by Samuel Robinson, who recalled that as a boy growing up in Garlieston, Scotland, "my fancy for a sea life was excited by the long yarns which James Cooper [an older schoolmate] used to spin to us after being a voyage to the West Indies." Thereafter "an irresistible desire for a seafaring life so completely carried me away, that it became a matter of perfect indifference to me where the ship went, if not to the bottom, provided I was aboard her—or in what trade engaged, if not a pirate." Robinson wanted not only to hear stories but to acquire the exotic experience that would allow him to tell them.[8]

An early-eighteenth-century London sailor named Walter Kennedy took the same route to a different end. Kennedy was known during his time in the Royal Navy to have a special love for pirate stories. He endlessly requested them of his shipmates, listened carefully to them, memorized them, and retold them himself, avidly and repeatedly. Then he acted on them. He found out in 1718 that Woodes

Rogers had been commissioned by the British government to sail to the Bahama Islands, a notorious pirate haunt, in order to reestablish proper British government and hang a pack of sea robbers there if need be. Kennedy signed on to the expedition, not to help Rogers establish good order in Providence but to desert him as soon as he got there and to join the pirates! This he did, sailing under the black flag for more than two years and indeed dying under it as the Jolly Roger was raised above the gallows on which he was hanged, back in London, on July 21, 1721.[9]

Yarns also served to socialize new workers into the social order of the ship by teaching basic knowledge about the ship in its technical or social dimensions. Sailors had to learn to face danger with courage and to live with want, to endure and survive in harsh, dangerous, often deadly conditions. Yarns might convey what a sailor should do in storms, in battle, or after shipwrecks. Stories would also help to promote common values, especially the necessity of cooperation and solidarity in such an insecure work environment, in which no one had much control over life and death, whether by disease, accident, weather, or warfare.[10]

Stories imparted useful information, as demonstrated again and again by William Dampier, the famous buccaneer turned explorer, naturalist, and popular writer, who led the historic process by which sailors' yarns appeared on the printed page. His book *A New Voyage Around the World*, first published in 1697 and reprinted many times thereafter, was one of the best-selling books of the era and indicative of how voyage literature was the single most popular genre of writing in the late seventeenth and early eighteenth centuries. In that book Dampier recounted an incident that took place on Mindanao in the Philippines, where a sailor found a special leaf, which he boiled and pounded to make "an excellent Salve," which many of the sailors used to treat skin ulcers with "great benefit." The man who found and prepared the leaves "had his first knowledge of them in the Isthmus of Darien, from one of the Indians there." Here was a kind of practical knowledge, embedded in a story, that circulated around the world, from Central America to East Asia, on board a ship, carried in the

of sail. Seamen had been tattooing each other long before specialized artists emerged in sailortown during the late nineteenth century to adorn the seafaring body. They pricked the skin repeatedly with needle or knifepoint, then rubbed into the small cuts a pigment, either ink or, more commonly, a compound made with gunpowder. The original purpose of the tattoo was deeper than decoration: many a sailor wanted a telltale mark on the body so that in the event of catastrophic death he could be identified and properly buried. The most common tattoo on the late-eighteenth- and early-nineteenth-century American sailor was his initials. But tattooing rapidly acquired other meanings. One was occupational: an anchor on the hand or forearm signaled initiation into the community of deep-sea sailors. Religious tars might visit Palestine and return home with a Jerusalem Cross, always a prompt to tell the story of the maritime pilgrimage. After Captain James Cook's historic voyages to the South Seas in the 1760s and 1770s, a newer Polynesian style of tattooing came to be popular among sailors, especially those who had made the grueling multiyear voyages to the Pacific and could therefore boast the marks as signs of cosmopolitanism. Tattooed hearts could prompt tales of loved ones back at home, while a liberty cap, pole, or tree could elicit a political rant about "liberty," a favorite theme among sailors in the age of revolution.[14]

Another aspect of the yarn was illuminated in a sweeping comment by the French philosopher Michel Foucault in a lecture of 1973. For the entirety of Western civilization, from the sixteenth century until the present, the ship—"a floating piece of space . . . closed in on itself"—was not only the "great instrument of economic development," it was at the same time "the greatest reserve of the imagination." Without ships, and presumably without yarns, said Foucault, "dreams dry up, espionage takes the place of adventure, and the police take the place of pirates." Within the enclosed, repressive space of the ship, an engine of capitalism, emerged dreams of freedom, stories of new ways of being, transcendent and sometimes utopian. Sailors spun yarns of gleaming gold (here we get close to the pirate tale), of abundant food, warm shelter, and human care, not unlike peasant tales of the same period, about the "Land of Cockaigne." Long voyages fostered fantasy—male fantasy in particular. Sailors' yarns therefore highlighted fighting, drinking, sex, virility, and masculinity. The dialectical shipboard imagination expressed itself as sailors gathered in an intimate space, sat in a circle on the main deck, among a group of messmates at mealtime, at night in the dark fo'c'sle, or even off the ship, on the dock or in the tavern, to spin a yarn. The sailor was a performer, especially when telling a "tall tale"—full of lies, humor, exaggeration, embellishment, and literally outlandish claims, as well as deep and necessary truths.[15]

The very dangers of life at sea encouraged among sailors a set of beliefs that are often derided as "superstition." Spirits loomed especially large, not least because of the high mortality that stalked life at sea. Ramblin' Jack Cremer noted that sailors all had a "fear of Aperishons [apparitions]." In a dangerous environment in which someone could be killed in an instant (falling from aloft, falling overboard, or being hit by falling gear), dead comrades frequently haunted the ship. Cremer relayed the story of "a man who was drownded two Voages past, and has been seen by Severall new-Shipt hands, but never but once to any body." On another occasion Cremer himself saw the apparition of a stranger sitting on his own sea chest.[16]

A common yarn among sailors in the late eighteenth century (when it entered written discourse) was the "Flying Dutchman." According to George Barrington in *A Voyage to Botany Bay* (1795), sailors told the tale of a Dutch man-of-war that went down in a storm off the Cape of Good Hope: "every soul on board perished." Its consort ship survived, refitted, and went back to sea, where in the very same latitude as before another fierce storm hit. Members of the night watch said they saw a vessel coming directly at them through the storm with a full press of sail "as though she would run them down." One sailor in particular swore it was their sunken consort ship, or her apparition. Later versions of the story claimed the ghost ship belonged to a mid-eighteenth-century Dutch captain who had defied the elements, was sunk and destroyed by his own arrogance, and now wandered the sea ever after as a punishment to himself and a warning to sailors. The glowing phantom ship represented the specter of death that haunted every deep-sea sailor, and yarns about it were many. In a dangerous, enchanted world sea stories had no small element of what we now call "magical realism."[17]

Many a yarn concerned sea monsters, symbols of the dangers of the ocean deep from antiquity through the age of sail. Cartographers had long drawn on seamen's stories to adorn their maps with strange sea creatures. Medieval Swedish mapmaker Olaus Magnus drew a rich and colorful map of Scandinavia in 1539, adorning the oceanic spaces with fantastical sea monsters, including the fearsome Kraken, which first appeared in the written historical record in the thirteenth century, in Iceland, and was subsequently spotted by Scottish seamen, Norwegian fishermen, and American whalemen in the North Atlantic, near Greenland, or in the North Sea, off the coasts of Norway, although French sailors encountered it off the coast of Angola. Seafarers' stories of Kraken inspired the literary imagination, moving John Milton to mention the monster "haply slumb'ring on the Norway foam" in *Paradise Lost* in 1667. Erik Pontoppidan, the Danish Bishop of Bergen, drew on the sailors' yarns as he wrote about Kraken in 1752, emphasizing that when the huge creature was submerged, a "dangerous swell of the sea" created a maelstrom that could pull a man-of-war straight to the bottom. Other tales had it that the creature was a mile and half long and that its back, when above the water line, could be mistaken for an island. Scientists listened to the sailors too: French naturalist Pierre Dénys de Montfort included Kraken in his *Histoire Naturelle Générale et Particulière des Mollusques* (1801). When the great Swedish taxonomist Carl Linnaeus included the creature in his *Systema Naturae* (1735), he gave it the name *Microcosmus marinus*, which was perfect in its way: among seamen, Kraken embodied in beastly form the dangers of the open, unmapped, deadly, and utterly terrifying oceans of the planet.[18]

It is of first importance that yarn spinning existed independently of the official hierarchy of power aboard the ship. In other words, the yarn spinner took his authority not from his privilege on land, nor from his rank or pay grade aboard the ship. He derived his authority from his own experience and that of his fellow tars—as long

Kraken, detail from map by Olaus Magnus. (Used with permission)

as he could speak to their commonalities in rich, compelling, and instructive ways. The haggard, weather-beaten, wise old salt might serve as a sort of griot on the ship, as a repository of occupational lore and living memory—about the ship, the officers, and the sailors' craft, all of which could be expressed in yarns long and short. What happened on any given vessel was always measured against the memory of "the oldest and most experienced man on the ship." The combination of experience, knowledge, resistance, and fantasy expressed in the yarn was critical to the self-understanding of a roving maritime proletariat.[19]

In order to last as a cultural form, the yarn had to be, first and foremost, consistent with the social realities of a sailor's life, which meant that it had to be mobile; it had to move with the men who moved restlessly from one job to another, one continent to another, one ocean to another. Part of its power lay in its flexible, democratic nature: anyone could tell a story, and everyone who was part of the group decided the meaning of the story. Another part of its power lay in its immateriality: the yarn was spoken and heard and repeated, but the storyteller's words were carried away by the wind over time, as they were on the very decks of ship. The yarn is therefore a fugitive form, and indeed this is the key to its success and significance as a means of communication. At the very same time it is what makes the yarn so difficult to study. In the distant past we never find it in its pure form, never as speech; we find it only after someone has taken the initiative to write some part of it down.

Yarns can therefore be found in unexpected places—for example, in depositions given by sailors in the High Court of Admiralty when summoned to testify about why a mutiny or murder had taken place on their ship. As the sailor spoke to the judge, in all likelihood repeating a story he had told many times before, a court scribe took down, and inevitably translated, his words. For example, one can almost hear the previous oral version of courtroom testimony when Phillip Brand explained in 1729 that a cruel mate named George Steel threatened his messmate, common seaman George Williams, with a beating. Williams, according to Brand, answered politely but firmly, drawing the line against mistreatment: "I never was beat by any Master yet and it will be very hard to be beat now." A yarn might thus be trapped in amber, so to speak: recolored by surrounding new circumstances but perhaps largely unchanged from its original expression.[20]

Yarns in Motion, or the Poetry of Salt Water

Where did the yarns go? They went all over the world, carried by sailors to sea and port city, up and down rivers, and into landed societies, and they went into print, into a most voluminous and popular form of eighteenth-century writing, the voyage narrative. Roughly two thousand accounts were published in England in that century to tell a ravenous reading public "the story of the voyage," to use the title of Phillip Edwards's important book on the subject. The maritime oral and printed traditions coexisted well into the nineteenth century.[21]

The seepage of yarns into printed form is exemplified, as suggested above, by the very book that made the voyage narrative one of the most popular genres of the eighteenth century: Dampier's *A New Voyage Round the World*. Dampier was conscious that the work, language, and culture of the sea shaped how he would tell the stories that made up the book: "As to my Stile, it cannot be expected, that a Seaman should affect Politeness." He explained that he had "divested my self of Sea Phrases, to gratify the Land Reader: for which the Seamen will hardly forgive me." And yet he admitted that he left many sea terms in the book, persuaded that if what he had to say was "intelligible, it matters not greatly in what words it is express'd." Many passages have the sound of well-rehearsed stories that made their way from yarn to print.[22]

Let me now give a few more examples of what I would call the migration of yarns, beginning with the lofty domain of philosophy. It will be recalled that one of the founding texts of Western philosophy, *Utopia* (1516) by Sir Thomas More, begins when a mariner named Raphael Hythloday returns from the sea to narrate the story of the new society without private property he has encountered in his travels, about which he spins a powerful yarn. Later in the same century, within the same humanist tradition, Michel de Montaigne wrote a famous essay entitled "Of Canibals," in which he concludes that the less civilized people in the meeting of Old World and New were not the Native Americans but rather the Europeans. He saw "Indians" not as savages, as did his contemporary fellow elites, but rather as noble and dignified people. Perhaps even more interesting is where Montaigne got his information about them—from a servant, a man who had worked for years as a sailor and voyaged to Brazil, where he met the indigenous people, later to spin yarns about them that would influence the famous humanist and his classic essay. What other great men learned from "the reports of illiterate men" populates a valuable book by William Brandon, *New Worlds for Old: Reports From the New World and Their Effect on the Development of Social Thought in Europe 1500–1800* (1986), about the profound effect the discovery of "primitive communism" had on Europe.[23]

Yarns have likewise had an enormous impact on the development of drama and literature worldwide. Shakespeare used the printed and oral tales of the deep-sea voyagers in writing *The Tempest* (1611). Kipling suggested that he got the main idea for the play from "a drunken sailor." Seafarers and their tales would shape many kinds of writing throughout the seventeenth century, poetic and literary, utopian and scientific, as English ships plied the oceans of the world. John Milton drew on voyage literature in imagining the rebellious Satan's empire in *Paradise Lost*. According to literary critic Margaret Cohen, Satan himself appeared as a "complete mariner." A new stage of influence emerged in the late seventeenth and early eighteenth centuries, when the mobile workers of the world inspired and fueled what we now call "the rise of the novel."[24]

Daniel Defoe, the writer usually credited with inventing the modern novel, drew heavily on sea narratives and the accounts of sailors as he produced a truly prodigious number of fictional and nonfictional works about sailors, pirates, shipwrecks, indeed about almost all things maritime. He paid special attention to Richard Hakluyt's *The Principal Navigations, Voyages, Traffiques and Discoveries of the English* (1589–1600) and Dampier's *New Voyage*. He was known to have forty-nine published accounts of voyages in his personal library and to seek out sailors to interview them for their valuable personal experience.[25]

Inspired by the adventures of the Scottish sailor Alexander Selkirk, marooned on a buccaneering voyage on the Juan Fernández Islands off Chile in 1704, then picked up by Woodes Rogers and his fellow privateers in 1709, Defoe in 1719 published the founding text of modern maritime fiction: *The Life and Strange Surprizing Adventures of Robinson Crusoe, of York, Mariner, Who lived Eight and Twenty Years, all alone in an un-inhabited Island on the Coast of America, near the Mouth of the Great River of Oroonoque; Having been cast on Shore by Shipwreck, wherein all the Men perished but himself, With An Account how he was at last as strangely deliver'd by Pirates*. Later known as *Robinson Crusoe*, the novel was an immediate and stunning success, rapidly appearing in dozens of editions (some of them pirated) in England and France and soon translated into twenty languages. The fictionalized account of the maritime marronage in turn inspired many other sea novels during the years following its publication. Defoe's picaresque stories drew their subjects and their energy from sailors and other workers in motion around the Atlantic and beyond.[26]

Defoe's contemporary and rival Jonathan Swift detested the notion of the adventurous sea hero, but he too was influenced by sailors and their writings, especially in his greatest work, *Travels into Several Remote Nations of the World, In Four Parts, By Lemuel Gulliver, First a Surgeon, and then a Captain of Several Ships*, published in London in 1726, and better known as *Gulliver's Travels*. Swift based the Yahoos on descriptions of Australian aborigines and may have based Lemuel Gulliver on Dampier himself. Even though Swift mercilessly satirized the popular sea voyage genre, he did so from within the form, and there can be no question that the popularity of his novel owed much to the public hunger for writing about sailors, the sea, and strange places abroad. Swift did not share Defoe's enthusiasm for merchants and empire, but he nonetheless affirmed the centrality of the sailor's oceanic labors—and stories—to his own epoch.[27]

The Scottish man of letters Tobias Smollett became a preeminent sea novelist courtesy of an early-life work experience as a lowly surgeon's second mate during the grandly named War of Jenkins' Ear in the Caribbean (1739–1748). Smollett served aboard HMS *Chichester*, a third-rate man-of-war with eighty cannon and a crew of six hundred. Here he saw cooperative labor, ferocious discipline, torture and terror, grisly sickness, and premature death, all on a massive scale. This set of experiences in turn formed the basis of his famous picaresque novel, *The Adventures of Roderick Random*, published in 1748, in which he graphically described the horror of the ship's sickroom:

> Here I saw about fifty miserable distempered wretches, suspended in rows, so huddled one upon another, that not more than fourteen inches space was allotted for each with his bed and bedding; and deprived of the light of the day, as well as of fresh air; breathing nothing but a noisome atmosphere of the morbid steams exhaling from their own excrements and diseased bodies, devoured with vermin hatched in the filth that surrounded them, and destitute of every convenience necessary for people in that helpless condition.

His description of the naval man-of-war applied equally well to a slave ship, although the sickroom in the latter was sometimes the entire lower deck. Smollett carried forward the maritime genre established by Defoe, in and through which the experience of seafaring animated the most popular novels of the era.[28]

In 1806 the sailors aboard the *Stirling* began the education of a seventeen-year-old American named James Fenimore Cooper. The vessel's crew was small but motley: its dozen hands included a Dane, a German, an Irishman, a Spaniard, and a Portuguese. On a transatlantic voyage to England, then to the Mediterranean, the novice seaman was taught "how to knot and splice, and other niceties of the calling." He heard yarns, saw sights, and learned about resistance as British press gangs came after his shipmates, including his friend "Philadelphia Bill," for service in the Napoleonic Wars. (Bill would serve as something of a model for Long Tom Coffin in Cooper's first sea novel, *The Pilot: A Tale of the Sea* [1823].) According to Cooper biographer Wayne Franklin, the voyage aboard the *Stirling* secured "the foundation for his future," and not merely his own: Cooper would pioneer the American sea novel and become an inspiration for a generation of European writers, including Frederick Marryat, Eugène Sue, and Victor Hugo. Best remembered for *The Last of the Mohicans* and other stories of the landed frontier, Cooper actually began his writing life with works about a different frontier, eastern and maritime, on which he wrote a third of his novels.[29]

Another example of the migration of yarns concerns the stories about the slave trade by dissident sailors told to an earnest young abolitionist gentleman named Thomas Clarkson, who had disguised himself as a sailor and walked the wharves of Liverpool to gather them. These sailors had sailed in slave ships, experienced the horror, and now wished to tell their stories. Clarkson's first informant was a black sailor named John Dean, who dramatically stripped off his shirt to show the gentleman the scars caused by a flogging he received while working on a slaver. This encounter, and others like it, had a profound effect on the abolitionist and on the movement that sought to educate the broader public about the terrors of the trade. Such yarns would circulate into Parliamentary reports, social movement propaganda, poetry (William Cowper and Robert Southey), literature (Samuel Taylor Coleridge), sermons (Joseph Priestley), and art (J. M. W. Turner). The "reports of illiterate men" were thus central to the social and intellectual origins of utopian literature, humanist philosophy, Renaissance drama, the rise of the novel, and the abolitionist movement, all because "Men of the greatest learning" went down to the docks to talk to sailors.[30]

The sailor's yarn was also crucial to community making from below as demonstrated on a grand scale in the Atlantic's age of revolution, especially the most revolutionary decade, the 1790s, as illustrated in two extraordinary works of scholarship, Julius Scott's "The Common Wind: Currents [note that: "currents"] of Afro-American Communication in the Era of the Haitian Revolution" and Niklas Frykman's "The Wooden World Turned Upside Down: Naval Mutiny in the Age of Revolution." These exemplary maritime histories reveal, each in its own way, how crucial events cannot be comprehended without attention to sailors' yarns as international means of communication.

Drawing on a classic account of communication from below—George Lefebvre's *The Great Fear*, about the role of rumor among self-organized rebellious peasants in late July and early August of 1789, in the French Revolution—Scott explains precisely how the related revolution in Saint-Domingue, led by Toussaint Louverture, became an Atlantic phenomenon, that is to say, precisely *how* this great slave revolt of half a million workers became the nightmare of every master class in every slave society in the Western Hemisphere. The agents of communication were sailors, black, white, and brown, part of what Scott calls the "masterless Caribbean" that spread from ship and seaport in North America, the West Indies, and northern South America. Sailors told the tale of revolution in the fo'c'sles and on the docks, key locations in the proletarian public sphere, to waterfront workers enslaved and free, to boatmen and pilots and other mobile workers, to "higglers," usually market women, and other small traders, who then carried the tales, news, and information inland, to the plantations, expanding geometrically the reach and political meaning of the uprising and expanding the worldwide antislavery movement from below.[31]

Niklas Frykman does something similar for the tens of thousands of sailors who engaged in mutiny in the 1790s—motley crews whose common history of resistance was previously hidden in narrowly national British, French, Dutch, and other histories. He shows that an upsurge from below—on the scale of the French and Haitian revolutions—took place at sea. He identifies structural causes of mutiny in all of the European navies of the day, but he also shows how the flow of experience, through common participants and common ideas, linked these most radical events. He details the history of the *Hermione*, on which a motley crew of 160 rose up in September 1797, somewhere between Saint-Domingue and Puerto Rico, killed ten officers, seized the ship, carried it to Caracas, surrendered it to Britain's enemy, Spain, then scattered with the Atlantic winds. Eventually thirty-five men would be tracked down, twenty-four of them executed, several because they could not resist telling yarns about the mutiny! It is inconceivable that naval mutiny could have exploded with such force and fury and on such a vast scale without the tales that were whispered on the lower decks of naval vessels far and wide, from Britain to France, to the West Indies, to South Africa.[32]

One of the big questions of the age of sail was: who can tell the story of the voyage? Sailors could, and did, but this posed a problem for the ruling classes of the day, who most decidedly did not want to depend on "the reports of illiterate men." This contradiction would lead to a series of important historical developments in the seventeenth and eighteenth centuries as reaction from above against this dependency: the rise of commercial newspapers; the rise of travel literature; the rise of the novel; the rise of maritime bureaucracies; the rise of vice-admiralty courts; the rise of state-sponsored scientific maritime expeditions; and the rise of modern cartography. These developments converged on a common point: seamen occupied a strategic position in the global division of labor, which in turn gave them mobile access to, and control of, certain kinds of knowledge, information, and ideas. Alternative sources and forms of knowledge, more securely generated by and controlled from above, would have to be developed in response.

Yarns were central to all of it. As the late, great labor historian David Montgomery used to say of the world of nineteenth- and twentieth-century industry: "the boss's brain was under the workman's cap." The same was true in the early modern era, in that workplace called the deep-sea sailing ship. The sailor's yarn, spun on merchant, naval, fishing, slave, privateering, and pirate ships, not only conveyed crucial information about a wide set of human issues, it shaped the very dynamics of world history in the age of sail.

TWO

✦

Edward Barlow,
"Poor Seaman"

Edward Barlow plied the oceans of the world for almost half a century. The only thing more remarkable than his ability to survive so long in a dangerous, often deadly occupation was the record he left of that survival. His journal, located in the National Maritime Museum in Greenwich, England, is an extraordinary work of 225,000 words and more than 150 drawings and color pictures. Self-educated in literacy and art ("I could not write before I came to sea"), Barlow wrote so that others might "understand what dangers and troubles poor seamen pass through." Even though he made no apparent efforts to publish his work in his lifetime, perhaps he had family or friends in mind; perhaps he wrote for posterity, which is to say, for us.[1]

Barlow sailed the seas during momentous times. His career (1659–1703) parallels almost perfectly England's "Commercial Revolution," the exponential and increasingly vital growth of trade between 1660 and the 1690s. During these years, unprecedented numbers of seamen were mobilized in the shipping industry in order to move the commodities of the world, and in navies in order to protect those profitable movements. Barlow was thus a member of one of the largest and most important occupational groups that comprised the first generation of international free wage laborers. He worked on the ship, where free and fully waged workers were employed, segregated, and taught the semiskilled work of using machinery within a complex division of labor, and where workers were disciplined to the task of orderly collective production. The concentration of labor on Barlow's ships was huge by the standards of the day, reaching as many as one thousand sailors on the largest man-of-war.[2]

Barlow's astonishing journal illuminates what it meant to be a sailor in the late seventeenth century. Here we can hear a man from the lower order speaking in his own voice; his words are not mediated or distorted by authorities—the merchants, naval officers, judges, and royal officials on whom we often depend for information about working people. We do not, for once, have to ask repression to recount the history of what it was repressing. Instead we can learn of the seaman's life as set down in the crooked hand of an autodidact, a man who valued his observations so much that for many years he carefully protected them from the elements in a wax-stopped joint of bamboo. His triumph over the voracious seas allows us to undertake an exercise in biography and identity formation from below.[3]

Early Life

Born in Prestwich, England (near Manchester), in 1642, Barlow early on had all the makings of a sailor. He had humble origins amid a large family of "poor people" who struggled as farmers. The family with six children had an annual income of eight or nine pounds (a little more than $1,200 in 2014 US dollars). "I never had any great mind to country work," admitted Barlow, "as ploughing and sowing, and making hay and reaping, nor also of winter work, as hedging and ditching and thrashing and dunging amongst cattle and suchlike drudgery." He had also worked in the coal pits. Without money or connections, Barlow was unable to get an apprenticeship to a decent trade: "the tradesmen would not take us without money or unless we would serve eight or nine years," an unreasonably long term. In any case, Edward never had a "mind to any trade [from the time he was] a child." Instead he had eyes that longed to see the world, and he had feet given to wandering. After hearing neighbors spin yarns about

Edward Barlow leaving his mother's house (National Maritime Museum)

their travels, he wanted to see places remote and "strange things in other countries."[4]

Although he did not know what a ship was the first time he saw one, he had in fact laid eyes upon his fate. Over the initial objections of family members, he signed an apprenticeship to a naval captain at the age of thirteen. He spent the remainder of his life working his way around the world, sailing merchant and naval vessels to Europe, the East Indies, and the New World. He spent many years living on the unforgiving element called the ocean, and left an unparalleled record of his working life.[5]

At Sea

Barlow's integration into the labor system of the wooden world upon the high seas was jarring. One of his earliest and most emotional comments about his new work life concerned his painful separation from loved ones. As he prepared to leave London, he ruefully noted, "Here hath the husband parted with the wife, the children from the loving parent, and one friend from another, which have never enjoyed the sight of one another again, and some by war and some in peace, and some by one sudden means and some by another." Work at sea meant painful distance from family and friends, in the short term and, for many, the long: all relationships involving sailors were haunted by the Grim Reaper—captains drew the death's head, a symbol of mortality, into their logs to record a sailor's end, far from home.[6]

Separated from kith and kin, Barlow had to adjust to the new spatial order of the ship. From the beginning of his long life at sea he compared the seaman's lot to that of the man who "endures a hard imprisonment." His sleeping place, for example, resembled nothing so much as a "Gentleman's dog kennel." And for good reason: after he was impressed into the navy in 1668, Barlow did not set foot on land for seven months. When he finally did feel the ground beneath his feet, it was in "a place where they knew I would not run away, it being a heathen country" (in North Africa). The Admiralty's fear of desertion, especially in wartime, made this a common fate among sailors. Long incarceration on a ship was a favorite complaint among naval sailors.[7]

Barlow soon began to see that the seaman's life was a running duel with fear. He discovered the hard way that the work of a maritime laborer was extremely dangerous. Before he had mastered "sea affairs," he suffered a serious accident: he fractured his skull while working at the capstan (a winch for heavy lifting). He also faced raging storms, including a hurricane, a fire in a ship with four hundred barrels of gunpowder, leaky vessels, cruel and abusive masters, capture by the Dutch navy and a Spanish privateer, and the ever-present threat injury, disease, and epidemic. Barlow counseled "young men to take any trade rather than go to sea, for though he work hard all day, he may lie safe at night." Lucky seamen might live as well "as many ordinary tradesmen, yet they must go through many more dangers." Peril and premature death, Barlow found, were the seaman's shadows while working on the vast and unpredictable ocean.[8]

Another important part of Barlow's initiation into the world of deep-sea sailing was learning to live on his wage, which he now required for subsistence itself. His family, although humble, always managed to produce a little food for themselves, but for Barlow and others aboard the ship, this fundamental fact of life had changed. He now depended upon that customary part of the wage that was food, always a topic of serious interest to Barlow, who dearly loved to eat. When he first went to sea, Barlow thought the food was better than what he had eaten among his poor rural family at home. But later he repented of such thoughts, recalling how he left his apprenticeship to a bleacher because of bad fare: "Though it was sometimes coarse, yet it might serve any ordinary man to live by, and many times since I could have wished for the worst bit of it." Compared to the sailor's traditional rotten salt beef and biscuit so full of vermin that it could self-locomote, his previous diet at times looked kingly. At sea he dreamed of the "pleasures those had in England who had their bellies full of good victuals and drink, though they never worked so hard for it."[9]

Barlow also complained about the monetary portion of his wage, especially after he had worked off his apprenticeship. He never considered his wages equal to his trouble and suffering, and worse, he found that he often had to fight for what was lawfully his. Many merchants, it turned out, bilked seamen of their wages in order to cover the cost of damaged cargo and oceanic transport. Barlow also discovered, much to his dismay, that the navy illegally held wages in arrears as a means of labor control, to prevent desertion. As we shall see, Barlow had serious misgivings about the ways in which money increasingly governed human relationships. His own dependence upon the wage taught many lessons on this score.[10]

All of these problems—isolation, incarceration, danger, and wage struggles—led Barlow to conclude: "There are no men under the sun that fare harder and get their living more hard and that are so abused on all sides as we poor seamen." He was even moved to write an imaginary dialogue with young men who were thinking of becoming sailors. He warned them away from the sea, saying that he found himself "wishing many times I had never meddled with it." He approvingly cited "the old saying": "whosoever putteth his child to get his living at sea had better a great deal bind him prentice to a hangman." He went

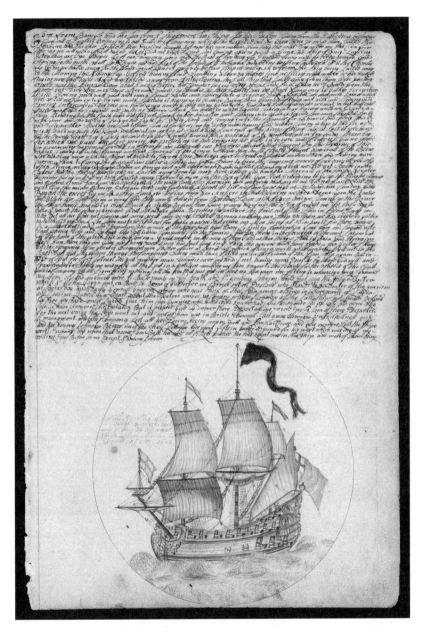

"East Indiaman Sceptre" by Edward Barlow (National Maritime Museum)

on to lament, "Yea, I always knew that the worst of prentices did live a far better life than I did, for they had Sundays and other holy days to rest upon and take their pleasures; but all days were alike to us, and many times it fell out that we had more work on a Sabbath day than we had on other days."[11]

This last comment is crucial, for it shows how the very necessities of work at sea weakened or stripped the seaman of attachments to local and regional land-based cultures. Life at sea, for example, nearly obliterated the plebeian calendar rich with holy days and breaks from work. By Barlow's reckoning, labor at sea even made difficult the observance of basic Christian rituals such as a proper Christmas dinner. Working as a seaman also had other, more subtle cultural effects. Barlow found that he had less control of his own time, his schedule, and his hours and activities of work, play, and rest. Seafaring, like disciplined wage labor in general, represented a brave new world.[12]

Since Barlow continually bemoaned his occupation, why didn't he leave the sea? At the end of each voyage Barlow faced the question anew. It seems his inability to leave the sea did not turn on lack of effort. Indeed, he felt his life at sea was a race against the clock, not least because he deeply feared having to go to sea after he reached forty years of age. Barlow kept trying to "drive a trade ashore," but he kept failing. He faced enormous obstacles. The English economy in the late seventeenth century offered little to the "swollen mass of the poor." The situation did not improve until late in the century, by which time Barlow was in his fifties and was unlikely to be able to switch occupations. His fears notwithstanding, Barlow was still battling the elements and "proud, imperious, and malicious" captains as he moved into his middle fifties. This was relatively uncommon among seamen, but far from unknown.[13]

Work and Thought

How did work at sea affect Barlow's consciousness and identity? Did it foster class consciousness? Did it foster national consciousness? International consciousness? How did he think about the world and his own place within it? We can answer these questions by analyzing the evidence of social conflict in Barlow's journal, and more specifically the language he uses to describe and discuss the power relationships that governed ever-roving travels around the globe.

Barlow took great pride in his global seafaring, which transformed him from a provincial farm laborer into a man of the world, a genuine cosmopolitan. Indeed he looked back from his worldly perch at sea to scorn his neighbors: "Some of them would not venture a day's journey from out of the smoke of their chimneys or the taste of their mother's milk; not even upon the condition that they might eat and drink of as good cheer as the best nobleman in the land, but they would rather stay at home and eat a little brown crust and drink a little whey." Barlow would return home as Walter Benjamin's man from afar to tell stories of strange and fascinating things he had seen overseas.[14]

One of Barlow's most dogged habits was his insistence upon blaming authorities for the problems he experienced. Whether his difficulties were personal or political, small or large, he usually managed to find a culprit. Not surprisingly, he always had special venom for those who exploited and oppressed "poor seamen." Actions by the lesser officers of the vessels on which he sailed rankled him from time to time, particularly with their privilege of first choice of the ship's food. When the officers took their cut of the salt beef, they "left for the poor men but the surloin next to the horns." They also left the tars "Hobson's choice"—that or nothing. Barlow also disliked the surgeons on the larger ships, whose prescriptions, he said, "doeth as much good to [the sick sailor] as a blow upon the pate with a stick." Even when Barlow became an officer later in his career, his view of the world reflected his origins on the lower deck.[15]

Barlow reserved special wrath for the purser, who stocked the king's ships with food and drink. This greedy figure "never buyeth that which His Majesty alloweth, but always buyeth the worst and putteth thee rest of the money in his own pocket." Corruption was rife throughout the Royal Navy. Even more galling—and dangerous—was a purser in unholy alliance with the ship's captain, for "if a poor seaman do but speak [his complaint], then he is in danger of being beaten, for the purser and captain holding together and sharing all the gains that cometh that way, a poor man must not be heard for that which is his right." Anyone who dared to speak for such right risked "twenty or thirty blows on the back." In extreme cases, "poor men's lives" were "taken away for speaking for what is their due."[16]

Masters and captains did not have to unite with pursers to excite Barlow's wrath, for oftentimes they were quite unbearable on their own. Barlow railed against "proud and ambitious masters" of merchant vessels, who cheated tars out of their lawful wages, made unreasonable demands, and found fault with every little thing the crew did. He had contempt for cowardly commanders of naval ships, "who can swagger and curse and swear, damn and damn, with their great periwigs and swords, huffing about when [none of their enemies] is near them." Such pretentious aristocrats, Barlow thought, belonged more in "some dung boat than in a good King's ship." Barlow was never reluctant to judge his "superiors," and his judgments were often harsh.[17]

Barlow aimed his most bitter denunciations at "merchants and owners of ships in England." These figures did not stock their vessels with enough food for transatlantic voyages, and they thereby profited from the sailor's "hungry belly." They also docked the seaman's hard-earned wages to pay for damaged cargo, even when the damage had been caused by a leaky ship, which a carpenter might fix but a common sailor could not. Barlow did not confine his criticism to single owners of ships or to small companies. He went after the East India Company, which he felt consistently took advantage of the "poor man" before the mast. To Barlow and his mates, the company's customs officers were always "as welcome to us as water into a ship which is about to sink." Barlow had nothing but a sneer for Sir Josiah Child, a leading light in the company and a leading mercantile thinker of the day. His fortune, not surprisingly, had come from being a merchant victualer to the Royal Navy in Portsmouth.[18]

Barlow occasionally ventured beyond the maritime world altogether in his expression of antagonism. He was not shy about criticizing "the rich," or at least some of them. He argued that "great Lords and earls" who lived in "pomp and vanity" amid their "moneys and pleasures"—and who were often "traitors" to their country—should have their property expropriated and given to "some poor true-hearted seaman that goes to sea for want of means." He also thought that "many of our English gentry and such as lie at home in their beds of down, in their ease and pleasure, eating up the fat of the land, and studying treacheries" should have to change places with seamen "for a month or two." Barlow fiercely detested the refusal of wealthy people to help "a poor lame or old seaman" who had "lost his limbs and suffered shipwreck and imprisonment" while defending the rich and their country and who was now reduced to begging. Barlow's desire to turn the world upside down by changing the places of rich and poor proceeded from his understanding that one of the primary functions of the state was to protect the wealthy and their property. Barlow several times referred to the misfortunes and dangers suffered by seamen on the high seas so that the rich "may lie glutting them-selves at home in all manner of pleasures." In fact, many were poor because a few were rich and vice versa, in his sophisticated concep-tion of the relations between classes.[19]

There was one last villain on Barlow's black list, and that was the English state itself. Barlow ranted against the "evil custom" of im-pressment, which affected so many seamen and so many of the poor as a whole. Throughout the seventeenth and eighteen centuries the Admiralty used forced labor to man the navy and fight the wars of empire. Many a "poor man" lost "his chest and clothes and several months pay" when pressed, all of which were "more to him than he can make good again in a twelvemonth time, considering his small wages and the uncertainty of it before he receiveth it." Barlow himself was impressed into the Royal Navy, as were many of his shipmates. They told their yarns of battle against the press gang. The state itself oppressed the tar by its use of coercive and involuntary labor.[20]

Barlow spoke of conflict largely in a religious idiom taken from the Bible. His contestants in conflict were sometimes "the rich" and "the poor," both Biblical concepts, but more often they were the powerful and the powerless, with the former designated according to position of power (merchant, captain, purser), and the latter as victim ("poor seaman," "poor man," "poor soul"). The notion of "the poor" is utterly central to Barlow's language of class. Barlow used "the poor" to designate not only the afflicted and the unfortunate in temporary need of relief, but all those with "want of means," those who had no independent way of getting a living, even though they did not, as in Barlow's case, lack employment. Barlow's poor were the laboring poor, who multiplied rapidly with enclosure of common lands and other forms of expropriation in seventeenth-century England. Living in a society fundamentally organized through patronage and preferment, Barlow's poor also lacked connections. When Barlow himself was on the verge of realizing a lifelong dream by setting up as captain and getting his own ship, his patron in the arrangement suddenly died: "It proves many times thus with a poor man, when he most depends upon the fair words and slippery performances of many men, their words being wind which passeth away without any hold to be taken of them." The "poor" or "ordinary" man, forced to sell his labor power for a wage because he owned no land, skills, or tools was thus repeatedly buffeted by forces beyond his control. This, along with the sheer weight of difficult material circumstances, led to a certain fatalism in Barlow's treatment of rich and poor. He noted that "riches always forget poverty," and that "he that is poor shall be poor still." Here as elsewhere Barlow paraphrased a common biblical observation: "For the poor always ye have with you."[21]

Alongside or within his beliefs about the ubiquity of "the poor," Barlow also had a certain leveling instinct, as he consistently expressed values of equality and justice in many of his complaints and critical reflections outlined above. For example, he placed rich and poor upon the same plane of spiritual equality. He believed that "there is no question that the Lord will hear the praise of the poor as well as the rich." God was "no respecter of persons," which meant that he did not favor the rich over the poor, men over women, white over black. He also pointed out that rich and poor were equally subject to "death's stroke." If Barlow could not always see how the poor might achieve parity with the rich, he was at least able to comfort himself with the evanescence of riches, which "have wings many times, and fly away from many." Barlow also expressed his leveling instinct in action. He returned to his hometown after years at sea, in clothes which, he said, were "too high for my calling." But the clothes had the desired effect: all of his old neighbors asked about the identity of the visiting "gentleman." Barlow snickered to himself: "if they had seen me many times before and since on such condition as I was many times in, they would sooner have asked what beggar or what gaol-bird I had been, or from what prison I had come out of."[22]

Barlow's attitude toward concentrated riches and the money that increasingly shaped England's social and political life was largely negative, sometimes violently so. His consciousness expressed a moral economy of fair treatment and decent subsistence for all. The advance of free, mobile, waged labor was part of a broad process of social change and polarization, part of the early establishment of capitalist relations of production in England and its empire. Such relations featured prominently in the merchant shipping industry and the Royal Navy, where Barlow and many thousands of others like him worked. As more men and women began to work for wages, money became more central to getting a living and thus to social life as a whole. Barlow found this process by which "all matters are balmed with money" to be deeply disturbing. The rapid accumulation of wealth was considered by many to be a corrosive, even illegitimate process. Barlow explained, "it is an old maxim, and I do believe a true one, that he that makes haste to be rich cannot be innocent." The lust for wealth thus produced an amoral drift in social life. Some men, Barlow said, "do anything for a little money, not caring how or which way they break their oath, so that they get gain." Although Barlow aimed these words at those who abused their authority in search of gain, they struck perilously close to home: many poor people found themselves in the desperate position of having to "do anything for a little money." Keeping body and soul together required it. But the real offenders to Barlow were not the poor, but rather the powerful. Merchant captains, Barlow insisted, "care not how much or what way they can get all to themselves, and care not what little other people get that are under them." Barlow clearly felt that proper social relations were being deranged by the advancing competition, materialism, and "possessive individualism" of the age.[23]

Near the end of his life, in 1703, Barlow issued a thundering damnation after a great storm that sank hundreds of vessels and killed thousands of his brother tars. To Barlow, the meaning of the storm was straightforward: it was a "warning of God's anger" and a sign of moral corruption. He wrote, "No man values his word or promise, or matters what he doth or saith, so that he can but gain and defraud his neighbour. All commanders and masters of ships are grown up with pride and oppression and tyranny." He concluded in frustration drawn from his own life experience: "I want words to lay out the business and unworthy dealings of many men I have met with, not acting like Christians." It would be no exaggeration to say that Barlow criticized, and often battled, ship captains throughout his long laboring life.[24]

Edward Barlow was not a radical, at least not according to the standard meaning of the term in the mid- to late-seventeenth century. He apparently harbored no antiroyalist sentiments; other than his complaints about impressment, he made no sustained critique of "kingly power." In fact he proclaimed the accession of Charles II in 1660 "with great joy." (It must be noted, however, that it is hard to tell how much of the joy came from satisfaction that the monarchy had been restored and how much came from the free wine, the piece of gold worth nine shillings and sixpence, and the extra month's pay given to the men in the Royal Navy to encourage their joy, celebration, and loyalty.) Barlow had no apparent association with the radical sects of the revolutionary era. He mentioned such groups only once, in 1661: there were "troubles arising about the Fifth Monarchy men, so called, and other disturbances, which put us in fear for the ships in Chatham, and we were forced to keep a watch very strictly every night."[25]

Despite such differences Barlow shared something of a mental and moral world with the radicals, for both were products of the same wrenching social changes that shook seventeenth-century England. Most significantly, both expressed great awareness and experience of social power and difference. The language used to discuss such matters fused politics and religion within a militant Christianity. Indeed Barlow sounded like the True Digger Gerrard Winstanley, one of the most radical voices of the English Revolution, when he wrote that the docking of seamen's wages was "a custom too long used in England to the oppression of poor seamen," depriving "the poor man of his lawful hire." Later in life, perhaps when his ability to fight his own battles had waned, Barlow invoked an angry and avenging God who "in His time will reward [the East India Company's] doings to oppress the poor and the hireling." It is of crucial significance that Barlow, like the most extreme of the radicals, identified not with "the people" (the middling elements of English society), but rather with "the poor."[26]

Like many of the radicals, Barlow considered himself both an English patriot and a Protestant internationalist, and as such he was often concerned with the doings and "plottings" of "papists." He called himself a patriot, a "true-hearted Englishman," a product of high civilization, and he tended to look down on the strange customs practiced in "heathen countries." It troubled him immensely—as Protestant, European, and free laborer—to hear about the selling of Christians as slaves in Algiers, where men were bought and sold "like so many sheep." He did not express the same objection to African slavery, though it must be noted that in his many voyages he never sailed in a slave ship, which must have reflected an important personal choice. He also expressed sympathy for the enslaved Africans who rebelled near Port Royal, Jamaica, in 1678: they "live under so much torture and hardship that rather than endure it they will run any hazard, for they are very hard worked."[27]

Yet Barlow's patriotism and Protestantism had limits. Like some radicals in the English revolutionary movement of the 1640s and 1650s, Barlow had doubts about the civilizing quest of the English empire. In 1689, after voyages to Brazil, China, and the East and West Indies, Barlow wondered about the world outside Europe: "But for foreign nations to come and plant themselves in islands and countries by force, and build forts and raise laws, and force the people to customs against the true natures and people of the said places, without their consent, how this will stand with the law of God and the religion we profess, let the world judge." His skepticism about the "civilizing" project of imperialism was palpable. Barlow also thought on occasion that England was "grown the worst kingdom in Christendom for poor seamen." His experience in the international maritime labor market undercut whatever nationalist sentiments he may have harbored.[28]

Another important commonality in the worldview of Barlow and many radicals was the utter absence of belief in "the dignity of labor." Despite his Protestant identity, Barlow gives not a shard of evidence to suggest that he attached any moral meaning whatsoever to work at sea. There was nothing dignified about the wage dependency and the harsh, degrading relations of authority Barlow experienced as a seaman. In fact, his condition seemed so bad at times that he likened the seaman's plight to that of the slave. He noted that "all the men in the ship except the master [were] little better than slaves, being under command." Barlow also fantasized about changing places with a beggar: "I was always thinking that beggars had a far better life of it and lived better than I did, for they seldom missed of their bellies full of better victuals than we could get, and also at night to lie quiet and out of danger in a good barn full of straw, nobody disturbing them, and might lie as long as they pleased." Of course "it was quite the contrary with us": Barlow never got his "belly full"; he never slept more than four hours (often it was less) because of the watch system at sea. Bitter comparisons to slaves and sweet fantasies of beggars are not the stuff of belief in the dignity of labor. Barlow saw work as "sweat and toil"; he got his living "by hard fare and sore labour."[29]

Conclusion

Christopher Hill has shown that seventeenth-century ideas about the dignity of labor were most popular among people of middling property, who, as independent farmers and craftsmen, owned their own land and tools, their means of independent subsistence. At the other end of the social scale there existed a contrary attitude, a hostility to wage labor and a desire to escape it. Hill writes, "Theories of the dignity of labour had little appeal for those who had evolved out of serfdom into wage labour." Further, the "antithesis of freedom was the stultifying drudgery of those who had become cogs in someone else's machine." This was precisely the situation in which Edward Barlow found himself. The drudgery was the monotonous and closely super-vised work in the wooden world; the machine was the ship; the some-one else to whom it belonged was the merchant and the shipowner, those ungodly people against whom he railed bitterly throughout his journal of four decades.[30]

In the end, Edward Barlow's precious account of his long life at sea offers a remarkable glimpse into the mind of a late-seventeenth-century sailor. Fundamentally shaped by his experience of labor, he combined in his thinking and doing a potent mix of the national and the international, the religious and the secular, the moral and the political. Given the present state of research, it is impossible to say whether Barlow was "typical" of his brother tars or English working people more generally. But we can say that his journal allows us to study a particular consciousness and set of beliefs in a concrete and nuanced way, to see how Barlow's work experience helped to create a personal disposition that included egalitarian, anti-authoritarian, and moralistic tendencies. It might be argued that in certain ways Barlow's thought reflects a form of plebeian antinomianism, a set of beliefs that by the late seventeenth century had lost both some of its millennial religious fervor and its overt political meaning. In any case, Barlow's journal illuminates a horizon of possibilities within a popular world of work and consciousness, a world still only poorly understood.[31]

✦

THREE

Henry Pitman,
"Fugitive Traitor"

Henry Pitman came from a prosperous Quaker family in Yeovil, Somersetshire, England, and was not therefore a typical participant in Monmouth's Rebellion of 1685. He was a physician and a member of the lesser gentry in an army made up almost entirely of the common sort, especially cloth workers, craftsmen, and agricultural laborers. People like Henry had kept their distance from uprisings, but Somerset itself, from which Monmouth drew most of his soldiers, had long been "the nursery of rebellion." It had a strong and variegated tradition of self-organization and struggle from below, encompassing commoners who fought to retain their rights to the marshes, "Clubmen" who opposed both Cavalier and Roundhead in the English Revolution, and cloth workers who did not hesitate to riot in the face of increasing immiseration. It was also a place of radical nonconformity (with sizable concentrations of Baptists and Quakers), republican conspiracy, and the persistence of "the good old cause," code words for the English Revolution, to which Henry was an heir.[1]

Henry also looks atypical when considered alongside the millions of servants, slaves, convicts, and sailors whose experiences are central to this book. He was a learned and literate man of privilege, but one who, because of the vicissitudes of war, found himself an astonished member of the Atlantic proletariat. As such he faced many of the "great sufferings" and "strange adventures" of other coerced workers, in his own time and after. Henry's account shows how the escape from bondage worked as a practical process, allowing us to see what kinds of knowledge and social relationships made it possible. It also suggests that escape is a rather different, and historically more important, kind of resistance than usually thought.

This point holds true even for the most highly developed historiography of escape to be found anywhere in the scholarly world: I refer to the extensive writing about running away from slavery in North America and the Caribbean in the seventeenth, eighteenth, and nineteenth centuries. In this rich, well-mined vein we find analyses of escape in relation to a plethora of variables: skill, acculturation, seasonality, geography, other forms of resistance. We have studies of *petit marronage* (temporary escape from slavery) and *grand marronage* (permanent escape). We have what the distinguished Caribbeanist N. A. T. Hall called "maritime marronage," of which Henry Pitman's escape is an example. But we have few examples of how it actually worked, concretely and in human terms, as a process.[2]

With all this in mind let us turn to the Monmouth rebel and his Atlantic adventure. His is a picaresque story of slavery and no less a story of self-emancipation from slavery. It is a story of violence, misery, and death, and it is equally a story of courage, strength, and luck (which is sometimes called providence). It is fundamentally a story of knowledge—technical knowledge, natural knowledge, and social knowledge. It might in the end tell us something about myths we have long told—and continue to tell—ourselves.

Capture

Henry came to misfortune by an odd combination of curiosity, compassion, and chance. Having recently returned from a voyage to Italy and happening to visit relatives in Sandford, Somersetshire, just as the Duke of Monmouth landed at Lyme Regis to launch his uprising, Henry decided to "to go and see whether his strength and number were answerable to what the common rumour had spread abroad."

He rode with family members to Taunton to satisfy his curiosity and promptly got himself caught between warring armies, Monmouth's rebels on the one side, Oxford's royalists on the other. He retreated to the former, among whom he met friends who asked him "to stay and take care of the sick and wounded men." Before long, "pity and compassion on my fellow creatures, more especially being my brethren in Christianity, obliged me to stay and perform the duty of my calling among them, and to assist my brother chirurgeons towards the relief of those that otherwise, must have languished in misery." Henry also treated the captured soldiers of the king, and he never actually took up arms in the cause, but his feelings of solidarity—with his fellow surgeons, fellow Christians, and fellow creatures (the last of these being a marker of radicalism from the 1640s and 1650s)— allied him with insurrection and ultimately treason. After the rout of Monmouth's forces at Sedgmoor on July 6, 1685, many of the rebel soldiers were hanged immediately. Henry tried to escape, was captured, robbed ("pockets rifled" and "my coat taken off my back"), and committed, with about four hundred others, to Ilchester gaol. He lay among the wounded, the gashed, and the bone-shattered in a filthy, overcrowded jail, where dozens would die of fever and small-pox. Henry survived.

Conviction and Exile

The bloodbath had only just begun. Soon came the "Bloody Assizes," presided over by the infamous hanging judge Lord Chief Justice George Jeffreys, whose natural violent irritability was at the moment made worse by kidney stones. The agents of King James visited the jails and prisons bulging with 1,300 men, promising grace and mercy in exchange for admissions of guilt. Many refused to play the game, whereupon twenty-eight were selected for trial at Dorchester, condemned, and "a warrant signed for their execution the same afternoon." After these hangings, most of the rest were sufficiently terrorized to plead guilty in hope of saving their lives. Most of those who did were quickly convicted and ordered "to be hanged, drawn, and quartered," but opposition arose from an unexpected quarter:

the hangmen protested that they could not carry out the number of executions being asked of them. (Their work standard was a dozen a day.) Another 230 prisoners were eventually executed, some of them making "no shew of repentance . . . but justified theyr treason and gloried in it." Bodies were disemboweled, heads severed, remains tarred and put on public display in what would be England's largest mass hangings since the 1550s. Henry's luck was stubborn: "The rest of us," he wrote, "were ordered to be transported to the Caribbee Islands." For him as for 850 other prisoners, the living death of slavery would be substituted for the literal death of hanging.

Henry, his brother William, and about a hundred other prisoners were given by the authorities to Catholic merchants, who immediately entered into negotiations with Henry's family for ransom. Fearing that Henry would not be released even if the money was paid, the family members hesitated, but relented when threatened that the brothers would be singled out for especially harsh treatment if they did not pay the required 120 pounds. Meanwhile, Henry was moved from Wells to Weymouth, where he and his "companions" (as he called them) were herded onto the *Betty*, a London ship now bound for Barbados. The five-week passage was "very sickly." Nine of the prisoners died and were buried in the sea. Those who survived would be linked in ways that were not yet clear to them. Henry's luck survived the transatlantic voyage to a strange land.

Slavery

Henry introduced his experience in Barbados by copying into his narrative the legislation passed by the colonial assembly in January 1686, just as he arrived, for the governing of political prisoners and transported felons such as himself. Fate had sent him to England's richest colony, a plantation society built on the gruesome exploitation of indentured servants and slaves who produced sugar for the world market. These workers, as one visitor noted, "perform their dreadful tasks and then expire," and indeed the death rate for workers black and white was high. Insatiable for labor power, the planters of Barbados were grateful to get Monmouth's rebels.[3]

The act of 1686 begins by denouncing the "monstrous villainy" of the traitors, who sought to turn the king's dominions into "theatres of blood and misery." Many "convict rebels" were justly hanged, the law announced, while others were sent, through his majesty's "unparalleled grace and clemency," to the colonies to serve ten-year terms of servitude. Henry observed sourly, "And thus we may see the buying and selling of Free-men into slavery, was beginning again to be renewed among Christians, as if that Heathenish Custom had been a necessary dependence on arbitrary power."[4]

The law spelled out exactly how the ruling class of Barbados thought Henry and his ilk would try to escape. They knew that some would try "to redeem themselves with money," and some would attempt to intermarry with free women on the island. They knew that some would feign death and try to get away in disguise, others would flee the island using "False Tickets under wrong names," still others would get shipmasters or anyone else they could to help them abscond. Some would get small craft and attempt to emancipate themselves by sailing away to freedom. (Some, the legislators knew, would die trying.) The legislation therefore preemptively forbade manumission through self-purchase or intermarriage, created a registry to keep track of the convicts, established a bevy of fines and imprisonments for any who assisted escape, regulated the use of all small vessels, and prescribed punishment for those who tried to run away: "Thirty-nine lashes on his bare body, on some public day, in the next Market town to his Master's place of abode: and, on another market day in the same town, to be set in the pillory, by the space of one hour; and be burnt in the forehead with the letters F.T. signifying Fugitive Traitor, so as the letters may plainly appear in his forehead." Henry considered this to be "an inchristian and inhuman *Act*." It reflected the class struggle over the mobility of bonded laborers.[5]

Exploitation

Despite the promises made to Henry's family by the merchants in England, Henry and his brother were sold to Robert Bishop, who showed "great unkindness," quashing all the petitions and entreaties for the freedom their family had paid for, refusing to give the servants proper clothes, and allowing them but a "very mean" diet, one that made Henry sick of "a violent flux." Henry tried to play upon his class background and professional skill in negotiating with his master: he "humbly recommended to his consideration my Profession and practice, which I hoped would render me deserving of better accommodation than was usually allowed to other Servants." His hopes were inappropriate to his new class condition and Bishop frankly told him so. Wounded, Henry declared, "I would choose rather to work in the field with the Negroes than to dishonour my Profession by serving him as Physician and Surgeon, and to accept the same entertainment as common Servants." Bishop flew into a rage, beat Henry with his cane until it splintered, then clapped him in the stocks "exposed to the scorching heat of the sun" for twelve hours.

Over the next fifteen months Henry experienced more cruel treatment by Robert Bishop, but soon the master fell into debt and Henry was sent back to the merchants who had originally sold him. The humiliation was complete: he was now "goods unsold." Tired of waiting for a pardon, angry about the endless abuse, and saddened by the recent death of his brother, Henry "resolved to attempt the making of my escape off the island." He would risk "a burnt forehead and a sore back," a branding and a whipping, but as it happened he was risking even more. As he later discovered, the planters of Barbados, once they learned of the collective escape, "were resolved, as they said, that I should be hanged!" The gallows would cast its shadow over Henry's adventure from beginning to end.

Planning

Henry mulled over various strategies of escape; all of them were dangerous. The one he chose entailed securing a small boat, organizing a group of fellow conspirators, gathering supplies, and slipping away in the middle of the night for the island of Curaçao, a voyage of six hundred miles, with the northeast trade winds at his back. (He chose a Dutch colony because he assumed that the officials of an English colonial government would capture and return him to Barbados immediately.) His relatives in England had facilitated the escape (perhaps unwittingly) by sending goods on consignment to a friend on the island who in turn sold them and gave the proceeds to Henry. Having money was a critical advantage, but it meant little without a series of alliances on which the whole endeavor would depend.

Henry began by working with a man named John Nuthall, who was not a prisoner, nor even a servant, but rather a free man, a wood carver in "mean circumstances": he had fallen into debt and wanted to leave the island, but he had no means to do so. Henry engaged Nuthall in a pact of secrecy and asked him to acquire the vessel for their common escape, in exchange for which he promised money, free passage, and eventually the boat itself once they had reached their destination. Henry gave him twelve pounds to buy the boat of "a Guiney man" lying at anchor in the harbor. This Nuthall did, but as soon as he registered the vessel (as required by the law) he aroused the suspicion of the authorities, who wondered where such a poor man got the money and how he intended to use the boat. Fearful that the magistrates might seize the boat, Henry got Nuthall to sink it offshore and lie low to allow suspicions to subside.

Henry now turned his attention to a second alliance. He brought into the plot two other transported felons who were political prisoners, Thomas Austin and John Whicker, the latter of whom had voyaged with him on the *Betty* from Weymouth to Barbados. These two gladly contributed what little money they had to the design. Whicker, a joiner, would be especially important to their voyage in a wooden vessel. Meanwhile, Henry continued to play the lead role in organizing the escape, since he had, in his employ, "more time and liberty" than Austin and Whicker. He and Nuthall met nightly on the waterfront at "some convenient place remote from town."

The next task was to gather supplies for the voyage. Henry compiled a detailed list of necessaries "so nothing might be forgotten": "A hundredweight of bread, a convenient quantity of cheese, a cask of water, some few bottles of Canary and Madeira wine and beer; these being for the support of Nature: and then for use, a compass, quadrant, chart, half-hour glass, half-minute glass, log and line, large tarpaulin, a hatchet, hammer, saw and nails, some spare boards, a lantern and candles." These he stored first at a friend's house near the waterside, then at the warehouse tended by Whicker close to their intended point of departure. Henry's preparations were thorough and careful.

In his third act of alliance Henry expanded the conspiracy further, bringing in another debtor, Thomas Waker, and four more fellow "convict rebels": Jeremiah Atkins (a husbandman from Taunton), Peter Bagwell (a thirty-three-year-old farmer from Colyton), John Cooke (from Chard), and William Woodcock (a nineteen-year-old cloth worker, a comber, imprisoned at Taunton). Bagwell and Cooke had been shipmates with Henry and John Whicker aboard the *Betty*. Old solidarities served a new design.

Henry found the right moment to escape when the governor of Nevis visited Barbados, whose own governor put on "a noble entertainment," parading the town's militia in arms, with "revelling, drinking, and feasting to excess." Henry sent out word to his comrades to meet, with whatever arms they could gather, by the wharf during this time of "drowsy security and carelessness." Meanwhile Nuthall arranged for "two lusty blacks" to refloat the boat and bring it to the point of embarkation, where, at 11:00 p.m. on the night of May 9, 1687, the men met to load their "necessaries of life." Their grand plan was unexpectedly interrupted when several watchmen strolled by, causing panic and flight, but they did not notice the boat and continued their rounds. Henry in particular was so terrified as to be "altogether unwilling to make a second attempt" until he remembered those "whom I had engaged in so much danger." Thomas Austin, fearful "of being cast away," refused in the end to make the voyage. At midnight eight men rowed softly—and closely—by the fort and a man-of-war anchored in the harbor. Their small craft began to fill with water, but they could not bail for fear of "making a noise to alarm our enemies." They made their escape to freedom in an unlikely vessel—a leaky old boat from a slave ship.

At Sea

Once they got clear of their enemies, they fell to work, emptying the boat of water, raising their mast, hoisting their sail, and setting their course southwest toward Grenada. The boat continued to leak despite their efforts to plug the gaping seams with tallowed linen and rags; someone had to be kept bailing "continually, day and night, . . . our whole voyage." Henry was at the helm "to guide and govern the boat," as he was the only one among the eight who knew navigation. Meanwhile, most of the rest of the crew were hanging over sides of the vessel, seasick. They began to grumble, "to wish themselves at Barbadoes again." Henry explained that there was no going back. This was literally true; the winds made it impossible. The following morning, when they were almost out of the sight of the island, "we began," according to Henry, "to be cheered up with the thoughts of our liberty, and the hopes of our safe arrival at our desired port."

The high spirits did not last, for that night crisis struck. A brisk gale arose, damaging the rudder, which split, suddenly forcing them to lower sail and use an oar "to keep our boat before the sea." John Whicker, the joiner, sprang into action, mending the helm by nailing two boards to it. "That done," Henry wrote, "we went cheerily on again."

Over the next few days the escape was aided by good weather but plagued by Henry's inability to take a true observation by his quadrant "because of the uneven motion of the sea, and the nearness of the sun to the zenith." He therefore steered a course from island to island, from Grenada to Los Testigos, to Margarita, where on the fifth day of the voyage, the men grew tired of their putrid water and wanted to go ashore for a fresh supply. Henry resisted the idea because he feared the "savage cannibals" they might encounter. But once they got to the north side of the island, which seemed to be free of the "inhuman man-eaters," Henry relented. They brought the boat to shore, got water, and soon directed their course for Saltatudos, or Salt Tortuga.

Late in the day (May 15) the wind stiffened "and a white ring encircled the moon," an omen of bad weather. Soon "a dreadful storm arose, which made us despair of ever seeing the morning sun. And now the sea began to foam, and to turn its smooth surface into mountains and vales." The boat "was tossed and tumbled from one side to the other"; it was "violently hurried and driven away by the fury of the wind and the sea." The men once again began to wish themselves back in Barbados or even on the island with the "savage cannibals" rather than face this "approaching ruin." At this point, Henry recalled, divine providence intervened. They heard "an unexpected voice," someone holloa-ing at them from a great distance. The violence of the winds and the furies of the raging waves ceased. With God's help, Henry thought, they had survived.

The next morning Margarita Island lay before them. They intended to go ashore to refresh themselves after the storm, to search for water, and to repair the leaks in the boat, whose timbers had been loosened by the pounding seas. They "stood in directly for shore, thinking it a convenient place to land," but then saw a canoe heading from the shore directly toward them. They reached immediately for their arms, blunderbusses and muskets, only to discover that they had left their bag of shot on the wharf as they escaped Barbados. So they loaded their barrels with pieces of glass and prepared for engagement. When they saw that the men in the canoe bearing down on them paddled like Indians, they decided to make haste and try to get away from them.

Pirates

The canoe kept gaining as Henry and his companions watched anxiously, ready to fire. Soon the approaching men "waved their hats and hailed us," by which gesture it was clear that they were not Indians, who did not wear hats. They seemed to be "white men." "We enquired," wrote Henry, "What they were?" They replied, "Englishman in distress, &c., and waited for an opportunity to go off the island." The men in the boat were no doubt relieved, but perhaps they should not have been. It turned out that the canoemen were something rather more than marooned Englishmen. They were pirates, all twenty-six of them on the island. Formerly part of a multiethnic crew with Captain Yanche, who marauded against the Spanish in the Caribbean, they had gone on a raid against Indians in Florida (to capture canoes), gotten separated from the rest, and come to Margarita in hopes of finding a vessel that would carry them back to an English port.

Henry and crew were, understandably, not exactly forthcoming about who they were and what they were doing. The pirates assumed they were debtors fleeing those to whom they owed money, as was common in the Caribbean at the time. Thomas Waker, who actually was a debtor, broke solidarity with his shipmates and sought to curry favor with the pirates by explaining that most of them were not debtors but rather rebels, thinking this would make the sea robbers more likely to take him over his shipmates. He miscalculated, badly. The pirates not only resented his treachery, they, according to Henry, "loved us the better, confessing they were rebels too," adding that "if the Duke of Monmouth had had 1,000 of them, they would soon have put to flight the King's army." Their affinity discovered, the pirates took the bedraggled men ashore and gave them fresh water and food and a chance to rest and recover from their hard voyage.

Later, when the escapees explained their intention to sail on to Curaçao, the pirates, said Henry, "endeavoured to persuade us from it: alleging the insufficiency of our boat, and the dangers we were so lately exposed unto." The pirates wanted Henry and his men to go marauding with them on the Spanish Main. Most of the gang from Barbados were willing, but not Henry, who was apparently inclined to risk his neck at sea for freedom but not upon the gallows for piracy. He in turn persuaded the others not to go. Not to be outdone in the argument, the pirates promptly burned their boat, "supposing then that we would choose rather to go with them" rather than stay on the island, where they would risk attack by the Spanish or starvation before anyone arrived to pick them up. Henry was undeterred, but he was worried about survival. He therefore paid the pirates thirty pieces of eight to leave behind an Indian they had captured in Florida. He would feed those who remained—the eight escapees and or pirates who decided to stay behind—with his ability to catch fish.[6]

Maroon

The privateers (a legal-sounding name for pirates) "had no sooner left us, but we found ourselves, of necessity, obliged to seek out for provisions." This was the new material reality for Henry and the others, who were now officially marooned. When he was narrating this part of his story, Henry's voice suddenly changed: he became something of a natural historian, describing in detail the island he had come by accident to inhabit—how it got its name, its geology and topography, and most crucially its resources, especially the salt deposits and how they were formed, and its animal and plant life. Henry knew that such descriptions were popular parts of the travel literature of his day. In any case, this was making the most of necessity: Henry and his fellow maroons had to figure how to feed themselves in this strange land. This required new kinds of knowledge and new forms of cooperation. There was an "art"—and a history—of marooning. Henry and his mates were suddenly, and literally, commoners. They had to wrest sustenance from an island commons with an unfamiliar ecology.[7]

In the first foray for food the escapees were "led by the example of those four privateers that stayed behind." These men had already lived on the island for a while, but more important, they had other kinds of knowledge that would prove invaluable, for buccaneers had long lived as hunting and gathering maroons, sometimes by choice, to escape various Caribbean authorities, and sometimes by necessity, as had happened to all of the men on Margarita. The crew immediately began "to turn turtle," that is, search during the nighttime hours for the amphibious creatures and flip them over on their backs, where they would remain until the hunters returned the following day to kill and eat them. Cooking was done in the old buccaneer manner, barbecuing the turtle meat on wooden spits (*boucans*, used to cook slaughtered wild cattle, whence the name *boucanier*). Any meat left over would be cut into long strips, salted, dried in the sun, and saved as their "winter store," as the buccaneers had long done. Henry called turtle flesh "very delightsome and pleasant to the taste, much resembling veal." The men also collected turtle eggs, their season fortunately being April, May, and June, beating the yolks in calabashes with salt before frying them, pancake-style, in tortoise fat.

A second major source of food lay in the fishing skill of the Native American whom Henry had retained. He "was so dextrous that with his bow and arrow, he would shoot a small fish at a great distance." He also caught crawfish and shellfish (whelks), which made for a welcome change of diet. This too reflected longstanding buccaneer tradition. West Indian freebooters had for decades worked out alliances with the multiethnic Miskito Indians from the coast of Nicaragua. The buccaneers would provide military assistance in the Miskito struggle against the Spanish; the Miskito would provide skilled fishermen who would sail with the buccaneers and provide food for them. Knowledge of the local ecology was prized.[8]

The next major task, since hurricane season was coming on, was "building houses to defend us from the stormy weather." They built simple structures and covered them with coarse grass that grew by the seaside. Their household goods consisted of two or three earthen jars left by the pirates, calabashes, and shells. The maroons spent much time in their "little huts or houses, . . . sometimes reading or writing." They were slowly making the island their own.

Henry turned his medical and scientific reading to new account on the island, searching out "vegetable productions" that would prove to be "of great service to us." He found a plant he called a "Turks' Head" that had a small nut that tasted like a strawberry, and another called the *curatoe* (agave) that had a variety of uses: its juice could be used as soap; its fibers made good thread; its leaves could be boiled to produce a "balsom [poultice] for wounds." The body of the plant, when heated and placed in a hole in the sand for five or six days, produced "a most pleasant and spiritous alcoholic liquor," which tasted like "the syrup of baked pears." Another pleasure was smoking a plant called "Wild Sage" in "a crab's claw." Despite Henry's inventiveness, however, island life remained "desolate and disconsolate."

Homecoming

After four months on the island, the maroons at last spied two vessels, a sloop and a man-of-war sailing toward them. Both were full of pirates. The captain of the warship learned from the four pirates on the island that one of their number was a doctor and sent for him. Henry was welcomed aboard the ship with trumpets, greeted by the captain and ship's doctor, and taken into the great cabin, where he was wined, fed, and given gifts. The conversation touched on the defeat of the Duke of Monmouth, which the pirates "seemed to deplore." They too were rebels against the English state. Henry had found compatriots on the western side of the Atlantic in the battle that had cost him his freedom in the first place.

Henry requested that he and his mates be taken to a port where they might find a ship bound for England, but the pirate captain informed him that the matter would have to be voted on by the crew, who met, debated, and decided to allow only Henry to sail with them, because they did not want to share the "rich prize" they had apparently just taken with the newcomers (which was their established practice). They did, however, entertain and give abundant provisions to the men on the island. Two days later, on May 25, 1687, they sailed away, Henry feeling "not a little grieved at my departure."

They sailed north, between Puerto Rico and Hispaniola, where they captured a ketch sailing from New York to Providence in the Bahamas, a place that had recently been resettled after a Spanish attack. Seafaring people, many of them formerly pirates, had erected a "little commonwealth," which was "under the Protection of no Prince." They built a small fort, made and enacted their own laws, and selected an Independent, "a very sober man," as their governor. The pirates were warmly received and liked the place so much that they ran their ship aground and burnt her, "giving the guns to the inhabitants to fortify the island."[9]

In two weeks Henry continued on with the crew of the ketch for Carolina and eventually to New York. There he met someone he knew in Barbados (who "would not discover me") who relayed the stories of how the runaways had been pursued by their masters, how colonial authorities throughout the Caribbean had been alerted of the escape, how promises of severe punishment had been made should they ever be returned, how rumors ran wild about their adventures, and how, in the end, it was "concluded that we had perished in the sea." From New York, Henry recrossed the Atlantic to Amsterdam, from there to the Isle of Wight, from there to Southampton, and eventually to his family, who greeted him "as one risen from the dead." Henry's final words were praise to God for preserving him against "all dangers and times of trial." These last he wrote "From my lodging, at the sign of the Ship, in Paul's Churchyard, London. June the 10th, 1689."

Conclusion

In the end Henry Pitman was typical of countless other rebels who in the seventeenth and eighteenth centuries found themselves flung to the edges of the Atlantic in the aftermath of a failed rebellion. Whenever authorities repressed a riot by an urban mob, a strike by workers, a mutiny by soldiers or sailors, or a revolt by servants or slaves, they often hanged a few of the rebels and sent a larger number into a miniature diaspora—such was the experience of defeat. What was unusual in Henry's case is that by the time he returned to England, those who had exiled him, the government of James II, had themselves been overthrown in the "Glorious Revolution" of 1688, by which means Henry the "convict rebel" suddenly became a heroic martyr of Protestant resistance to the "Arbitrary Power" of the dreaded papists. This change of political power is precisely what made the publication of Henry's narrative possible.[10]

As we have seen, many kinds of knowledge—technical, natural, and social—were necessary to his escape. First among these was navigation, without which the eight men could never have imagined trying to escape by sea to a destination six hundred miles away. Henry gathered a compass, a quadrant, a chart, a half-hour glass, a half-minute glass, and log and line for getting bearings and plotting his course. Henry did not say where he learned navigation, but it was almost certainly during a stint in the Royal Navy, a common career choice for young physicians in his day. He was not the only Monmouth rebel with valuable maritime experience. Indeed we know from accounts of other escapes made by the Monmouth rebels that seafaring skill was central to the design. A planter named Jeaffreson of Nevis wrote that he and other plantation owners had trouble keeping their new bonded laborers "who could jump on the first ship they found, find work, and sail away." The knowledge of medicine and of carpentry (Whicker) also came in handy.[11]

Related to technical knowledge was a necessary multifaceted knowledge of nature, which of course navigation itself demanded—of winds, tides, latitude (accurate ways to plot longitude had not been developed), and geography. Some of this was a matter of formal education, some of it a matter of experience. Henry knew the wind patterns of the southern Caribbean, he knew the locations of the various islands. He knew political geography—where English, Dutch, and Spanish colonies were located—and he knew economic geography, the patterns of ships as they engaged in the salt trade, for example. Equally important was the knowledge of nature once he and his mates were marooned on the island of Margarita, and here it is doubtful that they would have survived if not for the pirates who shared with them the buccaneer's knowledge of marooning amid the Caribbean ecology, and if not for the Native American whose fishing skill fed them. These were the Calibans to Henry's Prospero, to use Shakespeare's example of how the lowly fed and sustained one of higher station.[12]

Neither the technical nor the natural knowledge would have been sufficient without corresponding social knowledge—how to cooperate, how to make alliances. From the beginning Henry knew that his escape would depend on a broad and various lot of people, but even he could not have known just what a big and motley crew they would be: the indebted woodcarver John Nuthall; his fellow political prisoners and transported felons; two enslaved Africans; three shiploads of pirates; a Florida Indian; fellow maroons; and numerous crews of sailors who carried him hither and yon. The "shipmates" with whom he originally came over to the island, with whom he had suffered a deadly "middle passage" (and no doubt because of it developed strong bonds), were especially important as the core members of the conspiracy, but all of the above played essential roles. The pirates, with their own hard-won wisdom about survival and traditions of self-organization, were particularly instrumental. The circulation of proletarian knowledge and experience, not to mention simple mutual aid, was perhaps the linchpin of Henry Pitman's successful escape.

In the end, Henry's bid for freedom required that he and his mates know how two modes of production actually, concretely worked. The first was the capitalist economy as it operated in the Caribbean and across the Atlantic—the workings of plantations and ships, colonies and imperial metropolis. The second was the commoning noncapitalist economy of the uninhabited islands of the Caribbean such as Margarita. He had to know the resources of the latter and be able to find the "necessaries of life" there, while he had to know the commodities, connections, and variety of workers of the former. The central lesson of Henry's case is this: no matter how the story may be told, his escape, like almost all others, was not only *not* individualistic, it was collective and in this instance triply so—collective in the planning and execution by a group; collective in its sharing of knowledge; and collective in its dependence on cooperation in the division of labor.[13]

This conclusion takes on additional meaning if we compare Henry with Robinson Crusoe, the protagonist in Daniel Defoe's famous novel a generation later that would inspire a new generation of maritime novelists. The parallels between the real character and the fictional one are numerous: both were middling types who were enslaved and managed to escape in small open boats; both were subsequently marooned, in similar kinds of places, in similar geographic locations; both had minions, Henry his Indian, Robinson his Friday; both returned home to embrace the nation. None of this is accidental, as British historian Tim Severin has recently and convincingly shown. Although the marooned Scottish sailor Alexander Selkirk may have been the inspiration for Robinson Crusoe, Henry Pitman was the actual prototype, the literal model for the modern individualist hero. But notice what Defoe did in the translation of Henry's story: he makes Crusoe the solitary, independent individual, shorn of all natural ties, living outside society, involved only with nature.[14]

Crusoe would in turn pass into the classical political economy of Adam Smith, David Ricardo, and others as *homo economicus*, the progenitor and epitome of bourgeois individualism for the eighteenth century and after. This was, of course, as Karl Marx pointed out, an illusion and a deception, both of which were necessary to the mythology of capitalism. And here we find an odd parallel, for like Crusoe, the runaway slave, the person who dared to escape the peculiar institution to freedom, has been treated in the historiography of slave resistance as the individualist, over and against the collectivist who rose in insurrection. The story of Henry Pitman shows that both judgments, about Crusoe and about the escapee, are fundamentally wrong.[15]

✦

FOUR

Under the Banner
of King Death

Pirates

Writing to the Board of Trade in 1724, Governor Alexander Spotswood of Virginia lamented his lack of "some safe opportunity to get home" to London. He insisted that he would travel only in a well-armed man-of-war.

> Your Lordships will easily conceive my Meaning when you reflect on the Vigorous part I've acted to suppress Pirates: and if those barbarous Wretches can be moved to cut off the Nose & Ears of a Master for but correcting his own Sailors, what inhuman treatment must I expect, should I fall within their power, who have been markt as the principle object of their vengeance, for cutting off their arch Pirate Thatch [Teach, also known as Blackbeard], with all his grand Designs, & making so many of their Fraternity to swing in the open air of Virginia.[1]

Spotswood knew these pirates well. He had authorized the expedition that returned to Virginia boasting Blackbeard's head as a trophy. He had done his share to see that many pirates swung on Virginia gallows. He knew that pirates had a fondness for revenge, that they often punished ship captains for "correcting" their crews, and that a kind of "fraternity" prevailed among them. He had good reason to fear them.

Between 1716 and 1726 Atlantic pirates created an imperial crisis with their relentless and successful attacks upon merchants' property and international commerce. Accordingly, these freebooters occupy a grand position in the long history of robbery at sea. Their numbers, near five thousand, were extraordinary, and their plunderings were exceptional in both volume and value.[2] This chapter explores the social and cultural dimensions of piracy, focusing on pirates' experience, the organization of their ships, and their social relations and consciousness. It concludes with observations on the social and economic context of the crime and its culture. Piracy represented "crime" on a massive scale. It was a way of life voluntarily chosen, for the most part, by large numbers of men who directly challenged the ways of the society from which they excepted themselves. How did piracy look from the inside and what kinds of social order did pirates forge beyond the reach of traditional authority? Beneath the Jolly Roger, "the banner of King Death," a new social world took shape once pirates had, as one of them put it, "the choice in themselves." It was a world profoundly shaped and textured by the experiences of work, wages, culture, and authority accumulated in the normal, rugged course of maritime life and labor in the early eighteenth century.[3]

Contemporary estimates of the pirate population during the period under consideration placed the number between 1,000 and 2,000 at any one time. From records that describe the activities of pirate ships and from reports or projections of crew sizes, it appears that 1,800 to 2,400 Atlantic pirates prowled the seas between 1716 and 1718; 1,500 to 2,000 between 1719 and 1722; and 1,000 to 1,500, declining to fewer than 200, between 1723 and 1726. In the only estimate we have from the other side of the law, a band of pirates in 1716 claimed that "30 Company of them," or roughly 2,400 men, plied the oceans of the globe. In all, some 4,500 to 5,500 men went, as they called it, "upon the account." The pirates' chief military enemy, the British Royal Navy, employed an average of only 13,000 men in any given year between 1716 and 1726.[4]

These sea robbers followed lucrative trade and, like their predecessors, sought bases for their depredations in the Caribbean Sea and the Indian Ocean. The Bahama Islands, undefended and ungoverned by the crown, began in 1716 to attract pirates by the hundreds. By 1718 a torrent of complaints had moved George I to commission Woodes Rogers to lead an expedition to bring the islands under control. Rogers's efforts largely succeeded, and pirates scattered to the unpeopled inlets of the Carolinas and to Africa. They had frequented African shores as early as 1691; by 1718, Madagascar served as both an entrepôt for booty and a spot for temporary settlement. At the mouth of the Sierra Leone River on Africa's western coast, pirates stopped off for "whoring and drinking" and to unload goods. Theaters of operation among pirates shifted, however, according to the policing designs of the Royal Navy. Pirates favored the Caribbean's small, unsettled cays and shallow waters, which proved hard to negotiate for men-of-war in chase. But generally, as one pirate noted, these rovers were "dispers't into several parts of the World." Sea robbers sought and usually found bases near major trade routes, as distant as possible from the powers of the state.[5]

Backgrounds

Almost all pirates had labored as merchant seamen, Royal Navy sailors, or privateersmen. The vast majority came from captured merchantmen as volunteers, for reasons suggested by Dr. Samuel Johnson's observation that "no man will be a sailor who has contrivance enough to get himself into a jail; for being in a ship is being in jail with the chance of being drowned. . . . A man in jail has more room, better food, and commonly better company."[6] Dr. Johnson's class condescension aside, he had a point. Incarceration on a ship did not differ essentially from incarceration in a jail. Merchant seamen had an extremely difficult lot in the early eighteenth century. They got a hard, close look at death. Disease and accidents were commonplace in their occupation, natural disasters threatened incessantly, rations were often meager, and discipline was brutal, even murderous on occasion. Peacetime wages were low, fraud and irregularities in the distribution of pay general. A prime purpose of eighteenth-century maritime laws was "to assure a ready supply of cheap, docile labor." Merchant seamen also had to contend with impressment by the Royal Navy.[7]

Some pirates had served in the navy, where conditions aboard ship were no less harsh. Food supplies often ran short, wages were low, mortality was high, discipline severe, and desertion consequently chronic. As one officer reported, the navy had trouble fighting pirates because the king's ships were "so much disabled by sickness, death, and desertion of their seamen."[8] In 1722 the crown sent the *Weymouth* and the *Swallow* in search of a pirate convoy. Royal surgeon John Atkins, noting that merchant seamen were frequently pressed, underlined precisely what these sailors had to fear when he recorded that the "*Weymouth*, who brought out of *England* a Compliment [*sic*] of 240 Men," had "at the end of the Voyage 280 dead upon her Books." The same point was made by the captain of a man-of-war sent to Jamaica to guard against pirates in 1720–21. He faithfully recorded the names of the thirty-five seamen who died during the year of duty.[9] Epidemics, consumption, and scurvy raged on royal ships, and the men were "caught in a machine from which there was no escape, bar desertion, incapacitation, or death."[10] Or piracy.

Pirates who had served on privateering vessels knew well that such employment was far less onerous than on merchant or naval ships. Food was usually more plentiful, the pay considerably higher, and the work shifts generally shorter.[11] Even so, owing to rigid discipline and other grievances, mutinies were not uncommon. On Woodes Rogers's spectacularly successful privateering expedition of 1708–11, Peter Clark was thrown into irons for wishing himself "aboard a Pirate" and saying that "he should be glad that an Enemy, who could overpower us, was a-long-side of us."[12]

Most men became pirates when their merchant vessels were taken. Colonel Benjamin Bennet wrote to the Council of Trade and Plantations in 1718, setting forth his worries about freebooters in the West Indies: "I fear they will soon multiply for so many are willing to joyn with them when taken." The seizure of a merchant ship was followed by a moment of great confrontational drama. The pirate captain or quartermaster asked the seamen of the captured vessel who among them would serve under black colors, and frequently several stepped forward. Many fewer pirates originated as mutineers who had boldly and collectively seized control of a merchant vessel. But regardless of their methods, pirates necessarily came from seafaring employments, whether the merchant service, the navy, or privateering. Piracy emphatically was not an option open to landlubbers, since sea robbers "entertain'd so contemptible a Notion of Landmen."[13] Men who became pirates were grimly familiar with the rigors of life at sea and with a single-sex community of work.

Ages are known for 169 pirates active between 1716 and 1726. The range was 14 to 50 years, the mean 28.2, and the median 27; the 20–24 and 25–29 age categories had the highest concentrations, with 57 and 39 men, respectively. Almost three in five pirates were in their twenties. Compared with merchant seamen more broadly in the first half of the eighteenth century, there were fewer teenagers and more men in their thirties among the pirates, but not many. The age distribution among the outlaws was similar to that of the larger community of labor, suggesting that piracy held roughly equal attraction for sailors of all ages.[14] Though evidence is sketchy, most pirates seem not to have been bound to land and home by familial ties or obligations. Wives and children were rarely mentioned in the records of trials of pirates, and pirate vessels, to forestall desertion, often would "take no Married Man."[15] Almost without exception, pirates, like the larger body of seafaring men, came from the lower class of humanity. They were, as a royal official condescendingly observed, "desperate Rogues" who could have little hope in life ashore.[16] These traits served as bases of unity when men of the sea decided, in search of something better, to become pirates.

Shipboard Order Remade

These characteristics had a vital bearing on the ways pirates organized their daily activities. Contemporaries who claimed that pirates had "no regular command among them" mistook a different social order— different from the ordering of merchant, naval, and privateering vessels—for disorder.[17] This social order, articulated in the organization of the pirate ship, was conceived and deliberately constructed by the pirates themselves. Its hallmark was a rough, improvised, but effective egalitarianism that placed authority in the collective hands of the crew. A core value in the broader culture of the common tar, egalitarianism was institutionalized aboard the pirate ship.

A striking uniformity of rules and customs prevailed aboard pirate ships, each of which functioned under the terms of written articles, a compact drawn up at the beginning of a voyage or upon election of a new captain and agreed to by the crew. By these articles crews allocated authority, distributed plunder, and enforced discipline.[18] These arrangements made the captain the creature of his crew. Demanding someone both bold of temper and skilled in navigation, the men elected their captain. They gave him few privileges. He "or any other Officer is allowed no more [food] than another man, nay, the Captain cannot keep his Cabbin to himself."[19] Some pirates "messed with the Captain, but withal no Body look'd on it, as a Mark of Favour, or Distinction, for every one came and eat and drank with him at their Humour." A merchant captain held captive by pirates noted with displeasure that crew members slept on the ship wherever they pleased, "the Captain himself not being allowed a Bed."[20] The determined reorganization of space and privilege aboard the ship was crucial to the remaking of maritime social relations.

The crew granted the captain unquestioned authority "in fighting, chasing, or being chased," but "in all other Matters whatsoever" he was "governed by a Majority."[21] As the majority elected, so did it depose. Captains were snatched from their positions for cowardice, cruelty, or refusing "to take and plunder English Vessels."[22] One captain incurred the class-conscious wrath of his crew for being too "gentleman-like."[23] Occasionally, a despotic captain was summarily executed. As pirate Francis Kennedy explained, most sea robbers, "having suffered formerly from the ill-treatment of their officers, provided carefully against any such evil" once they arranged their own command. The democratic selection of officers echoed similar demands within the New Model Army in the English Revolution and stood in stark, telling contrast to the near-dictatorial arrangement of command in the merchant service and the Royal Navy.[24]

To prevent the misuse of authority, pirates delegated countervailing powers to the quartermaster, who was elected to represent and protect "the Interest of the Crew."[25] The quartermaster, who was not considered an officer in the merchant service, was elevated to a valued position of trust and authority. His tasks were to adjudicate minor disputes, to distribute food and money, and in some instances to lead the attacks on prize vessels. He served as a "civil Magistrate" and dispensed necessaries "with an Equality to them all," carefully guarding against the galling and divisive use of privilege and preferment that characterized the distribution of the necessaries of life in other maritime occupations.[26] The quartermaster often became the captain of a captured ship when the captor was overcrowded or divided by discord. This containment of authority within a dual and representative executive was a distinctive feature of social organization among pirates.[27]

The decisions that had the greatest bearing on the welfare of the crew were generally reserved to the council, the highest authority on the pirate ship. Pirates drew upon an ancient custom, largely lapsed by the early modern era, in which the master consulted his entire crew in making crucial decisions. Freebooters also knew of the naval tradition, the council of war, in which the top officers in a ship or fleet met to plan strategy. But pirates democratized the naval custom. Their councils called together every man on the ship to determine such matters as where the best prizes could be taken and how disruptive dissension was to be resolved. Some crews continually used the council, "carrying every thing by a majority of votes"; others set up the council as a court. The decisions made by this body were sacrosanct, and even the boldest captain dared not challenge a council's mandate.[28]

The distribution of plunder was regulated explicitly by the ship's articles, which allocated booty according to skills and duties. Pirates used the precapitalist share system to allocate their take. Captain and quartermaster received between one and a half and two shares; gunners, boatswains, mates, carpenters, and doctors, one and one-quarter or one and one-half; all others got one share each.[29] This pay system represented a radical departure from practices in the merchant service, Royal Navy, or privateering. It leveled an elaborate hierarchy of pay ranks and decisively reduced the disparity between the top and bottom of the scale. Indeed, this must have been one of the most egalitarian plans for the disposition of resources to be found anywhere in the early eighteenth century. The scheme revealingly indicates that pirates did not consider themselves wage laborers but rather risk-sharing partners. If, as a noted historian of piracy, Philip Gosse, suggested, "the pick of all seamen were pirates,"[30] the equitable distribution of plunder and the conception of the partnership were the work of men who valued and respected the skills of their comrades. But not all booty was dispensed this way. A portion went into a "common fund" to provide for the men who sustained injury of lasting effect.[31] The loss of eyesight or any appendage merited compensation. By this welfare system pirates attempted to guard against debilities caused by accidents, to protect skills, to enhance recruitment, and to promote loyalty within the group.

The articles also regulated discipline aboard ship, though "discipline" is perhaps a misnomer for a system of rules that left large ranges of behavior uncontrolled. Less arbitrary than that of the merchant service and less codified than that of the navy, discipline among pirates always depended on a collective sense of transgression. Many misdeeds were accorded "what Punishment the Captain and Majority of the Company shall think fit," and it is noteworthy that pirates did not often resort to the whip. Their discipline, if no less severe in certain cases, was generally tolerant of behavior that provoked punishment in other maritime occupations. Three major methods of discipline were employed, all conditioned by the fact that pirate ships were crowded; an average crew numbered near eighty on a 250-ton vessel. The articles of Bartholomew Roberts's ship revealed one tactic for maintaining order: "No striking one another on board, but every Man's Quarrels to be ended on Shore at Sword and Pistol." The antagonists were to fight a duel with pistols, but if both missed their first shots (which, given the state of pistol manufacture in their day, they probably did), they then seized swords, and the first to draw blood was declared the victor. By taking such conflicts off the ship (and symbolically off the sea), this practice promoted harmony in the crowded quarters below decks.[32] The ideal of harmony was also reflected when pirates made a crew member the "Governor of an Island." Men who were incorrigibly disruptive or who transgressed important rules were marooned. For defrauding his mates by taking more than a proper share of plunder, for deserting or malingering during battle, for keeping secrets from the crew, or for stealing, a pirate risked being deposited "where he was sure to encounter Hardships."[33] The ultimate method of maintaining order was execution. This penalty was stipulated (although apparently never enforced) for bringing on board "a Boy or a Woman" or for meddling with a "prudent Woman" on a prize ship, but was invoked to punish a captain who abused his authority.[34]

Some crews attempted to circumvent disciplinary problems by taking "no Body against their Wills."[35] By the same logic, they would keep no unwilling person. The confession of pirate Edward Davis in 1718 indicates that oaths of honor were used to cement the loyalty of new members: "at first the old Pirates were a little shy of the new ones, . . . yet in a short time the *New Men* being sworn to be faithful, and not to cheat the Company to the Value of a *Piece of Eight,* they all consulted and acted together with great unanimity, and no distinction was made between *Old* and *New.*"[36] Yet for all their efforts to blunt the cutting edge of authority and to maintain harmony and cohesion, conflict could not always be contained. Occasionally upon election of a new captain, men who favored other leadership drew up new articles and sailed away from their former mates.[37] The social organization constructed by pirates, although flexible, was unable to accommodate severe, sustained conflict. Those who had experienced the claustrophobic and authoritarian world of the merchant ship cherished the freedom to separate. The egalitarian and collective exercise of authority by pirates had both negative and positive effects. Although it produced a chronic instability, it also guaranteed continuity. The very process by which new crews were established helped to ensure a social uniformity and, as we shall see, a consciousness of kind among pirates.[38]

One important mechanism in this continuity can be seen by charting the connections among pirate crews. The accompanying diagram of connections among Atlantic pirate crews, arranged according to vessel captaincy, demonstrates that by splintering, by sailing in consorts, or by other associations, roughly 3,600 pirates—more than 70 percent of all those active between 1716 and 1726—fit into two main lines of genealogical descent. Captain Benjamin Hornigold and the pirate rendezvous in the Bahamas stood at the origin of an intricate lineage that ended with the hanging of John Phillips's crew in June 1724. The second line, spawned in the chance meeting of the lately mutinous crews of George Lowther and Edward Low in 1722, culminated in the executions of William Fly and his men in July 1726. It was primarily within and through this network that the social organization of the pirate ship took on its significance, transmitting and preserving customs and meanings and helping to structure and perpetuate the pirates' social world.[39]

Justice

Pirates constructed that world in defiant contradistinction to the ways of the world they left behind, in particular to its salient figures of power, the merchant captain and the royal official, and to the system of authority those figures represented and enforced. When eight pirates were tried in Boston in 1718, merchant captain Thomas Checkley told of the capture of his ship by pirates who "pretended," he said, "to be Robbin Hoods Men."[40] Eric Hobsbawm has defined social banditry as a "universal and virtually unchanging phenomenon," an "endemic peasant protest against oppression and poverty: a cry for vengeance on the rich and the oppressors." Its goal is "a traditional world in which men are justly dealt with, not a new and perfect world"; Hobsbawm calls its advocates "revolutionary traditionalists."[41] Pirates, of course, were not peasants, but they fit Hobsbawm's formulation in every other respect. Of special importance was their "cry for vengeance."

Spotswood told no more than the simple truth when he expressed his fear of pirate vengeance, for the very names of pirate ships made the same threat. Edward Teach, whom Spotswood's men cut off,

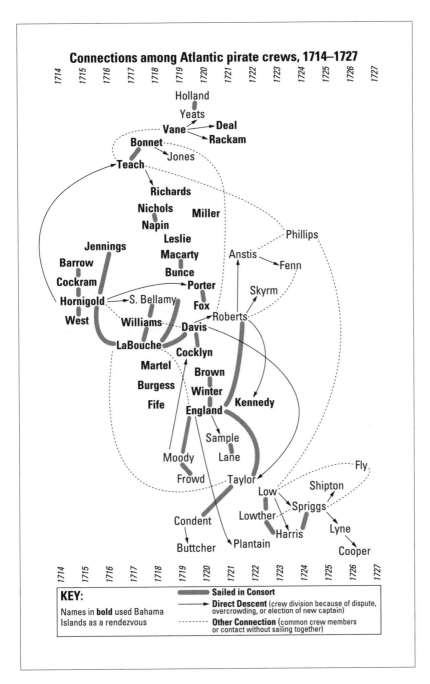

Connections among Atlantic pirate crews, 1714–1727

1714 1715 1716 1717 1718 1719 1720 1721 1722 1723 1724 1725 1726 1727

Holland
Yeats
Vane → Deal
Bonnet → Rackam
Jones
Teach

Richards
Nichols   Miller
Napin
Leslie   Phillips
Jennings   Macarty   Anstis
Barrow   Bunce   → Fenn
Cockram   → Porter
                        Skyrm
Hornigold → S. Bellamy   Fox
West   Williams → Davis → Roberts
           LaBouche   Cocklyn
           Martel   Brown
           Burgess   Winter
           Fife   England   Kennedy

Sample
Moody   Lane
Frowd   Taylor   Fly
                        Low   Shipton
                        Lowther → Spriggs
Condent   Harris   Lyne
Buttcher   Plantain   Cooper

KEY:

Names in **bold** used Bahama
Islands as a rendezvous

▬▬▬ **Sailed in Consort**

→ **Direct Descent** (crew division because of dispute, overcrowding, or election of new captain)

------- **Other Connection** (common crew members or contact without sailing together) called his vessel *Queen Anne's Revenge*; other notorious craft were Stede Bonnet's *Revenge* and John Cole's *New York Revenge's Revenge*.[42] The foremost target of vengeance was the merchant captain. Frequently, "in a far distant latitude," as one seaman put it, "unlimited power, bad views, ill nature and ill principles all concur[red]" in a ship's commander. Here was a man "past all restraint" who often made life miserable for his crew.[43] Spotswood also noted how pirates avenged the captain's "correcting" of his sailors. In 1722, merchant captains Isham Randolph, Constantine Cane, and William Halladay petitioned Spotswood "in behalf of themselves and other Masters of Ships" for "some certain method . . . for punishing mutinous & disobedient Seamen." They explained that captains faced great danger "in case of meeting with Pyrates, where we are sure to suffer all the tortures w[hi]ch such an abandoned crew can invent, upon the least intimation of our Striking any of our men."[44] Pirates acted the part of a floating mob with its own distinctive sense of popular justice.

Upon seizing a merchantman, pirates often administered the "Distribution of Justice," "enquiring into the Manner of the Commander's Behaviour to their Men, and those, against whom Complaint was made" were "whipp'd and pickled."[45] Bartholomew Roberts's crew considered such inquiry so important that they formally designated one of their men, George Willson, as the "Dispencer of Justice." In 1724 merchant captain Richard Hawkins described another form of retribution, a torture known as the "Sweat": "Between decks they stick Candles round the Mizen-Mast, and about twenty-five men surround it with Points of Swords, Penknives, Compasses, Forks &c in each of their hands: *Culprit* enters the Circle; the Violin plays a merry Jig; and he must run for about ten Minutes, while each man runs his Instrument into his Posteriors."[46] Many captured captains were "barbarously used," and some were summarily executed. Pirate Philip Lyne carried this vengeance to its bloodiest extremity, confessing when apprehended in 1726 that "during the time of his Piracy" he "had killed 37 Masters of Vessels."[47] The search for vengeance was in many ways a fierce, embittered response to the violent, personal, and arbitrary authority wielded by the merchant captain.

Still, the punishment of captains was not indiscriminate, for a captain who had been "an honest Fellow that never abused any Sailors" was often rewarded by pirates.[48] The best description of pirates' notions of justice comes from merchant captain William Snelgrave's account of his capture in 1719. On April 1, Snelgrave's ship was seized by Thomas Cocklyn's crew of rovers at the mouth of the Sierra Leone River. Cocklyn was soon joined by men captained by Oliver LaBouche and Howell Davis, and Snelgrave spent the next thirty days among 240 pirates.[49]

The capture was effected when twelve pirates in a small boat came alongside Snelgrave's ship, which was manned by forty-five sailors. Snelgrave ordered his crew to arms. They refused, but the pirate quartermaster, infuriated by the command, drew a pistol and then, Snelgrave testified, "with the but-end [he] endeavoured to beat out my Brains" until "some of my People . . . cried out aloud 'For God sake don't kill our Captain, for we never were with a better Man.'" The quartermaster, Snelgrave noted, "told me, 'my Life was safe provided none of my People complained against me.' I replied, 'I was sure none of them could.'"[50]

Snelgrave was taken to Cocklyn, who told him, "I am sorry you have met with bad usage after Quarter given, but 'tis the Fortune of War sometimes. . . . If you tell the truth, and your Men make no Complaints against you, you shall be kindly used." Howell Davis, commander of the largest of the pirate ships, reprimanded Cocklyn's men for their roughness and, by Snelgrave's account, expressed himself "ashamed to hear how I had been used by them. That they should remember their reasons for going a pirating were to revenge themselves on base Merchants and cruel commanders of Ships. . . . No one of my People, even those that had entered with them gave me the least ill-character. . . . It was plain they loved me."[51]

Snelgrave's men may not have loved him, but they surely did respect him. Indeed, Snelgrave's character proved so respectable that the pirates proposed to give him a captured ship with full cargo and to sell the goods for him. Then they would capture a Portuguese slaver, sell the slaves, and give the proceeds to Snelgrave so that he could "return with a large sum of Money to London, and bid the Merchants defiance."[52] Pirates hoped to show these merchants that good fortunes befell good captains. The proposal was "unanimously approved" by the pirates, but fearing a charge of complicity, Snelgrave hesitated to accept it. Davis then interceded, saying that he favored "allowing every Body to go to the Devil in their own way" and that he knew Snelgrave feared for "his Reputation." The refusal was graciously accepted, Snelgrave claiming that "the Tide being turned, they were as kind to me, as they had been at first severe."[53]

Snelgrave related another revealing episode. While he remained in pirate hands, a decrepit schooner belonging to the Royal African Company sailed into the Sierra Leone and was taken by his captors. Simon Jones, a member of Cocklyn's crew, urged his mates to burn the ship, since he had been poorly treated while in the company's employ. The pirates were about to do so when another of them, James Stubbs, protested that such action would only "serve the Company's interests," since the ship was worth but little. He also pointed out that "the poor People that now belong to her, and have been on so long a voyage, will lose their Wages, which I am sure is Three times the Value of the Vessel." The pirates concurred and returned the ship to its crew, who "came safe home to England in it." Captain Snelgrave also returned to England soon after this incident, but eleven of his seamen remained behind as pirates.[54] Snelgrave's experience revealed how pirates attempted to intervene against—and modify—the standard brutalities that marked the social relations of production in merchant shipping. That they sometimes chose to do so with brutalities of their own shows how they could not escape the system of which they were a part.

Snelgrave seems to have been an exceptionally decent captain. Pirates like Howell Davis claimed that abusive treatment by masters of merchantmen contributed mightily to their willingness to become sea robbers. John Archer, whose unusually long career as a pirate dated from 1718, when he sailed with Edward Teach, uttered a final protest before his execution in 1724: "I could wish that Masters of

Vessels would not use their Men with so much Severity, as many of them do, which exposes us to great Temptations."[55] William Fly, facing the gallows for murder and piracy in 1726, angrily announced, "I can't charge myself,—I shan't own myself Guilty of any Murder,— Our Captain and his Mate used us Barbarously. We poor Men can't have Justice done us. There is nothing said to our Commanders, let them never so much abuse us, and use us like Dogs."[56] To pirates revenge was justice; punishment was meted out to barbarous captains, as befitted the captains' crimes.

Terror

Sea robbers who fell into the hands of the state received the full force of penalties for crimes against property. The official view of piracy as crime was outlined in 1718 by Vice-Admiralty judge Nicholas Trott in his charge to the jury in the trial of Stede Bonnet and thirty-three members of his crew at Charleston, South Carolina. Declaring that "the Sea was given by God for the use of Men, and is subject to Dominion and Property, as well as the Land," Trott observed of the accused that "the Law of Nations never granted to them a Power to change the Right of Property." Pirates on trial were denied benefit of clergy, were "called *Hostis Humani Generis*, with whom neither Faith nor Oath" were to be kept, and were regarded as *"Brutes,* and *Beasts of Prey."* Turning from the jury to the accused, Trott circumspectly surmised that "no further Good or Benefit can be expected from you but by the Example of your Deaths."[57]

The insistence on obtaining this final benefit locked royal officials and pirates into a system of reciprocal terror. As royal authorities offered bounties for captured pirates, so too did pirates "offer any price" for certain officials.[58] In Virginia in 1720, one of six pirates facing the gallows "called for a Bottle of Wine, and taking a Glass of it, he Drank Damnation to the Governour and Confusion to the Colony, which the rest pledged." Not to be outdone, Governor Spotswood thought it "necessary for the greater Terrour to hang up four of them in Chains."[59] Pirates demonstrated an antinomian disdain for state authority when George I extended general pardons for piracy in 1717 and 1718. Some accepted the grace but refused to reform; others "seem'd to slight it," and the most defiant "used the King's Proclamation with great contempt, and tore it into pieces."[60] One pirate crew downed its punch, proclaiming, "Curse the King and all the Higher Powers."[61] The social relations of piracy were marked by vigorous, often violent, antipathy toward traditional authority. The pervasive antiauthoritarianism of the culture of the common seafarer found many expressions beneath the Jolly Roger.

Community

At the Charleston trial over which Trott presided, Richard Allen, attorney general of South Carolina, told the jury that "pirates prey upon all Mankind, their own Species and Fellow-Creatures without Distinction of Nations or Religions."[62] Allen was right in claiming that pirates did not respect nationality in their plunders, but he was wrong in claiming that they did not respect their "Fellow-Creatures." Pirates did not prey on one another. Rather, they consistently expressed in numerous and subtle ways a highly developed consciousness of kind. Here we turn from the external social relations of piracy to the internal in order to examine this consciousness of kind—in a sense, a strategy for survival—and the collectivistic ethos it expressed.

Pirates showed a recurrent willingness to join forces at sea and in port. In April 1719, when Howell Davis and crew sailed into the Sierra Leone River, the pirates captained by Thomas Cocklyn were wary until they saw on the approaching ship "her Black Flag"; then "immediately they were easy in their minds, and a little time after," the crews "saluted one another with their Cannon." Other crews exchanged similar greetings and, like Davis and Cocklyn, who combined their powers, frequently invoked an unwritten code of hospitality to forge spontaneous alliances.[63]

This communitarian urge was perhaps most evident in the pirate strongholds of Madagascar and Sierra Leone. Sea robbers occasionally chose more sedentary lifeways on various thinly populated islands, and they contributed a notorious number of men to the community of logwood cutters at the Bay of Campeche in the Gulf of Mexico. In 1718 a royal official complained of a "nest of pirates" in the Bahamas "who already esteem themselves a community, and to have one common interest."[64]

To perpetuate such community, it was necessary to minimize conflict not only on each ship but also among separate bands of pirates. Indeed, one of the strongest indicators of consciousness of kind is the manifest absence of discord between different pirate crews. To some extent, this was even a transnational matter: French, Dutch, Spanish, and Anglo-American pirates usually cooperated peaceably, only occasionally exchanging fire. Pirate crews consistently refused to attack one another.[65]

In no way was the pirate sense of fraternity, which Spotswood and others noted, more forcefully expressed than in the threats and acts of revenge taken by pirates. Theirs was truly a case of hanging together or being hanged separately. In April 1717, the pirate ship *Whidah* was wrecked near Boston. Most of its crew perished; the survivors were jailed. In July, Thomas Fox, a Boston ship captain, was taken by pirates who "Questioned him whether anything was done to the Pyrates in Boston Goall," promising "that if the Prisoners Suffered they would Kill every Body they took belonging to New England."[66] Shortly after this incident, Teach's sea rovers captured a merchant vessel and, "because she belonged to Boston, [Teach] alledging the People of Boston had hanged some of the Pirates, so burnt her." Teach declared that all Boston ships deserved a similar fate.[67] Charles Vane, reputedly a most fearsome pirate, "would give no quarter to the Bermudians" and punished them and "cut away their masts upon account of one Thomas Brown who was (some time) detain'd in these Islands upon suspicion of piracy." Brown apparently planned to sail as Vane's consort until foiled by his capture.[68]

In September 1720, pirates captained by Bartholomew Roberts "openly and in the daytime burnt and destroyed . . . vessels in the Road of Basseterre [St. Kitts] and had the audaciousness to insult H.M. Fort," avenging the execution of "their comrades at Nevis." Roberts then sent word to the governor that "they would Come and Burn the

Town [Sandy Point] about his Ears for hanging the Pyrates there."[69] In 1721 Spotswood relayed information to the Council of Trade and Plantations that Roberts "said he expected to be joined by another ship and would then visit Virginia, and avenge the pirates who have been executed here."[70] The credibility of the threat was confirmed by the unanimous resolution of the Virginia Executive Council that "the Country be put into an immediate posture of Defense." Lookouts and beacons were quickly provided and communications with neighboring colonies effected. "Near 60 Cannon," Spotswood later reported, were "mounted on sundry Substantial Batteries."[71]

In 1723 pirate captain Francis Spriggs vowed to find a Captain Moore "and put him to death for being the cause of the death of [pirate] Lowther," and, shortly after, similarly pledged to go "in quest of Captain Solgard," who had overpowered a pirate ship commanded by Charles Harris.[72] In January 1724, Lieutenant Governor Charles Hope of Bermuda wrote to the Board of Trade that he found it difficult to procure trial evidence against pirates because residents "feared that this very execution wou'd make our vessels fare the worse for it, when they happen'd to fall into pirate hands."[73] The threats of revenge were sometimes effective.

Pirates also affirmed their unity symbolically. Some evidence indicates that sea robbers may have had a sense of belonging to a separate, in some manner exclusive, speech community. Philip Ashton, who spent sixteen months among pirates in 1722–23 noted that "according to the Pirates usual Custom, and *in their proper Dialect*, asked me, If I would sign their Articles."[74] Many sources suggest that cursing, swearing, and blaspheming were defining traits of this style of speech, perhaps to an even greater extent than among the larger population of seafaring men. For example, near the Sierra Leone River, a British official named Plunkett pretended to cooperate with, but then attacked, the pirates with Bartholomew Roberts. Plunkett was captured, and Roberts

> upon the first sight of Plunkett swore at him like any Devil, for his Irish Impudence in daring to resist him. Old Plunkett, finding he had got into bad Company, fell a swearing and cursing as fast or

faster than Roberts; which made the rest of the Pirates laugh heartily, desiring Roberts to sit down and hold his Peace, for he had no Share in the Pallaver with Plunkett at all. So that by meer Dint of Cursing and Damning, Old Plunkett . . . sav'd his life.[75]

The symbolic connectedness, or consciousness of kind, extended to the domain of language.

The Black Flag

Certainly the best-known symbol of piracy is the flag, the Jolly Roger. Less known and appreciated is the fact that the flag was very widely used. No fewer, and probably a great many more, than 2,500 men sailed under it.[76] So general an adoption indicates an advanced state of group identification. The Jolly Roger was described as a "black Ensign, in the Middle of which is a large white Skeleton with a Dart in one hand striking a bleeding Heart, and in the other an Hour Glass."[77] Although there was considerable variation in particulars among these flags, there was also a general uniformity of chosen images. The flag's background was black, adorned with white representational figures.

Captain Jacob Bevan drew these skulls and crossbones in his ship's log to indicate the death of two of his seamen. On February 22, 1686, Bevan noted that a storm "kild 2 of our men out Right and broke our 3d Mat[e]s arme, our mans thigh and 5 more men brused." The symbol of the death's head was appropriated by pirates and used to emblazon the Jolly Roger, the notorious pirate flag. (British Library)

The most common symbol was the human skull, or "death's head," sometimes isolated but more frequently the most prominent feature of an entire skeleton. Other recurring items were a weapon—cutlass, sword, or dart—and an hourglass.[78]

The flag was intended to terrify the pirates' prey, but its triad of interlocking symbols—death, violence, limited time—simultaneously pointed to meaningful parts of the seaman's experience and eloquently bespoke the pirates' own consciousness of themselves as preyed upon in turn. Pirates seized the symbol of mortality from ship captains who used the skull "as a marginal sign in their logs to indicate the record of a death."[79] Seamen who became pirates escaped from one closed system only to find themselves encased in another. But as pirates—and, some believed, only as pirates—these men were able to fight back beneath the somber colors of "King Death" against those captains, merchants, and officials who waved banners of authority.[80] Moreover, pirates self-righteously perceived their situation and the excesses of these powerful figures through a collectivistic ethos that had been forged in the struggle for survival.

The self-righteousness of pirates was strongly linked to a world—traditional, mythical, or Utopian—"in which men are justly dealt with," as described by Hobsbawm.[81] It found expression in their social rules, their egalitarian social organization, and their notions of revenge and justice. By walking "to the Gallows without a Tear," by calling themselves "Honest Men" and "Gentlemen," and by speaking self-servingly but proudly of their "Conscience" and "Honor," pirates flaunted their certitude.[82] When, in 1720, ruling groups concluded that "nothing but force will subdue them," many pirates responded by intensifying their commitment.[83] Edward Low's crew in 1724 swore "with the most direful Imprecations, that if ever they should find themselves overpower'd they would immediately blow their ship up rather than suffer themselves to be hang'd like Dogs." These sea robbers would not "do Jolly Roger the Disgrace to be struck."[84]

The consciousness of kind among pirates manifested itself in an elaborate social code. Through rule, custom, and symbol, the code prescribed specific behavioral standards intended to preserve the social world that pirates had creatively built for themselves. As the examples of revenge reveal, royal officials recognized the threat of the pirates' alternative order. Some authorities feared that pirates might "set up a sort of Commonwealth"[85]—and they were precisely correct in their designation—in uninhabited regions, since "no Power in those Parts of the World could have been able to dispute it with them."[86] But the consciousness of kind never took national shape, and piracy was soon suppressed.

The End of Piracy

Contemporary observers usually attributed the rise of piracy to the demobilization of the Royal Navy at the end of the War of the Spanish Succession. A group of Virginia merchants, for instance, wrote to the Admiralty in 1713, setting forth "the apprehensions they have of Pyrates molesting their trade in the time of Peace."[87] The navy plunged from 49,860 men at the end of the war to 13,475 just two years later, and only by 1740 did it increase to as many as 30,000 again.[88] At the same time, the expiration of privateering licenses—bills of marque—added to the number of seamen on the loose and looking for work in the port cities of the empire. Such underemployment contributed significantly to the rise of piracy,[89] but it is not a sufficient explanation, since, as already noted, the vast majority of those who became pirates were working in the merchant service at the moment of their joining.

The surplus of labor at the end of the war had extensive, sometimes jarring social and economic effects. It produced an immediate contraction of wages; merchant seamen who made 45–55 shillings per month in 1707 made only half that amount in 1713. It provoked greater competition for seafaring jobs, which favored the hiring of older, more experienced seamen. And over time, it affected the social conditions and relations of life at sea, cutting back material benefits and hardening discipline.[90] War years, despite their deadly dangers, provided seafarers with tangible benefits. Atlantic seamen of 1713 had performed wartime labor for twenty of the previous twenty-five years and for eleven years consecutively.

Conditions did not worsen immediately after the war. As Ralph Davis explained, "the years 1713–1715 saw—as did immediate post-war years throughout the eighteenth century—the shifting of heaped-up surpluses of colonial goods, the movement of great quantities of English goods to colonial and other markets, and a general filling in of stocks of imported goods which had been allowed to run down."[91] This small-scale boom gave employment to some of the seamen who had been dropped from naval rolls. But by late 1715 a slump in trade began, to last into the 1730s. All of these difficulties were exacerbated by the intensification of maritime discipline over the course of the eighteenth century.[92] Many seamen knew that things had once been different and, for many, decisively better.

By 1726, the menace of piracy had been effectively suppressed by governmental action. Circumstantial factors such as the remobilization of the Royal Navy cannot account fully for its demise. The number of men in the navy increased from 6,298 in 1725 to 16,872 in 1726 and again to 20,697 in 1727, which had some bearing on the declining number of sea robbers. Yet some 20,000 sailors had been in the navy in 1719 and 1720, years when pirates were numerous.[93] In addition, seafaring wages only occasionally rose above 30 shillings per month between 1713 and the mid-1730s.[94] The conditions of life at sea did not change appreciably until war broke out in 1739.

The pardons offered to pirates in 1717 and 1718 failed to rid the sea of robbers. Since the graces specified that only crimes committed at certain times and in particular regions would be forgiven, many pirates saw enormous latitude for official trickery and refused to surrender. Moreover, accepting and abiding by the rules of the pardon would have meant for most men a return to the dismal conditions they had escaped. Their tactic failing, royal officials intensified the naval campaign against piracy—with great and gruesome effect. Corpses dangled in chains in British ports around the world "as a Spectacle for the Warning of others."[95] No fewer than 418, and probably between 500 and 600 Atlantic pirates were executed between 1716 and 1726 (see "The Hanging of Stede Bonnet"). The state also passed harsh legislation that criminalized all contact with pirates.

The hanging of pirate captain Stede Bonnet in Charleston, South Carolina, in 1719. Seamen looked on from the crow's nests of ships at anchor in Charleston's harbor. (London, 1724)

After 1721 anyone who "truck[ed], barter[ed], exchange[d]" with pirates, furnished them with stores, or even consulted with them might be punished with death.[96]

The campaign to cleanse the seas was supported by clergymen, royal officials, and publicists who sought through sermons, proclamations, pamphlets, and the newspaper press to create an image of the pirate that would legitimate his extermination. Piracy had always depended in some measure on the rumors and tales of its successes, especially among seamen and dealers in stolen cargo. After the capture and mass hanging of the crew of Black Bart Roberts in 1722 and another spate of executions and burst of propaganda in 1723–1724, the pirate population began to decline. By 1726, only a handful of the fraternity remained.

Pirates themselves unwittingly took a hand in their own destruction. From the outset, theirs had been a fragile social world. They produced nothing and had no secure place in the economic order. They had no nation, no home; they were widely dispersed; their community had virtually no geographic boundaries. Try as they might, they were unable to create reliable mechanisms through which they could either replenish their ranks or mobilize their collective strength. These deficiencies of social organization made them, in the long run, vulnerable to attack by the imperial state.

Conclusion

The pirate was, perhaps above all else, an unremarkable man caught in harsh, often deadly circumstances. Wealth he surely desired, but a strong social logic informed both his motivation and his behavior. Emerging from proletarian backgrounds and maritime employments, and loosed from familial bonds, pirates developed common symbols and standards of conduct. They forged spontaneous alliances, refused to fight each other, swore to avenge injury to their own kind, and even retired to pirate communities. They erected their own ideal of justice, insisted upon an egalitarian, if unstable, form of social organization, and defined themselves against other social groups and types. So, too, did they perceive many of their activities as ethical and justified, not unlike the eighteenth-century crowds described by E. P. Thompson.[97] But pirates, experienced as cooperative seafaring laborers and no longer disciplined by law, were both familiar with the workings of an international market economy and little affected by the uncertainties of economic change. Their experience as free wage laborers and as members of an uncontrolled, freewheeling subculture gave pirates the perspective and occasion to fight back against brutal and unjust authority and to construct a new social order where King Death would not reign supreme. Theirs was probably a contradictory pursuit. For many, piracy, as a strategy of survival, was ill fated.

Piracy, in the end, offers us an extraordinary opportunity. Here we can see how a sizable group of workers—poor men in canvas jackets and tarred breeches—constructed a social world where they had "the choice in themselves."[98] The choice did not exist on the merchant ship or the man-of-war. The social order and practices established by pirates recalled several key features of ancient and medieval maritime life. They divided their money and goods into shares; they consulted collectively and democratically on matters of moment; they elected a quartermaster, who, like the medieval "consul," adjudicated the differences between captain and crew.[99]

Pirates constructed a culture of masterless men. They were as far removed from traditional authority as any men could be in the early eighteenth century. Beyond the church, beyond the family, beyond disciplinary labor, and using the sea to distance themselves from the powers of the state, they carried out a strange experiment. The social constellation of piracy, in particular the complex consciousness and egalitarian impulses that developed once the shackles were off, provides valuable clarification of more general social and cultural patterns among seamen in particular and the laboring poor in general. Here we can see aspirations and achievements that under normal circumstances were heavily muted, if not in many cases rendered imperceptible altogether, by the power relationships of everyday life.

The final word on piracy must belong to Barnaby Slush, the man who understood and gave poetic expression to so many aspects of the common seaman's life in the early eighteenth century:

> *Pyrates* and *Buccaneers*, are Princes to [Seamen], for there, as none
> are exempt from the General Toil and Danger; so if the Chief have
> a Supream Share beyond his Comrades, 'tis because he's always the
> Leading Man in e'ry daring Enterprize; and yet as bold as he is
> in all other Attempts, he dares not offer to infringe the common
> laws of Equity; but every Associate has his due Quota . . . thus these
> *Hostes Humani Generis* as great robbers as they are to all besides, are
> precisely just among themselves; without which they could no more
> Subsist than a Structure without a Foundation.[100]

Thus did pirates express the collectivistic ethos of life at sea by the
egalitarian and comradely distribution of life chances, the refusal to
grant privilege or exemption from danger, and the just allocation
of shares. Their notion of justice—among themselves and in their
dealings with their class enemies—was indeed the foundation of
their enterprise. Equally, piracy itself was a "structure" formed upon
a "foundation" of the culture and society of Atlantic deep-sea sailors
in the eighteenth century.

✦

A Motley Crew in the American Revolution

In October 1765 a mob of sailors wearing blackface and masks, and armed with clubs and cutlasses, visited the home of wealthy Charleston merchant Henry Laurens. Eighty strong and warm with drink and anger, they had come to protest the Stamp Act, recently passed by Parliament to raise tax revenues in the American colonies. Responding to the rumor that Laurens had stored in his home the stamped paper everyone would be forced to buy in order to conduct the business of daily life, they chanted, "Liberty, liberty, and stamped paper!" and demanded that he turn it over so that they could destroy it in an act of defiance. Laurens was rattled, as he later explained: they "not only menaced very loudly but now & then handled me pretty uncouthly." Finally convinced that Laurens did not have the paper, the men dispersed across the waterfront, shedding their disguises and straggling into the smoky taverns and bare boardinghouses, onto the damp wharves and creaky ships.

Their protest had consequences. Parliament, taken aback by colonial protests, would soon repeal the Stamp Act. And in Charleston, one thing led to another, as a mob met in January 1766 to cry again for liberty. This time the protesters were African slaves, whose action caused greater fear and "vast trouble throughout the province."

Armed patrols stalked the city's streets for almost two weeks, but the tumult continued. Since Charleston's harbor was crowded with ships, the seafarers were soon "in motion and commotion again," styling themselves, said a cynical Laurens, the "Protectors of Liberty." South Carolina governor William Bull looked back over the events of late 1765 and early 1766 and blamed Charleston's turmoil on "disorderly negroes, and more disorderly sailors."[1]

Laurens and Bull identified a revolutionary subject, often described by contemporaries as a "motley crew." Rarely discussed in the American Revolution, the history of the motley crew extends from the piracies of the 1710s and 1720s to the slave revolts and urban insurrections of the 1730s and 1740s. The defeat of these movements allowed slavery and maritime trade to expand, as gangs of slaves extended plantation acreage and gangs of sailors manned ever-growing fleets of naval and merchant vessels. Britain confirmed its place as the world's greatest capitalist power by defeating France in the Seven Years' War in 1763, protecting and expanding its lucrative colonial empire and opening vast new territories in North America and the Caribbean for the hewing of wood and the drawing of water. And yet at the very moment of imperial triumph, slaves and sailors opened a new cycle of rebellion.[2]

Operations on sea and land, from mutiny to insurrection, made the motley crew the driving force of a revolutionary crisis in the 1760s and 1770s. They helped to destabilize imperial civil society and pushed America toward the world's first modern colonial war for liberation. By energizing and leading the movement from below, the motley crew shaped the social, organizational, and intellectual histories of the era. Their stories·demonstrate that the American Revolution was neither an elite nor a national event, because its genesis, process, outcome, and influence depended on the circulation of proletarian experience around the Atlantic. Such circulation would continue into the 1780s, as the veterans of the revolutionary movement in America would carry their knowledge and experience to the eastern Atlantic, initiating pan-Africanism, advancing abolitionism, and helping to revive dormant traditions of revolutionary thought and action in England and Europe more broadly. The motley crew would help to break apart the first British empire and inaugurate the Atlantic's age of revolution.

Two meanings of "motley crew" appear in this chapter. The first meaning refers to an organized gang of workers, a squad of people performing similar tasks or performing different tasks contributing to a single goal. The gangs of the tobacco and sugar plantations were essential to the accumulation of wealth in early America. Equally essential were the crews assembled from the ship's company, or ship's people, for a particular, temporary purpose, such as sailing a ship, making an amphibious assault, or collecting wood and water. These crews knew how to pull together, or to act in unison, not least because they labored beneath the whip. The first meaning, then, is technical to plantation and seafaring work. The economies of the eighteenth-century Atlantic depended on this unit of human cooperation.

The second meaning describes a social-political formation of the eighteenth-century port city. "Motley crew" in this sense was closely related to the urban mob and the revolutionary crowd, which, as we shall see, was usually an armed agglomeration of various crews and gangs that possessed its own motility and was often independent of leadership from above. It provided the driving force from the Stamp Act crisis to the "Wilkes & Liberty" riots, to the series of risings of the American Revolution. The revolts of the eighteenth-century Atlantic depended on this broader social form of cooperation.

To say that the crew was motley is to say that it was multiethnic. This was characteristic of the recruitment of ships' crews since trans-oceanic voyaging began with Columbus and Magellan. Its diversity was an expression of defeat—consider the deliberate mixing of languages and ethnicities in the packing of slave ships—but defeat was transformed into strength by agency, as when a pan-African, and then African American, identity was formed of the various ethnicities and cultures. Originally "ethnic" designations, such as the "free-born Englishman," could become generalized, as shown by the case of the African sailor Olaudah Equiano.

This chapter will show how the second (political) meaning emerges from the first (technical) one, broadening the cooperation, extending the range of activity, and transferring command from overseers or petty officers to the group. We will observe the transition from one to the other in the actions of the motley crew in the streets of the port cities. As sailors moved from ship to shore, they joined waterfront communities of dockers, porters, and laborers, freedom-seeking slaves, footloose youth from the country, and fugitives of various kinds. At the peak of revolutionary possibility, the motley crew appeared as a synchronicity or an actual coordination among the "risings of the people" of the port cities, the resistance of African American slaves, and Indian struggles on the frontier. Tom Paine feared precisely this combination, but it never materialized. On the contrary, the reversal of revolutionary dynamics, toward Thermidor, shifted the milieu of the motley crew, as refugees, boat people, evacuees, and prisoners became the human form of defeat.

Sailors

Sailors were prime movers in the cycle of rebellion, especially in North America, where they helped to secure numerous victories for the movement against Great Britain between 1765 and 1776. They led a series of riots against impressment beginning in the 1740s, moving Tom Paine (in *Common Sense*) and Thomas Jefferson (in the Declaration of Independence) to list impressment as a major grievance. Their militancy in port grew out of their daily work experience at sea, which combined daring initiative and coordinated cooperation. Sailors engaged in collective struggles over food, pay, work, and discipline, and brought to the ports a militant attitude toward arbitrary and excessive authority, an empathy for the grievances of others, and a willingness to cooperate for the sake of self-defense. As Henry Laurens discovered, they were not afraid to use direct action to accomplish their goals. Sailors thus entered the 1760s armed with the traditions of what we call "hydrarchy," a tradition of self-organization of seafaring people from below. They would learn new tactics in the age of revolution, but so too would they contribute the vast amount they already knew.[3]

Part of what sailors knew was how to resist impressment. This tradition had originated in thirteenth-century England and continued through the Putney Debates and the English Revolution, into the late seventeenth century, with the expansion of the Royal Navy, and on to the eighteenth century and its ever-greater wartime mobilizations. When, after a quarter century's peace, England declared war against Spain in 1739, sailors battled and often defeated press gangs in every English port. Fists and clubs flew in American ports as well, in Antigua, St. Kitts, Barbados, Jamaica, New York, and New England.⁴ Admiral Peter Warren warned in 1745 that the sailors of New England were emboldened by a revolutionary heritage: they had, he wrote, "the highest notions of the rights and liberties of Englishmen, and indeed are almost Levellers," referring to one of the most radical groups of the English Revolution.⁵

During the 1740s sailors began to burn the boats in which press gangs came ashore to snatch bodies, cutting their contact with the man-of-war and making "recruitment" harder, if not in some cases impossible. Commander Charles Knowles wrote in 1743 that naval vessels pressing in the Caribbean "have had their Boats haul'd up in the Streets and going to be Burned, & their Captains insulted by 50 Arm'd Men at a time, and obliged to take shelter in some Friends House." After Captain Abel Smith of the *Pembroke Prize* had pressed some men near St. Kitts, a mob of seamen "came off in the road and seized the Kings boat, hawled her up . . . and threatned to burn her, if the Captain would not return the Prest Men, which he was obliged to do to save the Boat, & peoples Lives, to the great Dishonour of Kings Authority (especially in Foreign Parts)." These attacks on the property and power of the British state were intimidating: by 1746 the captain of HMS *Shirley* "dared not set foot on shore for four months for fear of being prosecuted . . . or murdered by the mob for pressing."⁶

The struggle against impressment took a creative turn in 1747, when, according to Thomas Hutchinson, there occurred "a tumult in the Town of Boston equal to any which had preceded it." The commotion began when fifty sailors, some of them New Englanders, deserted Commander Knowles and HMS *Lark.* In response, Knowles sent a press gang to sweep the Boston wharves. A mob of three hundred seamen swelled to "several thousand people," seized officers of the *Lark* as hostages, beat a deputy sheriff and slapped him into the town's stocks, surrounded and attacked the provincial council chamber, and posted squads at all piers to keep naval officers from escaping back to their ship. The mob soon faced down Massachusetts Governor William Shirley, reminding him of the murderous violence visited upon sailors by the press gang in 1745 and threatening him with the example of Captain John Porteous, the despised leader of Edinburgh's City Guard, who after murdering a member of a protesting crowd in 1736 was seized and "hanged upon a sign post." Governor Shirley beat a hasty retreat to Castle William, where he remained until the riot ran its course. Meanwhile, armed sailors and laborers considered burning a twenty-gun ship being built for His Majesty in a local shipyard, then picked up what they thought was a naval barge, carried it through town, and set it aflame on Boston Common. Commodore Knowles explained their grievance:

> The Act [of 1746] against pressing in the Sugar Islands, filled the Minds of the Common People ashore as well as Sailors in all the Northern Colonies (but more especially in New England) with not only a hatred for the King's Service but [also] a Spirit of Rebellion each *Claiming a Right* to the same Indulgence as the Sugar Colonies and declaring they will maintain themselves in it.

As sailors defended liberty in the name of right, they captured the attention of a young man named Samuel Adams, Jr. Using what his enemies called "serpentine cunning," and understanding "Human Nature, in low life" very well, Adams watched the motley crew defend itself and then translated its "Spirit of Rebellion" into political discourse. He used the Knowles Riot to formulate a new "ideology of resistance, in which the natural rights of man were used for the first time in the province to justify mob activity." Adams saw that the mob "embodied the fundamental rights of man against which government itself could be judged," and he justified violent direct action against oppression. The motley crew's resistance to slavery produced a break-through in revolutionary thought.[7]

Adams thus moved from "the rights of Englishmen" to the broad-er, more universal idiom of natural rights and the rights of man in 1747, and one likely reason why may be found in the composi-tion of the crowd that instructed him. Adams faced a dilemma: how could he watch a crowd of Africans, Scotsmen, Dutchmen, Irish-men, and Englishmen battle the press gang and then describe them as engaged simply in a struggle for "the rights of Englishmen"? How could he square the apparently traditional Lockean ideas in his Harvard master's thesis of 1743 with the activities of "Foreign Sea-men, Servants, Negroes, and other Persons of mean and vile Con-dition" who led the riot of 1747?[8] The diversity of the rebellious subject forced his thought toward a broader justification. Adams would have understood that the riot was, literally, a case of the people fighting for their liberty, for throughout the eighteenth century the crew of a ship was known as "the people," who once ashore were on their "liberty."[9]

The mass actions of 1747 moved Adams to found a weekly publica-tion called the *Independent Advertiser*, which expressed a remarkable, even prophetic variety of radical ideas during its brief but vibrant life of less than two years. The paper reported on mutiny and resistance to the press gang. It supported the natural right to self-defense and vigorously defended the ideas and practices of equality, calling, for example, for popular vigilance over the accumulation of wealth and an "Agrarian Law or something like it" (a Digger-like redistribution of land) to support the poor workers of New England. It announced that "the reason of a People's Slavery, is . . . *Ignorance of their own Power.*" Perhaps the single most important idea to be found in the *In-dependent Advertiser* appeared in January 1748: "All Men are by Nature on a Level; born with an equal Share of Freedom, and endow'd with Capacities nearly alike." These words reached back exactly a century to the English Revolution and the Levellers' Agreement of the Peo-ple, and simultaneously looked forward to the opening words of the Declaration of Independence of 1776.[10]

Another connection between 1747 and 1776 appeared in Jonathan Mayhew's sermon *A Discourse Concerning Unlimited Submission and Non-Resistance to the Higher Powers*, delivered and published in Boston in early 1750. The eminent clergyman delivered his sermon at a time when the riot and its consequences were still on the minds of towns-people, especially the traders and seafaring people who made up his own West Church. By 1748 Mayhew's preachings were considered heretical enough to get one listener, a young Paul Revere, a whip-ping by his father for his waywardness. By early 1749 Mayhew was tending toward what some saw as sedition, saying that it was not a sin to transgress an iniquitous law, such as the one that legalized impress-ment. Mayhew defended regicide in his sermon of January 30, the anniversary of the execution of Charles I, which was to him no day of mourning but rather a day for remembering that Britons will not be slaves. Like Adams before him he argued passionately for both civil disobedience and a right to resistance that utilized force; indeed, pas-sive nonresistance, Mayhew claimed, was slavery. Mayhew's influential defense of the right to revolution could not have been made without the action of the riot and its discussion among Sam Adams and the readers of the *Independent Advertiser*.[11]

The ideas and practices of 1747 were refined and expanded dur-ing the 1760s and 1770s, when Jack Tar took part in almost every port-city riot, especially after the end of the Seven Years' War (1763), when the demobilization of the navy threw thousands out of work. For those who remained at sea, the material conditions (food, wages, discipline) of naval life deteriorated, causing many to desert. The Ad-miralty responded with terror. In 1764 deserters John Evans, Nicho-las Morris, and John Tuffin took seven hundred lashes on the back; Bryant Diggers and William Morris were hanged. Admiral Alexander Colvill admitted that these were, for desertion, "the most severe pun-ishments I ever knew to have been inflicted." Such deadly punish-ments at sea imparted a desperate intensity to shoreside resistance once the press gang resumed its work.[12]

Sailors revived their attack on the king's naval property. They re-captured pressed men, forced naval captains to make public apology, and successfully resisted efforts in court to convict any member of the mob of wrongdoing. Soon after, another mob of maritime workers in Casco Bay, Maine, seized a press boat, "dragged her into the middle of Town," and threatened to burn it unless a group of pressed men were freed.[13] In Newport in 1765 a mob made up of sailors, youths, and African Americans seized the press tender of HMS *Maidstone*, carried it to a central location in town, and set it ablaze. As popular antagonism toward the customs service rose in the late 1760s, sailors began to attack *its* vessels. Thomas Hutchinson wrote that in Boston in 1768, "A boat, belonging to the custom-house, was dragged in triumph through the streets of the town, and burnt on the Common." Seamen threatened or actually torched other vessels belonging to the king in Wilmington, North Carolina, and in Nevis in 1765, in Newport again in 1769 and 1772, and twice in New York in 1775. Sailors thus warned local leaders not to sign press warrants as they twisted the longest and strongest arm of state power.[14]

In the late 1760s sailors linked movements in England and America by engaging in revolts that combined workers' riots over wages and hours with protests about electoral politics ("Wilkes and Liberty," in which the London mob supported John Wilkes, the journalist and ruling-class renegade, in his battles with King and Parliament). The sailors of London, the world's largest port, played leading roles in both movements and in 1768 struck (took down) the sails of their vessels, crippling the commerce of the empire's leading city and adding the strike to the armory of resistance. Seamen's strikes would subsequently appear on both sides of the Atlantic with increasing frequency, as would struggles over maritime wages, especially after the reorganization of British customs in 1764, when officials began to seize the nonmonetary wages of seamen, the "venture" or goods they shipped on their own account, freight free, in the hold of each ship.[15] In leading the general strike of 1768, sailors drew upon traditions of hydrarchy to advance a proletarian idea of liberty. One writer, looking back on the uprising, explained: "Their ideas of liberty are the entering into [of] illegal combinations." Such combinations were "a many headed monster which every one should oppose, because every one's property is endangered by it; nay, the riches, strength, and glory of this kingdom must ever be insecure whilst this evil remains unchecked."[16]

Sailors also continued the struggle against impressment, battling the press gangs in the streets of London in 1770 (during the war against Spain) and 1776 (during the war against the American colonies, not a popular cause among sailors). "Nauticus" observed the clashes between seamen and the navy in London in the early 1770s and wrote *The Rights of the Sailors Vindicated*, in which he compared the sailor's life to slavery and defended the right to self-defense. He echoed the Putney Debates more than a century earlier when he imagined a sailor asking a magistrate, "I, who am as *free-born* as yourself, should devote my life and liberty for so trifling a consideration, purely that such wretches as you may enjoy your possessions in safety?" Like Sam Adams, Nauticus went beyond the rights of Englishmen, pitting the rights of private property against common rights and the "natural rights of an innocent subject." John Wilkes also began to argue for the right to resist impressment in 1772.[17]

The motley crew helped to create an abolitionist movement in London in the mid-1760s by setting in motion the eccentric but zealous Granville Sharp, who became one of slavery's most implacable foes. The key moment was a meeting in 1765 in a queue at a London medical clinic between the obscure, flinty clerk and musician, Sharp, and a teenager named Jonathan Strong, formerly a slave in Barbados who had been pummeled by his master into a crippled, swollen, nearly blind indigent. Sharp and his brother, a surgeon, nurtured him back to health, but two years later his former master imprisoned and sold him. To prevent such inhumanity, the African sailor Olaudah Equiano pushed Sharp to study the law and the writ of habeas corpus, the most powerful legacy of the "free-born Englishman," because it prohibited imprisonment or confinement without due process of law and trial by jury, and thus might be employed against impressment and slavery alike. Sharp believed that the law should be no respecter of persons and concluded in 1769 that "the common law and custom of England . . . is always favourable to liberty and freedom of man." He was especially moved by the struggles of black sailors on the waterfront; he used *habeas* to defend several who struggled to resist reenslavement, often by the press gang. Sharp won a lasting victory in his legal defense of James Somerset in 1772, which limited the ability of slaveowners to possess and exploit their human property in England. Habeas corpus, however, was suspended in 1777, although not without opposition. Meanwhile, the police magistrate, John Fielding, founded the "Bow Street Runners," an urban metropolitan parallel to the notorious slave "padrollers" of the southern plantations. He paid close attention to the motley crew in London and observed their westward circulation back to Caribbean insurrections.[18]

Sailors and the dockside proletariat attacked slavery from another angle in 1775, when they went on strike in Liverpool, as three thousand men, women, and children assembled to protest a reduction in wages. When the authorities fired upon the crowd, killing several, the strike exploded into open insurrection. Sailors "hoisted the red flag," dragged ships' guns to the center of the city, and bombarded the mercantile exchange, leaving "scarce a whole pane of glass in the neighborhood." They also trashed the property of several rich slave-trading merchants. One observer of the strife in Liverpool wrote, "I could not help thinking we had Boston here, and I fear this is only the beginning of our sorrows."[19]

There was a literal truth to the observation that Boston, the "Metropolis of Sedition," had popped up in English ports on the eve of the American Revolution. An anonymous eyewitness noted that multiethnic American sailors "were among the most active in the late tumults" of London in 1768. They were "wretches of a mongrel descent," the "immediate sons of Jamaica, or African Blacks by Asiatic Mulatoes." When such seamen chanted "No Wilkes, No King!" during the river strike of 1768, they displayed the independent revolutionary spirit that informed their actions ocean-wide. An escaped indentured servant named James Aitken, better known as "Jack the Painter," took part in the Boston Tea Party, then returned to England to wage revolutionary arson in 1775 against the king's ships and shipyards, for which he was captured and hanged. The mobility of sailors and other maritime veterans ensured that both the experience and the ideas of opposition carried fast. If the artisans and gentlemen of the American Sons of Liberty saw their struggle as but "one episode in a worldwide struggle between liberty and despotism," sailors, who had a much broader experience of both despotism and the world, saw their own as part of a long Atlantic struggle between slavery and freedom.[20]

"A Sailor and His Hammock" (National Maritime Museum)

Slaves

A new wave of struggle against slavery was inaugurated in Jamaica in 1760 by Tacky's Revolt, which was, according to sugar planter and historian Edward Long, "more formidable than any hitherto known in the West Indies." The revolt began, significantly, on Easter, in St. Mary's parish and spread like cane fire to involve thousands island-wide. The rebels were not motivated by Christianity (Jamaican Baptism and Methodism lay in the future, and the Moravian mission, established in 1754, was tiny) but rather by the mysterious Akan religion, which, despite prohibition since 1696, stressed spirit possession, access to supernatural powers, and a lively presence of the dead. Practitioners, or obeahmen, conferred immortal powers upon the freedom fighters, who shaved their heads to signify solidarity.[21] Their idea was to seize the forts and arms, and destroy the mills. One of the leaders, Aponga (a.k.a. Wager) had been a sailor aboard HMS *Wager* and may have witnessed the battles between the press gang and the mob of sailors in Boston in 1745. In Kingston a female slave, Cubah, was dubbed the Queen. The main leader, "Tacky" (whose name meant chief in Akan), was said to catch bullets in his hand and hurl them back at the slavemasters. The rebellion raged for several months, until a military force, including the Scott's Hall maroons, was organized by land and sea against the rebels. Tacky was captured and decapitated, his head exhibited on a pole in Spanish Town. When his head was recaptured by night, Edward Long admitted that "such exercises in frightfulness proved of doubtful value." Guerrilla fighting continued for a year. The carnage was among the greatest yet witnessed in a slave revolt: as many sixty whites killed and five hundred of the enslaved killed in battle, dead of suicide when their cause became hopeless, or executed. Accompanying the terror was legislation and policing, tighter control of meetings, registration of free blacks, permanent fortification in each parish, and the death penalty for those who practiced obeah.[22]

Control was reestablished in Jamaica but apparently with little help from the merchant seamen who found themselves in Jamaica when the revolt broke out and who were quickly herded into the local militias to help put down the uprising. Thomas Thistlewood explained that as sailors wandered from one plantation to another, the grog and silver spoons of the terrified sugar planters seemed to disappear. Edward Long claimed that in the middle of the revolt a captured leader of the slave rebels told a Jewish militia guard: "As for the sailors, you see they do not oppose us, they care not who is in possession of the country, Black or White, it is the same to them." The rebel was convinced that after the revolution, the sailors would "bring us things from t'other side the sea, and be glad to take our goods in payment."[23]

Like the Knowles Riot of 1747, Tacky's Revolt revived and contributed to a tradition of revolutionary thought that stretched back to Gerrard Winstanley and the English Revolution. In 1760, after the rebellion had broken out but before it was suppressed, a writer known to us only as J. Philmore wrote a pamphlet entitled *Two Dialogues on the Man-Trade*. Considering himself more "a citizen in the world" than a citizen of England, Philmore insisted that "all of the human race, are, by nature, upon an equality" and that one person simply could not be the property of another. He denied the worldly superiority of Christianity and thought the slave trade to be organized murder. Philmore had probably learned of Tacky's Revolt by way of merchant seamen, for he made it his business to frequent the docks. Much of the great deal he knew of the slave trade came "from the mouths of some sailors."[24]

Philmore supported the efforts of Tacky and his fellow rebels "to deliver themselves out of the miserable slavery they are in." His principal conclusion was clear, straightforward, and revolutionary:

> so all the black men now in our plantations, who are by unjust force deprived of their liberty, and held in slavery, as they have none upon earth to appeal to, may lawfully repel that force with force, and to recover their liberty, destroy their oppressors: and not only so, but it is the duty of others, white as well as black, to assist those miserable creatures, if they can, in their attempts to deliver themselves out of slavery, and to rescue them out of the hands of their cruel tyrants.

Philmore thus supported these freeborn people engaged in revolutionary self-defense, calling for immediate emancipation, by force if necessary, and asking all good people to do the same. Even though Philmore's ideas must have caused pacifist Quakers to shudder (Anthony Benezet drew on Philmore but carefully deleted his argument about repelling force with force), they nonetheless had broad influence. He wrote that "no legislature on earth, which is the supreme power in every civil society, can alter the nature of things, or make that to be lawful, which is contrary to the law of God, the supreme legislator and governour of the world." His "higher law" doctrine would over the next century become central to the transatlantic struggle against slavery. His inclusive, egalitarian conception of "the human race" had been inspired by the mass actions of rebellious slaves.[25]

Tacky's Revolt may have helped to generate another breakthrough in abolitionist thought, in the same seaport where Sam Adams had earlier learned to oppose impressment. When James Otis Jr. made his 1761 oration against the writs of assistance that allowed British authorities to attack the trade carried on between New England and the French West Indies, he went beyond his formal subject to "assert the rights of the Negroes." Otis delivered his electrifying speech immediately after Tacky's Revolt, which had been covered in a series of articles in Boston newspapers. John Adams later recalled that Otis was, that day, "a flame of fire," a prophet with the combined powers of Isaiah and Ezekiel. He gave a "dissertation on the rights of man in a state of nature," an antinomian account of man as "an independent sovereign, subject to no law, but the law written on his heart" or lodged in his conscience. No Quaker in Philadelphia ever "asserted the rights of negroes in stronger terms." Otis called for immediate emancipation and advocated the use of force to accomplish it, causing the cautious Adams to tremble. When Otis published *The Rights of the British Colonies Asserted and Proved* (1764), he claimed that all men, "white or black," were "by the law of nature freeborn," thereby broadening and de-racializing the idiom of the "free-born Englishman."[26] Whether Otis had read Philmore's pamphlet or had simply drawn similar conclusions from Tacky's Revolt, abolitionist thought would never be the same. Otis, whose echoes of the 1640s caused some to compare him to Masaniello, "was the first who broke down the Barriers of Government to let in the *Hydra* of Rebellion."[27]

Baptist church in Georgia, was evacuated by the British to Kingston, Jamaica, where he established another church.[30]

Revolutionary ideas circulated rapidly in the port cities. Runaway slaves and free people of color flocked to the ports in search of sanctuary and a money wage and took work as laborers and seamen. Slaves also toiled in the maritime sector, some with ship masters as owners, others hired out by the voyage. By the middle of the eighteenth century, slaves dominated Charleston's maritime and riverine traffic, in which some 20 percent of the city's adult male slaves labored. The independence of Charleston's "boat negroes" had long worried the city's rulers, especially when they took up subversive activities, as alleged against Thomas Jeremiah, a river pilot, in 1775. Jeremiah was arrested for stockpiling guns as he waited for the imperial war that would "help the poor Negroes." "Two or three White people," probably sailors, were also arrested, then released for lack of evidence, and finally driven from the province. Black pilots were "a rebellious lot, particularly resistant to white control."[31]

The political effects of slave resistance were contradictory, fueling fear and repression (police and patrols) on one side and new opposition to slavery on the other. This was especially true for the years leading up to the American Revolution, which marked a new stage in the development of an abolitionist movement. Benezet, America's leading Quaker abolitionist, chronicled slave uprisings around the world and tirelessly disseminated the news of them through correspondence, pamphlets, and books. His work, in tandem with resistance from below, led to new attacks on the slave trade in Massachusetts in 1767 and in Rhode Island, Delaware, Connecticut, Pennsylvania, and the Continental Congress by 1774. The first formal antislavery organization in America was established in Philadelphia in 1775.[32]

Two of the revolution's most popular pamphleteers were moved by the militancy of slaves in the 1770s to attack slavery as they made larger arguments for human freedom. John Allen, a Baptist minister who had witnessed the riots, trials, hangings, and diaspora of London's Spitalfields silk weavers through the 1760s, delivered (and then published) *An Oration on the Beauties of Liberty* after the burning of the revenue cutter *Gaspee* by sailors in 1773. In the fourth edition of his pamphlet, which was read to "large Circles of the Common People," Allen denounced slavery, not least for the frequent and recent revolts of slaves, which "so often occasion streams of blood to be shed." Thomas Paine, another man fair of pen and smitten with liberty, wrote against slavery immediately upon his arrival in America in 1774. He repeated in diluted form Philmore's argument for self-liberation: "as the true owner has a right to reclaim his goods that were stolen, and sold; so the slave, who is proper owner of his freedom, has a right to reclaim it, however often sold." Paine signaled his awareness of the upswing in African American resistance by referring to slaves as "dangerous, as they are now." The struggles of African American slaves between 1765 and 1776 increased the commotion and sense of crisis in every British colony in the years leading up to the revolution. Within the Baptist Allen and the half-Quaker Paine, they awakened an antinomian abolitionism from a previous revolutionary age.[33]

Mobs

The trajectories of rebellion among sailors and slaves intersected in seaport mobs, the rowdy gatherings of thousands of men and women that created the revolutionary crisis in the North American colonies. Sailors and slaves fraternized in grogshops, dancing cellars, and "disorderly houses," in Philadelphia's Hell Town and elsewhere, despite efforts by authorities to criminalize and prevent such meetings.[34] They had gathered together in Boston's north-side and south-side mobs since the 1740s. Indeed, perhaps the single most common description of mobs in revolutionary America was "a Rabble of boys, sailors, and negroes." Moreover, on almost every occasion when a crowd went beyond the planned objectives of the moderate leaders of the patriot movement, sailors and often slaves led the way. Motley mobs were central to protests against the Stamp Act (1765), the Quartering Acts (1765, 1774), the Townshend Revenue Act (1767), the increased power of the British customs service (1764–1774), the Tea Act (1773), and the Intolerable Acts (1774), and therefore to the revolutionary rupture itself.[35]

Multiracial mobs helped to win numerous victories for the revolutionary movement. In 1765, "Sailors, boys, and Negroes to the number of above Five Hundred" rioted against impressment in Newport, Rhode Island, and in 1767 a mob of "Whites & Blacks all arm'd" attacked Captain Jeremiah Morgan in a press riot in Norfolk. A mob of sailors, "sturdy boys & negroes" rose in the *Liberty* riot in Boston in 1768. Jesse Lemisch has noted that after 1763, "armed mobs of whites and Negroes repeatedly manhandled captains, officers, and crews, threatened their lives, and held them hostage for the men they pressed." Authorities like Cadwallader Colden of New York knew that royal fortifications had to be "sufficient to secure against the Negroes or a mob."[36]

Why did African Americans fight the press gang? Some probably considered impressment a death sentence and sought to avoid the pestilence and punishment that ravaged the men of the Royal Navy. Others joined anti-impressment mobs to preserve bonds of family or some degree of freedom they had won for themselves. Many may have been drawn to the fight by the language and principles of the struggle against impressment, for on every dock, in every port, everywhere around the Atlantic, sailors denounced impressment as slavery plain and simple. Michael Corbett and several of his brother tars fought against being forced on board a man-of-war in the port of Boston in 1769, claiming that "they preferred death to such a life as they deemed slavery." John Allen reiterated what countless sailors had expressed in action and what Sam Adams had written years before: the people "have a right, by the law of God, of nature, and nations, to reluct at, and even to resist any military or marine force." Allen then compared one form of enslavement to another. The press gang, he insisted, "ought ever to be held in the most hateful contempt, the same as you would *a banditti of slave-makers on the coast of Africa*." Salt was the seasoning of the antislavery movement.[37]

The motley crew led a broad array of people into resistance against the Stamp Act, which taxed the colonists by requiring stamps for the sale and use of various commodities. Since the act affected all classes of people, all were involved in the protests, though sailors were singled out by many observers for their leadership and spirit. The refusal to use stamped paper (and to pay the tax) slowed commerce, which meant that idle sailors, turned ashore without wages, became a volatile force in every port. Royal officials everywhere would have agreed with the customs agent in New York who saw the power of "the Mob . . . daily increasing and gathering Strength, from the arrival of seamen, and none going out, and who are the people that are most dangerous on these occasions, as their whole dependence for subsistence is upon trade." Peter Oliver observed that after the Stamp Act riots, "the *Hydra* was roused. Every factious Mouth vomited out curses against *Great Britain*, & the Press rung its changes against Slavery."[38]

Boston's mob took angry action against the property of stamp distributor Andrew Oliver on August 14, 1765, then twelve days later turned an even fiercer wrath against the house and refined belongings of Thomas Hutchinson, who cried out at the mob, "You are so many Masaniellos!" Others who detested the crowd later singled out its leader, Ebenezer MacIntosh, as the incarnation of the shoeless fisherman of Naples. Sailors soon carried the news and experience of the tumults in Boston to Newport, where loyalists Thomas Moffat and Martin Howard Jr. suffered the same fate as Hutchinson on August 28. In Newport, where the mercantile economy depended upon the labor of sailors and dockworkers, the resistance to the Stamp Act was led by John Webber, probably a sailor and according to one report "a deserted convict." A band of sailors known as the "Sons of Neptune" then led three thousand rioters in an attack on New York's Fort George, the fortress of royal authority. They followed the example of the insurrection of 1741 when they tried to burn it to the ground. In Wilmington, North Carolina, a "furious Mobb of Sailors &c." forced the stamp distributor to resign. Sailors also led mass actions against the Stamp Act in Antigua, St. Kitts, and Nevis, where they "behaved like young Lions." Mob action continued in resistance to the Townshend Revenue Act and the renewed power of the British customs service in the late 1760s and early 1770s. Seamen drew on maritime custom to add a weapon to the arsenal of justice, the tarring and feathering used to intimidate British officials. The clunk of the brush in the tar bucket echoed behind Thomas Gage's observation in 1769 that "the Officers of the Crown grow more timid, and more fearfull of doing their Duty every Day."[39]

The burning of the customs schooner *Gaspee* in Newport in 1772 proved to be another decisive moment for the revolutionary movement. "Lawless seamen" had long taken direct action against customs men, in Newport and elsewhere. After the *Gaspee* ran aground, sixty to seventy men swarmed out of three longboats to board the ship, capture the despised Lieutenant William Dudingston, take him and his crew ashore, and set the vessel afire. These men were charged with "high treason, viz.: levying war against the King," which the sailors' burning of the king's vessels had long signified. Merchants, farmers, and artisans may have been involved in the *Gaspee* affair, but sailors were clearly the leaders, as concluded by Daniel Horsmanden, who had presided over the trials of the rebels in New York in 1741 and now headed the King's commission to investigate the *Gaspee* incident. The act, he wrote, was "committed by a number of bold, daring, rash enterprising sailors." Horsmanden did not know if someone else had organized them or if these men of the sea had simply "banded themselves together."[40]

Seamen also led both the Golden Hill and Nassau Street riots of New York City and the King Street Riot, remembered as the Boston Massacre. In both ports sailors and other maritime workers resented the British soldiers who labored for less than customary wages along the waterfront; in New York they also resented the soldiers' attacks on their fifty-eight-foot liberty pole (a ship's mast). Rioting and street fighting ensued. Thomas Hutchinson and John Adams believed that the events in New York and Boston were related, perhaps by common participants. Adams, who defended Captain Thomas Preston and his soldiers in trial, called the mob that assembled on King Street on "the Fatal Fifth of March" nothing but "a motley rabble of saucy boys, negroes and molattoes, Irish teagues, and out landish Jack Tarrs." Their leader was Crispus Attucks, a runaway slave of African American and Native American descent whose home was the small free black community of Providence in the Bahama Islands. Seamen also took part in the direct actions of the several Tea Parties, after which Thomas Lamb in New York exclaimed, "We are in a perfect Jubilee!"[41]

By the summer of 1775 seamen and slaves had helped to generate an enthusiasm described by Peter Timothy: "In regard to War & Peace, I can only tell you that the Plebeians are still for War—but the noblesse [are] perfectly pacific." Ten years of insurrectionary direct action had brought the colonies to the brink of revolution. As early as the Stamp Act protests of 1765 General Thomas Gage had recognized the menace of mob action: "This Insurrection is composed of great numbers of Sailors headed by Captains of Privateers" and those from the surrounding area, the whole amounting to "some thousands." Late in 1776 Lord Barrington of the British army claimed that colonial governments in North America "were overturned by insurrections last summer, because there was not a sufficient force to defend them." Sailors, laborers, slaves, and other poor workingmen provided much of the spark, volatility, momentum, and sustained militancy for the attack on British policy after 1765. During the revolutionary war, they took part in mobs that harassed Tories and blunted their political effectiveness.[42]

The motley crew thus provided an image of revolution from below that proved terrifying to Tories and moderate patriots alike. In his famous but falsified engraving of the Boston Massacre, Paul Revere tried to make the "motley rabble" respectable by leaving black faces out of the crowd and putting into it entirely too many gentlemen. The South Carolina Council of Safety complained bitterly of the attacks of sailors—"white and black armed men"—in December 1775.[43] Elite colonists reached readily for images of monstrosity, calling the mob a "Hydra," a "many-headed monster," a "reptile," and a "many-headed power." Many-headedness implied democracy, as Joseph Chalmers explained: a government that was too democratic "becomes a many-headed monster, a tyranny of many." Against the revolutionary soldiers and sailors who fought beneath the banner of the serpent and the motto "Don't Tread on Me," John Adams proposed Hercules as the symbol for the new nation.[44]

Multiracial mobs under the leadership of maritime workers thus

helped to create the imperial crisis of the 1770s and simultaneously helped to create a revolutionary solution to it. The militancy of
multiracial workers in Boston, Newport, New York, and Charleston
led to the formation of the Sons of Liberty, the earliest intercolonial
organization to coordinate anti-imperial resistance. Richard B. Morris wrote that New York's sailors "were organized as the Sons of Neptune, apparently antedating the Sons of Liberty, for whom they may
well have provided the pattern of organization." The commotion
around the *Gaspee* incident in 1772 set in motion a new round of
organization, for in the aftermath of this bold action, another revolutionary organization, the committee of correspondence, was established throughout the colonies."[45] And if the motley crew shaped the
organizational history of the American Revolution, it had, as we have
seen, an even greater impact upon the intellectual history, influenc-
ing the ideas of Samuel Adams, J. Philmore, James Otis Jr., Anthony
Benezet, Thomas Paine, and John Allen. Action from below taken in
Boston, St. Mary's Parish, Jamaica, and London perpetuated old ideas
and generated new ones that would circulate around the Atlantic for
decades to come.

One of the main ideas kept alive by multiracial seaport crowds was
the antinomian notion that moral conscience stood above the civil
law of the state and therefore legitimized resistance to oppression,
to a corrupt minister of empire, a tyrannical slave owner, or a violent
ship captain. David S. Lovejoy has convincingly shown that a leveling
spirit and an antinomian disdain of laws and government lay within
the rising "political enthusiasm" of the revolutionary era. Explosive
mobs consistently expressed such enthusiasm, moving Benjamin
Rush to name a new type of insanity: *anarchia*, the "excessive love
of liberty." Eventually the higher-law doctrine historically associated
with antinomianism appeared in secular form in the Declaration of
Independence, which was denounced in its own day as an instance
of "civil antinomianism."[46]

In its struggle against impressment in the 1760s and 1770s, the
motley crew drew on ideas from the English Revolution, when Thomas Rainborough and the revolutionary movement of the 1640s had

denounced slavery. In the second *Agreement of the Free People of England* (May 1649), the Levellers explained the antinomian basis of their opposition to impressment: "We the free People of England" declared to the world that Parliament had no power to press any man into war, for each person must have the right to satisfy his conscience about the justice of the war. Thus they made man and his conscience (not the citizen) the subject of declaration, life (not the nation) its object. Peter Warren was correct when he claimed that the sailors of New England were "almost Levellers." As such, they expressed their opposition to impressment and to slavery more broadly, influenced Jefferson, Paine, and a whole generation of thinkers, and showed that the 1640s—not 1688—were precedent to the events of 1776.[47]

Counterrevolution

If the motley crew's audacious actions gave motion to the multiclass movement toward independence, they also generated commotion *within* it—fear, ambivalence, and opposition. In New York, for example, the Sons of Liberty came into being as a reaction against the "threatened anarchy" of autonomous risings against the press and the Stamp Act in 1764 and 1765. Everywhere the Sons began to advertise themselves as the guarantors of good order, as the necessary counterpoint to the upheaval within which they themselves had been born. By 1766 the propertied opponents of British policy had declared themselves for "ordered resistance." In the aftermath of the Boston Massacre in 1770, John Adams defended the redcoats and made an explicitly racist appeal in court, claiming that the looks of the Afro-Indian sailor Crispus Attucks "would be enough to terrify any person." But in 1773 he wrote a letter about liberty, addressed it to Thomas Hutchinson, and signed it "Crispus Attucks." Adams dreaded the motley crew, but he knew that they had made the revolutionary movement.[48]

Similar contradictions haunted Thomas Jefferson, who acknowledged the motley crew but feared its challenge to his own vision of America's future. Jefferson included in the Declaration of Independence the complaint that King George III "has constrained our fellow

Citizens taken Captive on the high seas to bear Arms against their Country, to become executioners of their friends and Brethren, or to fall themselves by their Hands." He (and Congress) included sailors in the revolutionary coalition but tendentiously simplified their history and role within the movement, leaving out the war of classes and emphasizing only the war of nations. The passage also lacked the graceful wording and lofty tone of the rest of the Declaration. It is awkward and confused, especially in its indecision about classifying the sailor (citizen, friend, brother?). Jefferson employed "the most tremendous words," as Carl Becker said of the draft passage concerning African slavery, but "the passage somehow leaves us cold." There is in it "a sense of labored effort, of deliberate striving for an effect that does not come." As it happened, Jefferson added the words about impressment as an afterthought, squeezing them into his rough draft of the Declaration. He knew that the labor market in a mercantile age was a serious problem and that commerce would depend on sailors whether America was to remain within the British Empire or not.[49]

Tom Paine knew it too. He also denounced impressment but was more concerned in *Common Sense* to reassure American merchants about the maritime labor supply after the revolution. "In point of manning a fleet, people in general run into great errors; it is not necessary that one fourth part should be sailors. . . . A few able and social sailors will soon instruct a sufficient number of active landmen in the common work of a ship." This had been his own experience aboard the *Terrible*, privateer, during the Seven Years' War, which led him to argue that sailors, shipbuilders, and the maritime sector as a whole constituted a viable economic basis for a new American nation. (He failed to mention that the crew of the vessel was motley and mutinous.) The only question remaining was how to obtain independence: should it be done from above, by the legal voice of Congress, or should it be done from below, by the mob? Here Paine shared the attitudes of others of his station: he feared the motley mob (though he would think differently in the 1790s). The multitude, he explained, was reasonable in 1776, but "virtue" was not perpetual. Safeguards were necessary lest "some Massanello may hereafter arise,

the next year that neither free blacks nor slaves would be eligible for military service. Scarcity of labor would force reconsideration of the issue, especially later in the war. While five thousand African Americans fought for liberty, the American political and military leadership battled the British and some of their own soldiers to protect the institution of slavery.[52]

The sailor would be encouraged to serve in the Continental Navy, but he was not, according to James Madison, a good citizen for a republic. What little virtue he may have had was deadened by his life as a dumb drudge at sea: "Though traversing and circumnavigating the globe, he sees nothing but the same vague objects of nature, the same monotonous occurrences in ports and docks; and at home in his vessel, what new ideas can shoot from the unvaried use of the ropes and the rudder, or from the society of comrades as ignorant as himself." Madison's own ignorance, arrogance, or denial caused him to invert the truth, but he was right about something else: the greater the number of sailors in a republic, he suggested, the less secure the government. Madison was joined in these attitudes by many, including the "Connecticut Wits" (David Humphreys, Joel Barlow, John Trumbull, and Dr. Lemuel Hopkins), who in 1787 wrote a poem entitled "The Anarchiad" in response to Shays' Rebellion and in memory of the cycle of rebellion in the 1760s and 1770s. The poets expressed their hatred for mobs and their ideas. They sneered at "democratic dreams," "the rights of man," and the goal of reducing all "To just one level." One of their darkest nightmares was what they called a "young DEMOCRACY from *hell*." They had not forgotten the role of sailors in the revolution. In their imagined state of anarchy, the "mighty Jacktar guides the helm." He had been "Nurs'd on the waves, in blust'ring tempests bred, / His heart of marble, and his brain of lead." Having sailed "in the whirlwind" as a part of his work, this hard-hearted, thick-headed man naturally "enjoys the storm" of revolution. The poets alluded to the revolutionary acts of sailors when they referred to "seas of boiling tar."[53]

During the 1780s such thinking came to prevail among those who made up the emerging political nation—merchants, professionals, shopkeepers, artisans, slave owners, and yeoman farmers. Sailors and slaves, once necessary parts of the revolutionary coalition, were thus read out of the settlement at revolution's end. Of the five working-men killed in the Boston Massacre in 1770 John Adams had written: "the blood of the martyrs, right or wrong, proved to be the seed of the congregation." Yet had Crispus Attucks—slave, sailor, and mob leader—survived the fire of British muskets, he would not have been allowed to join the congregation, or new nation, he had helped to create. The exclusion of people like Attucks epitomized a sudden, re-actionary retreat from the universalistic revolutionary language that had been forged in the heat of the 1760s and 1770s and permanently emblazoned in the Declaration of Independence. The reaction was institutionalized in the US Constitution, which gave the new federal government the power to suppress domestic insurrections. James Madison was worried in 1787 about "a levelling spirit" and an "agrar-ian law."[54] The Constitution also strengthened slavery by extending the slave trade, providing for the return of fugitive slaves, and giving national political power to the plantation master class.[55] Meanwhile, an intensive debate about the nature and capacity of "the negro" raged between 1787 and 1790. Many Baptists and Methodists backed away from antislavery commitments and sought instead "a gospel made safe for the plantation."[56] The new American ruling class rede-fined "race" and "citizenship" to divide and marginalize the motley crew, legislating in the 1780s and early 1790s a unified law of slavery based on white supremacy. The actions of the motley crew, and the reactions against them, help to illuminate the clashing, ambiguous nature of the American Revolution—its militant origins, radical mo-mentum, and conservative political conclusion.[57]

Vectors of Revolution

And yet the implications of the struggles of the 1760s and 1770s could not easily be contained by the Sons of Liberty, Jefferson, Paine, Ad-ams, or the new American government. Soldiers who fought in the war circulated the news, experience, and ideas of the revolution. Sev-eral veterans of the French regiments deployed in North America, including Henri Christophe and André Rigaud, would later lead the next major revolution of the western Atlantic, in Haiti beginning in 1791. Other veterans returned to France and may have led a series of revolts against feudal land tenure that accelerated revolution in Europe during the 1790s. The news carried by Hessian soldiers back to their homeland eventually propelled a new generation of settlers toward America. But it was the motley crew, the sailors and slaves who were defeated in America and subsequently dispersed, who did the most to create new resistance and to inaugurate a broader age of revolution throughout the world.[58]

Sailors were a vector of revolution that traveled from North America out to sea and southward to the Caribbean. The sailors of the British navy grew mutinous after 1776, inspired in part by the battles against the press gangs and the king's authority in America. An estimated 42,000 deserted naval ships between 1776 and 1783. Many who went to sea got a revolutionary education. Robert Wedderburn, born to a slave woman and a Scottish plantation owner in Jamaica, joined the mutinous navy in 1778, and thereafter worked as a sailor, a tailor, a writer, and a preacher of jubilee as he took part in maritime protests, slave revolts, and urban insurrection. Julius Scott has shown that sailors black, white, and brown connected with slaves in the British, French, Spanish, and Dutch port cities of the Caribbean, exchanging information about slave revolts, abolition, and revolution, generating rumors that became material forces in their own right. It is not known for certain if sailors carried the news of the American Revolution that helped to inspire slave rebels in Hanover Parish, Jamaica, in 1776. It is known that a motley crew, "fifty or sixty men of all colors," including an "Irishman of prodigious size," attacked British and American ships in the Caribbean in 1793, apparently in league with the new revolutionary government of Haiti.[59]

The slaves and free blacks who flocked to the British army during the revolution and who were then dispersed around the Atlantic after 1783 constituted a second, multidirectional vector of revolution. Twelve thousand African Americans were transported out of Savannah, Charleston, and New York with the army in 1782 and 1783, while another eight to ten thousand departed with loyalist masters. They went to Sierra Leone, London, Dublin, Nova Scotia, Bermuda, East Florida, the Bahamas, Jamaica, the Mosquito Shore, and Belize. Free people of color from North America caused problems throughout the Caribbean in the later 1780s, especially in Jamaica and the Windward Islands, where they created new political openings and alignments in slave societies and helped to prepare the way for the Haitian Revolution. By 1800 Lord Balcarres, governor of Jamaica, wrote of the "Pandora's Box" that had been opened in the West Indies: "Turbulent people of all Nations engaged in illicit Trade; a most abandoned class of Negroes, up to every scene of mischief, and a general levelling spirit throughout, is the character of the lower orders in Kingston." Here, he explained, was a refuge for revolutionaries and a site for future insurrection, a place that might "in a moment . . . be laid in ashes."[60]

A third powerful vector of revolution hurtled eastward toward the abolitionist movement in England. Sailors and slaves, some of them sailors who had been slaves, proved to be strategic links to the abolition movement's most important leaders, Granville Sharp and Thomas Clarkson. During the 1780s the African sailor Olaudah Equiano mobilized Sharp on the case of the *Zong*, wherein captain Luke Collingwood threw 132 living Africans overboard in an effort to collect insurance money. Soon thereafter dissident sailors such as John Dean and others in Liverpool and Bristol educated Clarkson about the nature of the slave trade.[61]

A fourth and final vector pointed toward Africa. The African Americans in diaspora after 1783 would originate modern pan-Africanism by settling, with the help of Equiano and Sharp, in Sierra Leone. Their dispersal after the American Revolution, eastward across the Atlantic, was similar to the dispersal of radicals after the English Revolution, a century and a half earlier, westward across the Atlantic. Both movements had posed challenges to slavery but were defeated. The earlier defeat permitted the consolidation of the plantation and the slave trade, while the latter defeat allowed the slave system to expand and gather new strength. Yet the long-term consequences of the second defeat would be a victory, the ultimate undoing of the slave trade and plantation system. The theory and practice of antinomian democracy, which had been generalized around the Atlantic in the seventeenth-century diaspora, would be revived and deepened in the eighteenth. What went out in whiteface came back in blackface, to end the pause in the discussion of democratic ideas in England and to give new life to worldwide revolutionary movements. What goes around comes around, by the circular winds and currents of the Atlantic.

The failure of the motley crew to find their place in the new American nation forced them into broader, more creative forms of identification. One of the phrases often used to capture the unity of the age of revolution was "citizen of the world." J. Philmore described himself this way, as did others, including Thomas Paine. The real citizens of the world, of course, were the sailors and slaves who instructed Philmore, Paine, Jefferson, and the rest of the middle- and upper-class revolutionaries. This multiethnic proletariat was "cosmopolitan" in an original meaning of the word. Reminded that he had been sentenced to exile, Diogenes, the slave philosopher of antiquity, responded saying he sentenced his judges to stay at home. "Asked where he came from, he said, 'I am a citizen of the world'"—a cosmopolitan. Transatlantic workers both created and made real the concept in the age of revolution.

✦

SIX

African Rebels

From Captives to Shipmates

The man refused to eat. He had been sick, reduced to a "mere skeleton." He had apparently made a decision to die. Captain Timothy Tucker was outraged, and probably fearful that his example might spread to the other two-hundred-plus captives aboard his ship, the *Loyal George*, as it made its way across the Atlantic to Barbados in the year 1727. The captain turned to his black cabin boy, Robin, and commanded him to fetch his whip. This was no cat-o'-nine-tails, but rather something much bigger, a horse whip. He tied up the man and lashed him: "From his neck to his ancles, there was nothing to be seen but bloody wounds," said Silas Told, an apprentice seaman and crew member who recounted the story years later. All the while, the man made no resistance and said nothing, which incensed the captain, who now threatened him in his own language: "he would *tickeravoo* him," that is kill him, to which the man answered, "*adomma*," so be it.[1]

The captain then left the man "in shocking agonies" to take his dinner on the quarterdeck, eating "like a hog," thought Told. After he had finished his meal, Captain Tucker was ready to resume the punishment. This time he called another ship's boy, John Lad, to bring him two loaded pistols from his cabin. Captain Tucker and John Lad then walked forward on the main deck, approaching the nameless hunger striker, who was sitting with his back against the larboard gunnel of the ship. With a "malicious and virulent grin," Tucker pointed a pistol at the man and repeated that he would kill him if he did not eat. The man answered simply, as before: "*adomma*." The captain put the barrel of the pistol to the man's forehead and pulled the trigger. The man "instantly clapped his hands to his head, the one behind, the other before," and stared the captain directly in the face. Blood gushed from the wound, like the "tapping [of] a cask," but he did not fall. The captain, infuriated, cursed, turned to the cabin boy, and screamed, "This will not kill him," so he clapped the other pistol to the man's ear and fired again. To the utter amazement of Told and surely everyone else who looked on, "nor did he drop, even then!" Finally the captain ordered John Lad to shoot the man through the heart, whereupon "he then dropt down dead."

In consequence of the murder, the rest of the male captives rose in vengeful wrath "upon the ship's company with full purpose to slay us all." The crew scrambled to retreat behind the barricado. Once there they took up their positions at the swivel guns, raking the main deck with shot and sending the rebels flying in all directions. Some of the men dove below deck seeking cover, while others jumped overboard. As soon as the crew had regained control of the main deck, they took to the boats to save the men in the water, but were able to rescue only one or two from "violence of the sea" and the men's own concerted efforts to drown themselves. A large but unknown number perished. Thus did an individual act of resistance spark a collective revolt, and one form of resistance give rise to another. The refusal to eat had led to a kind of martyrdom, an insurrection, and, once that failed, to mass suicide.[2]

Scenes like this played out on one slave ship after another, showing that the transoceanic ship was a site of fierce resistance. These scenes epitomized a deep dialectic of discipline and resistance—on the one hand, extreme violence enacted by the captain against an enslaved individual, with an expectation that the resulting terror would help him to rule the others; and in response from the enslaved, extreme opposition to that violence and terror, individually and in the end collectively. Beneath the response, however, lay a question: how did a multiethnic mass of several hundred Africans, thrown together in a slave ship, learn to act collectively? From the time they were first brought aboard the ship, they were socialized into a new order, one designed to objectify, discipline, and individualize the laboring body through violence, medical inspection, numbering, chaining, "stowing" below decks, and various social routines, from eating and "dancing" to working. Meanwhile, the captives communicated among themselves and fought back, individually and collectively, which meant that each ship contained within it a process of culture stripping from above and an oppositional process of culture creation from below. In the shadow of death the millions who made the great Atlantic passage in a slave ship forged new forms of life—new language, new means of expression, new resistance, and a new sense of community. Herein lay the maritime origins of cultures that were at once African American and pan-African, creative and hence indestructible. Crucial social processes occurred at sea.[3]

Resistance: Refusing to Eat

If the common experiences of expropriation and enslavement, including the violent, densely communal regimentation of the slave ship, created the potential for community among African prisoners, and if social practices—working, communicating, and singing—helped to realize it, nothing was more important to the collective project of creating group identity than resistance. This was in itself a new language, a language of action employed every time people refused food, jumped over the side of the ship, or rose up in insurrection. It was a universal language, which everyone understood regardless of cultural background, even if they chose not to speak it actively themselves. Every act of resistance, small or large, rejected enslavement and social death as it embraced creativity and a different future. Each refusal bound people together, in ever deeper ways, in a common struggle.[4]

The Atlantic slave trade was, in many ways, a four-hundred-year hunger strike. From the beginning of the waterborne human commerce in the early fifteenth century to its end in the late nineteenth century, enslaved Africans routinely refused to eat the food given to them. When some of the enslaved came on board the ship, they fell into a "fixed melancholy," a depression in which they responded to nothing their captors said or demanded, including instructions to eat. Others got sick and were unable to eat even if they had wanted to. And yet even among some of the depressed and the sick, and among a much larger group that was neither, the refusal to eat was a conscious choice, which served several important purposes among the enslaved. Because the captain's main charge from the merchant was to deliver as many live, healthy African bodies as possible to the New World port, anyone who refused sustenance, for any reason whatsoever, endangered profits and subverted authority. Refusing to eat was therefore first and foremost an act of resistance, which in turn inspired other acts of resistance. Second, it proved to be a tactic of negotiation. Mistreatment could trigger a hunger strike. Third, it helped to create a shipboard culture of resistance, a "we" against a "they." Among the messages of the hunger strike were: we will not be property; we will not be labor power; we will not let you eat us alive.

On John Riland's ship the *Liberty*, in 1801, several of the enslaved rejected their food. The officer on watch swore he would throw them overboard if they did not eat, then he threatened them with the cat (of nine tails), which seemed to work, or so he thought: "The slaves then made a show of eating, by putting a little rice into their mouths; but whenever the officer's back was turned they threw it into the sea." Seaman James Morley also saw slaves pretend to eat, holding food in their mouths "till they have been almost strangled." The officers would damn them "for being sulky Black b———." They would try to force them to eat, using the cat, the thumbscrews, a "bolus knife" or a stick (to open the mouth), and a *speculum oris* or a "horn" to force food down obstinate throats.[5]

Anyone who resisted food posed a direct challenge to the captain's powers, as the example might spread with disastrous results. This was made chillingly clear by seaman Isaac Parker when he testified before the House of Commons committee investigating the slave trade in

1791. Aboard the *Black Joke* in 1765, a small child, whose mother was on board, "took sulk, and would not eat," refusing both the breast and standard fare of rice mixed with palm oil. Captain Thomas Marshall flogged the child with the cat as enslaved men looked on through the crevices of the barricado: they made "a great murmuring" in protest. Still the child refused to eat, and day after day the captain punished with the cat, but also by tying a mango log, eighteen to twenty inches long and twelve to thirteen pounds in weight, around its neck by a string. "The last time he took the child up and flogged it," explained Parker, he "let it drop out of his hands" to the deck, saying, "Damn you . . . I will make you eat, or I will be the death of you." In less than an hour the child died. In a final act of cruelty the captain commanded the child's mother to throw the small corpse overboard. When she refused, he beat her. Eventually she complied, and afterwards, "She seemed very sorry, and cried for several hours." Even the smallest rebel, a nine-month-old child who refused to eat, could not be tolerated aboard the *Black Joke*.[6]

What captains like Marshall feared, the contagion of resistance, was illustrated in a case that came before the High Court of Admiralty in 1730. James Kettle, captain of the *City of London* (owned by the South Sea Company), charged that seaman Edward Fentiman was too violent in his carriage toward the enslaved. He had beaten an unnamed slave woman, after which all of the others—and there were 377 on board—refused to take sustenance. This in turn earned Fentiman a beating from Kettle, who explained to the court that what had happened here was one instance of a larger problem: it is "the nature & disposition of Negroes & so frequently happens on board of Merchant Ships that when any one of them have been beat or abused for the whole Company of them on Board to resent it & grow Sullen and refuse to eat and many of them thereby to pine away and die."[7]

Dr. T. Aubrey reinforced Captain Kettle's point and raised it to a higher level of generalization. In his vade mecum for slave-trade surgeons, he explained that the violent mistreatment of the enslaved often resulted in their refusal to eat. Once they stopped, "then they lose their Appetites, and perhaps fall sick, partly thro' fasting, and partly with Grief to see themselves so treated." More tellingly still, once they had taken their resistance to heart, "all the Surgeon's Art will never keep them alive; they will never eat any thing by fair Means, or foul, because they choose rather to dye, than be ill treated." He referred, of course, to the various violent means used to make people eat. These would be resisted, in his view, and would in the end be useless against the will to refuse all sustenance. Like Kettle, Aubrey made it clear that the hunger strike was a tactic employed in the struggle that raged aboard every slave ship.[8]

The hunger strike aboard the *Loyal George*, as recalled by Silas Told, led directly to an insurrection and, once that failed, to mass suicide. The process of resistance also worked the other way, as hunger strikes often followed failed insurrections. After the captives rose aboard the *Ferrers Galley* in 1721, "near eighty" were killed or drowned. Most of those who survived, wrote Captain William Snelgrave, "grew so sullen, that several of them were starved to death, obstinately refusing to take any Sustenance." After an uprising on an unnamed vessel in the Bonny River in 1781, three of the wounded leaders "came to the resolution of starving themselves to death." They were threatened, then beaten, but "no terrors were effectual, for they never tasted any sustenance after their resolution, and they died in consequence of it." Likewise aboard the *Wasp* in 1783, when two insurrections took place. Following the first, in which the women captives seized the captain and tried to throw him overboard, twelve died of wounds and the refusal to eat. Following the second, even bigger explosion, fifty-five Africans died of "bruises, swallowing salt water, chagrins at disappointment, and abstinence."[9]

Jumping Overboard

Perhaps an even more dramatic form of resistance than self-starvation was jumping overboard. Some jumped in the hope of escape while docked in an African port, while others chose drowning over starvation as a means to terminate the life of the body meant to slave away on New World plantations. This kind of resistance was widely practiced and just as widely feared by the organizers of the trade.

Merchants warned captains about it in their instructions, formal and informal. Captains in turn made sure their ships had nettings all around. They also had the male captives chained to a ring bolt whenever they were on the main deck, and at the same time made sure that vigilant watches were always kept. When the enslaved did manage to get overboard, captains like Timothy Tucker urgently dispatched emergency rescue parties, in boats, to catch and bring them back aboard.

African women had greater freedom of movement on the ship than men, so they played a prominent role in this kind of resistance. In 1714, four women, one of them "big with child," jumped overboard as the *Florida* departed Old Calabar. As a man on board noted, they "shew'd us how well they could swim, & gave us ye slip." The crew immediately went after them but caught only the pregnant one, because she "could not shift so well as the rest." In Anomabu on the Gold Coast in 1732, Captain James Hogg discovered in the middle of the night that six women had jumped overboard and afterward was sure that only a brisk effort from the crew prevented the rest from following. Such escapes were dangerous, even for expert swimmers, as many of the enslaved from coastal regions happened to be. Anyone retaken in the water (and most who jumped overboard were) could expect severe punishment, even in some cases death (as a deterrent to others), once back aboard the ship. Even if the fugitives got to shore, chances were that their African captors would catch them and return them to the slaver. Finally, many of the waterways near shore where people jumped overboard were shark infested. Captain Hugh Crow recalled two Igbo women who went over the side of one of his vessels, only to be torn apart immediately by sharks.[10]

Some captives went overboard spontaneously, in response to a specific event, rather than in a calculated bid for freedom. In 1786 a gang of six, "enraged or terrified" at seeing the corpse of their deceased countryman cut open by a ship's doctor for anatomical analysis, "plunged into the sea, and were instantly drowned." A couple of years before, another forty of fifty jumped into the sea during a "scramble," a deliberately terrifying manner of selling slaves on the ship's deck in Jamaica. One hundred men jumped off the *Prince of Orange* after they had been released from chains upon the docking of the vessel at St. Kitts in 1737. Thirty-three refused assistance from the sailors and drowned. They were "resolv'd to die, and sunk directly down." The cause of the mass action, according to Captain Japhet Bird, was that one of the countrymen of the enslaved came aboard and "jokingly" told them they would be blinded and eaten by the white men.[11]

One of the most illuminating aspects of these suicidal escapes was the joy expressed by people once they had gotten into the water. Seaman Isaac Wilson recalled a captive who jumped into the sea and "went down as if exulting that he got away." Another African man, who knew that the nettings had been loosened to empty the lower deck's "necessary tubs," got free of a group of sailors and "darted himself through the hole overboard." When the sailors went after him, and almost caught him, the man dived down and popped up again some distance away, eluding his would-be captors. All the while, recalled the ship's surgeon, he "made signs which it is impossible for me to describe in words, expressive of the happiness he had in escaping from us." Finally, he again went down again, "and we saw him no more." After a bloody insurrection had been suppressed aboard the *Nassau* in 1742, the captain ordered all injured slaves on deck: everyone whose wounds made recovery doubtful was ordered "to jump into the sea," which many of them did, going to their deaths with "seeming chearfulness," according to the person who had been the cabin boy on the voyage. The same thing happened aboard the infamous *Zong*. As Captain Luke Collingwood ordered 122 sick captives thrown overboard, another ten jumped of their own accord.[12]

Hunger strikes and jumping overboard were not the only means of self-destruction. Some sick people refused medicine because "they want to die." Two women found ways to strangle themselves to death aboard the *Elizabeth* in 1788–1789. Others cut their own throats, with hard-edged tools, sharp objects, or their own fingernails. A sailor named Thompson noted that he "has known all the slaves [locked below deck] unanimously [to] rush to leeward in a gale of wind, on purpose to upset the ship, choosing to drown themselves, than to continue in their situation, or go into foreign slavery."[13]

The least common but most spectacular mass suicides involved blowing up the entire ship. In January 1773, the enslaved men below deck aboard the *New Britannia*, using tools slipped to them by the more mobile boys, cut through the bulkheads and got into the gun room, where they found weapons and used them to battle the crew for more than an hour, with significant loss of life on both sides. When they saw that defeat at the hands of the crew was inevitable, "they set fire to the magazine, and blowed the vessel up," killing almost everyone on board, as many as three hundred altogether. When Captain James Charles learned in October 1785 that Gambian captives had successfully captured a Dutch slaver (and killed the captain and crew), he resolved go after the vessel, not least because the insurgents, if defeated, might become his property. After a chase of three hours and an indecisive engagement, a party of his own crew volunteered to board the self-emancipated people's craft under fire. Ten men and an officer went aboard and, after a smart contest on deck, "drove the mutinous slaves into the hold." As the battle continued, someone apparently blew the vessel up "with a dreadful explosion, and every soul on board perished." Part of the wreckage fell upon the deck of Captain Charles's vessel, the *Africa*.[14]

Even though suicides run like a blood-red thread through the documentation of the slave trade, it is impossible to be sure how common they were. One measure, for a limited time period, may be found in the journals that slave-ship surgeons were required to keep in the aftermath of the Dolben Act, or Slave Carrying Bill, of 1788. For the period 1788 to 1797, physicians for eighty-six vessels recorded in their journals the cause of death for all of the Africans under their charge, and in these suicide looms rather large. Twenty-five surgeons recorded what appeared to be one or another kind of self-destruction: eight ships had one or more person jump overboard; three others listed captives "missing" (no doubt overboard) after an insurrection; three others experienced nonspecific forms of suicide; and another twelve gave causes such as "lost," "drowned," "sulkiness," and "abortion." Almost one third of the vessels in the sample witnessed a suicide, and even this is likely a serious understatement as surgeons had vested interests in not reporting suicides in this era of charged debate about the inhumanity of slave ships.[15] Another reason to reduce or conceal the number of suicides was the ruling of an English court, Judge Mansfield presiding, in Trinity Term 1785: insurance companies would be required to pay for insured slaves who died in an insurrection but would not be required to pay for those who died of chagrin, abstinence, or despair. More specifically, "all who died by leaping into the sea, were not to be paid for."[16]

Rising Up

Hundreds of bodies packed together below deck were a potent source of energy, as could be seen in material emanation anytime a slave ship sailed through cool, rainy weather. On these occasions steam billowed up from the mass of hot bodies on the lower deck, through the gratings, onto the main deck where the crew worked. Aboard the slave ship *Nightingale* in the late 1760s seaman Henry Ellison saw "steam coming through the gratings like a furnace." Not infrequently, the human furnace down below exploded—into open insurrection. The peculiar war that was the slave trade would now be waged openly on the ship.[17]

Yet insurrection aboard a slave ship did not happen as a spontaneous natural process. It was, rather, the result of calculated human effort—careful communication, detailed planning, precise execution. Every insurrection, regardless of its success, was a remarkable achievement, as the slave ship itself was organized in almost all respects to prevent it. Merchants, captains, officers, and crew thought about it, worried about it, took practical action against it. Each and all assumed that the enslaved would rise up in a fury and destroy them if given half a chance. For those who ran the slave ship, an insurrection was without a doubt their greatest nightmare. It could extinguish profits and lives in an explosive flash.

Collective action began in communication among people who identified common problems and searched together for common solutions. They began to converse in small groups, probably twos and threes, literally conspiring in the dank, fetid air below deck, probably at night, away from the ears of captain and crew. The lower deck was usually crowded, but mobility among the enslaved was possible, even among the shackled and manacled men, so potential rebels could move around, find each other, and talk. Once they had formulated a plan, the core conspirators might take a "sangaree," an "Oath to stick by each other, and made by sucking a few Drops of one another's Blood." They would then organize others, mindful of a dangerous contradiction: the greater the number of people involved in the plot, the greater the chance of success, but at the same time the greater the chance that someone would snitch. Many would therefore opt for a smaller number of more committed militants, wagering that once the insurrection was under way, others would join them. Most conspirators would proceed carefully and wait for their moment to strike.[18]

Everyone involved in running the slave trade assumed, correctly, that the most likely insurrectionists were African men, who were therefore fettered and chained at almost all times, whether on the lower or main deck. But women and children had important roles to play as well, not least because of their greater mobility around the ship. Indeed, women sometimes played leading parts in uprisings, as, for example, when they seized Captain Richard Bowen aboard the *Wasp* in 1785 and tried to throw him overboard. The captives on board the *Unity* (1769–1771), like those aboard the *Thomas* (1797), rose up "by the means of the women." On other occasions women used their proximity to power and freedom of movement to plan assassinations of captains and officers, or to pass tools to the men below. The boys on board the *New Britannia*, anchored in Gambia, passed to the men down below "some of the carpenter's tools wherewith they ripped up the lower decks, and got possession of the guns, beads, and powder."[19]

Crucial to any uprising was the previous experience of those involved. Some of the men (like the Gola), and perhaps a few of the women (from Dahomey), had been warriors, and hence had spent their lives mastering the courage, discipline, and skills of warfare.

They would have been trained to fight at close quarters, to act in co-ordinated ways, and to hold position, not retreat. Others had valuable knowledge of Europeans, their ways, even their ships. Seaman William Butterworth described several captives "who, by living at Calabar and the neighbouring towns, had learned the English tongue so as to speak it very well; men who, for the commission of some misdemeanour, had forfeited their freedom, and who, desirous of regaining

Insurrection on a slave ship (Library Company of Philadelphia)

their liberty at any risk, had for some time been sowing the seeds of discontent in the minds of the less guilty, but equally unfortunate slaves, of both sexes." Such savvy men and women from the port cities could "read" their captors in ways others could not, and some could even read their ships. A special port city denizen was the African seafarer, skilled in the ways of the deep-sea sailing ship and probably the most valuable person to an insurrectionary attempt. The Kru of the Windward Coast and the Fante of the Gold Coast were known to be especially knowledgeable about European ships and sailing, as were lots of other coastal and riverine peoples. For these reasons, captives known to have come from the waterside were considered by slave ship captains to be special security risks.[20]

Knowledge of European arms was evident aboard the *Thomas*, which lay in the Gambia River in March 1753. All eighty-seven of the enslaved "privately got off their Irons," came upon deck, and threw the chief mate overboard. Alarmed, the seamen fired their small arms and drove the rebels back below. But some of the captives noticed that the seamen's firearms were not working properly, whereupon they picked up "Billets of Wood, and Pieces of Board" and came back upon deck, battling the crew, who numbered only eight at the moment, driving them to the longboat, in which they escaped, leaving "the Sloop in Possession of the Slaves"—who suddenly were slaves no longer. When two slave ship captains tried to recapture the sloop, they got a blistering engagement, "the Slaves making use of the Swivel guns, and trading Small Arms, seemingly in an experienced Manner against them." Such use of firearms was not uncommon, provided the enslaved could get to them.[21]

Certain cultural groups were widely known for their rebelliousness. Several observers noted that captives from the Senegambia region had a special hatred for slavery, which made them dangerous on board the ships. According to Royal African Company employee William Smith: "the Gambians, who are naturally very idle and lazy, abhor Slavery, and will attempt any Thing, tho' never so desperate, to obtain Freedom." The Fante of the Gold Coast were ready to "undertake any hazardous enterprise," including insurrection, noted

Dr. Thomas Trotter based on his experience of the 1780s. Alexander Falconbridge agreed: those from the Gold Coast were "very bold and resolute, and insurrections happen more frequently among them, when on ship-board, than amongst the negroes of any other part of the coast." The Ibibio of the Bight of Biafra, also known as "Quaws" and, in America, the "Moco," were, according to Captain Hugh Crow, "a most desperate race of men," always "foremost in any mischief or insurrection amongst the slaves" in the late eighteenth century. They killed many crew members and were known to blow up ships. "The females of this tribe," added Crow, "are fully as ferocious and vindictive as the men." Indeed the Ibibio were considered so dangerous that captains were careful "to have as few of them as possible amongst their cargoes." When they did take them aboard, they "were always obliged to provide separate rooms for these men between decks." The Ibibio were the only group known to warrant special quarters for their rebelliousness, which the captains sought to contain by isolation.[22]

Each line of recruitment, among women, boys, and cultural groups, contained within it potential divisions. Numerous were the times when either the men or the women rose up in insurrection, unsupported by the other, which of course made it much easier for the crew to put down the uprising. The men, for example, did not act when the women attacked Captain Bowen of the *Wasp* in 1785, while the women did not rise up with the men on the *Hudibras* in 1786. Boys were known to pass not only hard-edged tools to the enslaved men, but information to the crew about designs afoot below deck. And if certain African groups were inclined to rebellion, it did not necessarily follow that their militant ways were agreeable to others on the ship. The Ibibio and Igbo were called "mortal enemies," the Chamba despised the Fante, and during the middle of an insurrection in late 1752 Igbo and Coromantee insurgents began to fight each other. It is not always clear in any given case whether the divisions arose from previous history, inadequate communication and preparation, or disagreement about insurrection as a goal.[23]

Uprisings required knowledge of the ship, hence one of the things that people whispered about was what they knew of the hold, the lower deck, the main deck, the captain's cabin, the gun room, and how they should therefore proceed based on this knowledge. They found that they needed three specific kinds of knowledge about Europeans and their technologies, and that these were related to three distinct phases of the uprising: how to get out of the chains, how to find and use weapons against the crew, and how to sail the ship if they were successful. Insurrections tended to break down and suffer defeat at one of these moments in the process.

The iron technology of manacles, shackles, and chains was largely effective for its purpose, as its continued use, for centuries, on the enslaved and on all kinds of other prisoners, makes perfectly clear. But it is also clear that male captives on the lower deck regularly found ways to get out of these fetters. Sometimes the irons fit too loosely and the enslaved could, with lubrication and effort, simply squirm out of them. In other cases they used nails, picks, slivers of wood, and other instruments to pick the locks or a hard-edged tool of some kind (saw, adze, knife, hammer, chisel, hatchet, or ax, likely passed below by one of the women or boys) to cut or break through the iron. An additional challenge was to use the tools quietly so as not to be discovered in the process of breaking free. Once the chains were off, the rebels had to get through the fortified gratings, which were always locked overnight. Surprise at the morning opening frequently represented the best opportunity, unless someone could trick a member of the crew to open the gratings overnight.[24]

The next step was to unleash the explosive energy from below decks, the sounds of which were, to a terrified crew member, "an uncommon uproar" and "several dreadful shrieks," perhaps "from a sailor being killed." African war cries would pierce the morning quiet. Striking with speed, surprise, force, and fury was important, because it could shock the crew into running for the longboat in an effort to escape the insurrection. Meanwhile, hand-to-hand combat engulfed the forward part of the ship, and if a substantial number of the enslaved managed to get out of their irons, they would have had a decided numerical advantage over the sailors assigned to guard them. The sailors, however, had cutlasses, and the insurgents had no weapons other than what they could pick up from the deck, such as belaying pins, staves, perhaps an oar or two. If the women had risen in coordination with the men, fighting would have broken out in the aft part of the ship, behind the barricado, where they would have had access to better implements such as fish gigs and the cook's hatchet. Most insurrectionists found themselves in the situation of a group who had burst onto a moonlit deck at midnight: "They had no fire arms, and no weapons, except the loose articles which they could pick up on the deck."[25]

As all hands rushed on deck to quell the uprising, they picked up pistols and muskets and took their positions at the barricado, firing through the peepholes at the men. They also manned the swivel guns at the top of the barricado, which allowed them to sweep the deck with shot. This was a decisive moment. If the enslaved had any hope of victory, they had to breach the barricado, not least to get into the gun room, which was located as far from the men's section as possible, in the stern of the vessel, near the captain's cabin, where crew members would be around to guard it. Many insurrectionists therefore tried to crash through the small door of the barricado or scale its wall, which ranged from eight to twelve feet high with spikes at the top. If they managed to get through or over, if they could fight their way to the gun room and break it open, and if they knew how to use European firearms (as many African men with military experience did), they might have an outcome like that of the enslaved aboard the ship *Ann* in 1750: "the Negroes got to the Powder and Arms, and about 3 o'Clock in the Morning, rose upon the Whites; and after wounding all of them very much, except two who hid themselves: they run the Vessel ashore a little to the Southward of Cape Lopez, and made their Escape."[26]

As the fighting raged on, the rebels would act on previous planning. What would they do about the crew? They usually had a straightforward answer: they would kill them. Such would appear to have been the choice on an unnamed vessel out of Bristol when, in 1732, the enslaved "rose and destroyed the whole Crew, cutting off the Captain's Head, Legs and Arms." This issue was complicated, however, by another one—that is, whether the Africans had any among them who knew how to sail the ship. The absence of such knowledge was always considered by Europeans to be one of their greatest bulwarks against insurrection once the ship was out at sea, as John Atkins pointed out in 1735: "it is commonly imagined, the *Negroes* Ignorance of Navigation, will always be a Safeguard." Some insurrectionaries therefore made it a point to keep several crew members alive, to assist with navigation and sailing the ship back to Africa.[27]

Insurrections aboard slave ships usually had one of four outcomes. The first of these was exemplified in 1729 aboard the *Clare* galley. Only ten leagues out to sea off the Gold Coast, the enslaved "rose and making themselves Masters of the Gunpowder and Fire Arms," drove the captain and crew into the longboat to escape their wrath and took control of the ship. It is not clear whether the successful rebels sailed the vessel or simply let it drift toward the shore, but in any case they made landfall and their escape to freedom not far from Cape Coast Castle. An even more dramatic rising occurred off the Windward Coast in 1749. The enslaved picked the locks of their shackles, grabbed large billets of wood off the deck, fought the crew, and after two hours overpowered them, forcing them to retreat to the captain's cabin and lock themselves inside. The following day, as the captives ripped open the quarterdeck, five members of the crew jumped overboard in an attempt to escape but discovered the hard way that some among the captives knew how to use firearms; they were shot and killed in the water. The successful insurrectionists then ordered the rest of the crew to surrender, threatening to blow up the powder room if they refused. The vessel soon ran aground, and before leaving the victors plundered it. Some of them went ashore, not in the nakedness required on the ship, but now clad in the clothes of the crew.[28]

Sometimes an insurrection resulted in the mutual destruction of the contending sides. Such would appear to have been the case aboard a "ghost ship" discovered adrift in the Atlantic in 1785 by another vessel. The unnamed slave schooner had sailed about a year earlier with a Newport, Rhode Island, crew to the coast of Africa. Now it had no sails and no crew, only fifteen Africans on board and they were in "very emaciated and wretched condition." It was supposed by those who found them that they had "been long at sea." It was also supposed that the enslaved had waged an insurrection on board, "had rose and murdered the Captain and crew," and that during or after the rising "many of the Blacks must have died." Perhaps no one knew how to sail the vessel and some slowly starved to death.[29]

By far the most common outcome of shipboard rebellion was defeat, which always featured torture, torment, and terror in its aftermath. Those who had played a leading role in the insurrection would be made examples to the rest. They would be variously flogged, pricked, cut, razored, stretched, broken, unlimbed, and beheaded, all according to the overheated imagination of the slave ship captain. The war would continue through these savage punishments, the insurgents refusing to cry out when they were whipped or going to their deaths calmly, as the Coromantee notoriously did, despising "Punishment, even death it self." Sometimes the body parts of the defeated would be distributed among the remaining captives throughout the ship as a reminder of what happened to those who dared to rise up. It was proven again and again that the slave ship was a well-organized fortress for the control of human beings. It was, by design, extremely difficult for its prisoners to capture it and sail to freedom.[30]

The main cause of slave revolts was slavery. And indeed Africans themselves offered their own explanations aboard the ship that proved the observation true. Seaman James Towne, who knew the primary trading language of the Windward Coast "nearly as well as English," conversed with the enslaved and learned their grievances. Asked by an MP in 1791 whether he had ever known them to attempt an insurrection on board a slave ship, he said that he had. He was then asked, "Did you ever inquire into the causes of such insurrections?" He replied, "I have. The reasons that were given me were 'What business had we to make Slaves of them, and carry them away from their own country? That they had wives and children, and wanted to be with them.'" Other considerations that made insurrection more likely on any given ship were, for some, proximity to shore (worries about navigation once the vessel was out to sea) and poor health or lax vigilance among the crew. The captives' previous experience in Africa of warfare in the expansion of slaving operations would add to the likelihood of insurrection.[31]

Historian David Richardson has shown that insurrections aboard slave ships materially affected the conduct of the trade. They caused losses, raised shipping costs, and created disincentives for investors, as a writer in the *Boston News-Letter* recognized in 1731: "What with the Negroes rising, and other Disappointment, in the late Voyages thither [Gold Coast], [we have witnessed] a great Reducement in our Merchants Gains." Richardson estimates that as many as one in ten vessels experienced an insurrection, that the average number of deaths per insurrection was roughly twenty-five, and that, all told, 100,000 valuable captives died as a result. Insurrections also generated other economic effects (higher costs, lower demand) that "significantly reduced the shipments of slaves" to America—by a million over the full history of the slave trade, by 600,000 in the period from 1698 to 1807.[32]

Insurrections also affected the reading public, as newspapers on both sides of the Atlantic endlessly chronicled the bloody uprisings of the enslaved. Alongside and sometimes within this coverage, opponents of the slave trade also gave voice to the struggles from the lower deck, noting the "desperate resolution, and astonishing heroism" displayed by the enslaved. They often insisted that the prisoners were trying to recapture their "lost liberty," their natural right. Moreover, when public debate about the slave trade exploded in Britain and the United States after 1787, abolitionists repeatedly used the resistance of the enslaved to disprove everything the slave-trading interest said about the decency of conditions and treatment aboard the ships. If slave ships were what merchants and captains said they were, why would the enslaved starve themselves to death, throw themselves over the side of the vessel, or rise up against long odds and suffer likely death in insurrection?[33]

Thomas Clarkson wrote of the "Scenes of the brightest Heroism [that] happen repeatedly in the Holds or on the Decks of the Slave-Vessels." So great and noble were these acts that the "Authors of them often eclipse by the Splendour of their Actions the celebrated Character both of Greece and Rome." He continued:

> But how different is the Fate of the one and of the other. The Actions of the former are considered as so many Acts of Baseness, and are punished with Torture or with Death, while those of the latter have been honoured with publick Rewards. The Actions of the former again are industriously consigned to oblivion, that not a trace, if possible, may be found, while those of the latter have been industriously recorded as Examples for future Times.[34]

Clarkson was right about the heroism, the torture, the death, and about the endless glorification of the history of Greece and Rome, but he was wrong about the legacy of the rebels. The effect of insurrection was probably greatest upon the enslaved aboard the ship, and this despite their various degrees of participation in the project. Those who refused to accept slavery initiated a struggle that would go on for hundreds of years. As martyrs they would enter the folklore and long memory of those on the lower deck, the waterfront, and the slave plantation. The rebels would be remembered and the struggle would continue.[35]

"Going Home to Guinea"

The experience of death and the impulse to all forms of resistance were linked to a broadly held West African spiritual belief. From the beginning of the eighteenth century to the time of abolition most captives seem to have believed that in death they returned to their native land. This allowed them to "meet their fate with a fortitude and indifference truely their own." The belief seems to have been especially prominent among peoples from the Bight of Biafra, but it was also present among those of Senegambia, the Windward Coast, and the Gold Coast. It persisted long after the Middle Passage. Among people of African descent in North America and the West Indies, funerals often featured rejoicing, even rapture, because the deceased was "going home to Guinea."[36]

Early in the century an unnamed observer noted of those dying aboard his ship, "Their opinion is that when they dye, they go to their own country, which made some of them refuse to eat their victuals. Striving to pine themselves, as [most ex]peditious way to return home." A woman of Old Calabar who starved herself to death aboard a slaver in the 1760s said to other women captives the night before she died that "She was going to her friends." Late in the century, Joseph Hawkins wrote that after death the Ibau "must return to their own country, and remain forever free of care or pain." Abolitionists knew of the belief in the transmigration of souls, as explained by Thomas Clarkson: "It is an opinion, which the Africans universally entertain, that, as soon as death shall release them from the hands of their oppressors, they shall immediately be wafted back to their native plains, there to exist again, to enjoy the sight of their beloved countrymen, and to spend the while of their new existence in scenes of tranquility and delight: and so powerfully does this notion operate upon them, as to drive them frequently to the horrid extremity of putting a period to their lives." When someone died, the other Africans said, "*he has gone to his happy country.*"[37]

A European observer who talked to various captives aboard his ship noted that among the majority, this belief was "so gross [ignorant] as to allow them to inhabit the same country with the same bodies." Some even thought they would go back to life just as it was before, and even inhabit their "old dwellings." Others (denominated the "more intelligent" Africans) thought they would return to "a portion of this vast continent which alive they can never know." In an "African paradise" they would enjoy the joys and luxuries of life with none of its fears. The Islamic slaves on board the slave ship referred to the "law . . . which is to be the inheritance of all true Musselmen!" But they seemed to have a difference of opinion about who would accompany them into the afterlife, whether they would "carry their old wives along with them" or "blew eyed virgins." According to the man who collected the lore, the anthropological foray led nowhere: "Their opinion of this matter however must be acknowledged to be so dark and unintelligible as scarce to deserve our attention."[38]

Slave-trade merchants and ship captains begged to differ. They gave the belief a great deal of attention, in contemplation and action.

They not only hooked up the nettings to prevent suicides and readied the implements of forced feeding, they resorted to studied terror. Since many Africans believed that they would return to their native land in their own bodies, captains terrorized the dead body, and all who would look upon it, as a "preventative." One captain brought all of the enslaved onto the main deck to witness as the carpenter cut off the head of the first slave who died, throwing the body overboard and "intimating to them, that if they were determined to go back to their own country, they should go back without their heads." He repeated the grisly ritual with each subsequent death. Captain William Snelgrave had the same idea. After decapitating a man who had been executed for leading an insurrection, he explained, "This last part was done, to let our Negroes see, that all who offended thus, should be served in the same manner, For many of the Blacks believe, that if they are put to death and not dismembred, they shall return again to their own Country, after they are thrown overboard." Hugh Crow knew that the belief often led to the "the utter annihilation of the culprit." To the many roles played by the slave ship captain in the burgeoning capitalist economy of the Atlantic must be added another: terrorist.[39]

The determination to "go home to Guinea" also suggests that the goal of an insurrection was not always the capture of the ship. The objective on many occasions was collective suicide, as Thomas Clarkson explained: the captives often "determine to rise upon the crew, hoping by those means to find that death which they have wished for, and indulging a Hope at the same time, that they shall find it at the Expence of some of the Lives of their Oppressors." Given this objective, a much larger number of insurrections must be counted as successful from the point of the view of those who made them. In death and spiritual return, insurgents reversed their expropriation, enslavement, and exile.[40]

Bonding

The violence of expropriation and enslavement shattered the structures of kinship that had ordered the lives of almost all of the people who had been forced aboard the slave ship. As deep, disruptive, and disorienting as this was, the enslaved did not suffer it passively. They did everything they could to preserve whatever may have survived of these kin relations, and, just as important, they set about building new ones, on the ship if not earlier, in the coffles, "slave-holes," factories, and fortresses along their way to the ship. Olaudah Equiano developed new connections to his "countrymen," a word that could refer to his fellow Igbo or to all of the African people with whom he found himself sharing the ship. What anthropologists have called "fictive kinship" was actually an endlessly reproduced series of miniature mutual aid societies that were formed on the lower deck of the slave ship. The kindred would call themselves "shipmates."

The first point to be emphasized about kinship is that it was real and commonplace aboard the slave ship. Husbands and wives, parents and children, siblings, members of families both extended and nuclear, found themselves on the same ships, as one observer after another pointed out. One of the primary means of enslavement in Africa made this likely. The "grand pillage" of entire villages, set afire in the middle of the night, meant that families, indeed clans and sometimes communities, were swept up by marauding enemy forces, carried to the coast, and often sold together as "prisoners of war." As John Thornton has written, "An entire slave ship might be filled, not just with people possessing the same culture, but people who grew up together."[41]

Kinfolk met regularly aboard the slavers. An Igbo man, an embrenché "styled of the higher class," encountered on the main deck of his vessel a woman of similar "countenance and color," his sister. The two then "stood with silence and amazement," looked at each other with the greatest affection, and "rushed into each other's arms." An "extremely clever and intelligent" fifteen-year-old girl was brought aboard another slaver only to find, three months later, that a "girl with similar features," her eight-year-old sister, had been forced to join her. "They very soon embraced each other, and went below." It happened repeatedly on slave ships that "relations are brought on board, such as Brothers and Sisters, Wives and Husbands, and these at Separate Times." Brothers messed together, as did sisters. But because men and women were separated, it was not easy for all kin to maintain contact. Communication between husbands and wives, for example, "was carried betwixt them by the boys which ran about the decks."[42]

Slowly, in ways surviving documents do not allow us to see in detail, the idiom of kinship broadened, from immediate family, to messes, to workmates, to friends, to countrymen and women, to the whole of the lower deck. Central to the process was the additive nature of many West African cultures, as explained by John Matthews: the people of Sierra Leone had an extraordinary "facility with which they form new connexions." Captain James Bowen described the bonding process among the enslaved. On his ship, there were among the Africans "many relations." These were not, he made clear, traditional kin relations, but something of more recent formation. These were people "who had discovered such an attachment to each other, as to have been inseparable, and to have partaken of the same food, and to have slept on the same plank during the voyage." They had, in short, shared violence, terror, and difficult conditions, as well as resistance, community, and finally survival on the lower deck of the slave ship. They built "new connexions": they were shipmates.[43]

Dr. Thomas Winterbottom explained the significance of the term. He worked as a physician in the Sierra Leone colony in the early 1790s and observed the connection between kinship in Africa, aboard the ship, and in the New World. He noted that at a certain age, "the title of pa, or father, is prefixed to the names of the men, as a token of respect," and the "title of ma, or mother, is also added to the names of the women." This, he noted, was "also practised among the slaves in the West Indies." Then he showed how the ship provided a link: "it is worthy of remark, that those unfortunate people who have gone to the West Indies in the same vessel, ever after retain for each other a strong and tender affection: with them the term *ship-mate* is almost equivalent to that of brother or sister, and it is rarely that matrimonial connections take place between them." This phenomenon prevailed throughout the Atlantic colonies: in the Dutch colonies, those who came over on the same ship called each other "sibbi" or "sippi." In Portuguese Brazil, the word for seafaring kinship was "malungo." In French Caribbean Creole, it was "bâtiment." And from Virginia to Barbados, Jamaica, and beyond, it was "shipmate." Such kinship would be extended when those who sailed together on the ship would later instruct their children to call their shipmates uncle or aunt. Speaking of the changed social relationships aboard his own ship during the Middle Passage, seaman William Butterworth noted how "much were things altered in a few weeks sailing."[44]

Evidence of such bonds appeared in the extreme anxiety and pain of shipmates as they were sold and separated at the end of the voyage. Part of their agitation was of course the fear of the unknown that lay ahead on the plantation, but part of it was losing what had been built, in anguish and desperate hope, aboard the ship. In the House of Commons hearings on the slave trade between 1788 and 1792, surgeon Alexander Falconbridge and seaman Henry Ellison were asked the same question by an MP: "Have you ever known the Slaves on board your ship to appear exceedingly distressed when they were sold in the West Indies?" They agreed, yes, "they seemed sorry to be parted from one another." Falconbridge had witnessed four such sales, while the long-experienced Ellison had seen ten. Between them, they had seen more than four thousand Africans sold off the ships. They spoke not just of formal kin, who would have been in a small minority in any case; rather they generalized about the enslaved of each ship as a whole.[45]

Others added depth to the observation. Dr. Thomas Trotter wrote that the people from his ship "were crying out for their friends with all the language of affliction at being parted." He added that "on this occasion some husbands and wives were parted," but also noted that there were "many other relations of different degrees of kindred"—in other words, from closest family to extended kin, to fellow villagers, to countrymen, to new shipmates. Captain Bowen tried to keep together for group sale (in a scramble) those "connected by consanguinity or attachments," but he failed in his design. With "shrieking and dismay," even fainting, the attached were parted, probably, the captain thought, never to meet again. A final sale and separation involved three young girls "of the same country" whose vessel docked in Charleston, South Carolina, in 1804. This produced "the most piercing anguish" among one of the three, who was "overloaded with horror and dismay at the separation from her two friends." They in turn "looked wistfully at her, and she at them. At last they threw themselves into each others arms, and burst into the most piteous exclamations.—They hung together and sobbed and screamed and bathed each other with their tears." At last they were torn apart, whereupon one of the girls took "a string of beads with an amulet from her neck, kissed it, and hung it on her friend's."[46]

Another instance of a shipboard community in formation appeared in the comments of Captain Thomas King, veteran of nine Guinea voyages between 1766 and 1780. Captain King had witnessed instances in which "religious Priests" of certain groups had been brought aboard among the captives and had proceeded to encourage insurrection. These spiritual leaders induced others "to make those attempts, with the expectation that they should get the ship to some shore, where they would form a little community of their own." Here, on the ship, was a new community in formation. It began when the African Adam and Eve—the first man and woman—came aboard and it would continue in plantation, maroon, church, and urban communities. Here was the alchemy of chains mutating, under the hard pressure of resistance, into bonds of community. The mysterious slave ship had become a place of creative resistance for those who now discovered themselves to be "black folks." In a dialectic of stunning power, the community of mortal suffering aboard the slave ship gave birth to defiant, resilient, life-affirming African American and pan-African cultures.[47]

SEVEN

✦

"Black Pirates"

The Amistad Rebellion, 1839

The story began with a sensational headline: "A Suspicious Sail—a Pirate." The *New York Morning Herald* announced on August 24, 1839, that a pilot boat had spotted a mystery ship about twenty-five miles off the coast of New York. On deck were "a number of negroes, twenty five or thirty, . . . almost or quite naked; some were wrapped in blankets, and one had on a white coat." They were a "strange crew," all the stranger for brandishing machetes, pistols, and muskets. One sailor "had a belt of dollars round his waist; another called the captain, had a gold watch. They could speak no English, but appeared to talk in the negro language." Black pirates, armed and flush with plunder, were cruising the coast of Long Island.[1]

The vessel itself was in eerie disrepair: "Long grass was growing upon her bottom, and her sails were much torn, as if she had been driving about at the mercy of the gale, with her sails set and no one at the helm." Here, declared the *Morning Herald*, was the "Flying Dutchman," the ghost ship that wandered the seas endlessly as a portent of doom. Indeed, doom seemed already to have struck the vessel, which once upon a time had been a slave ship: "It was supposed that the prisoners had risen upon the captain and his assistants and captured her." Having murdered the master and crew, those aboard could

146

not navigate the vessel. They "are now drifting about bound for no particular port."

Over the next few days, other newspapers offered new accounts of the vessel, many of them short on reliable information and long on overheated speculation. One reported that this "black, rakish, suspicious sail" was full of "black piratical wretches" who had "undoubtedly robbed several vessels, and perhaps committed murder." Another had no doubt: the crew "had murdered all the white men." They were, moreover, rife with riches: "there is money and jewels on board of the value of $40,000." Another wrote, "Some accounts say, that there are two hundred thousand dollars in coin stowed away in her hold." Yet another claimed they had "three tons of money on board."[2]

Thus began the story of the *Amistad* in America's penny press, with lurid tales of gore and gold. These articles made "the long, low, black schooner" a popular sensation. The nation's two leading penny newspapers, the *Morning Herald* and the *New York Sun*, known for their interest in crime stories, especially murder, and for their ability to convey the news cheaply to the "great masses of the community," took an avid interest in the case of the "black pirates." So did the older commercial newspapers, the *New York Commercial Advertiser* and the *New York Journal of Commerce*. Southern newspapers such as the *Richmond Enquirer*, the *Charleston Courier*, and the *New Orleans Bee*, republished articles from the Northern press, sometimes editing out inconvenient information about the slave rebellion and adding fearful rhetoric of their own, demanding the gallows for murderous "African pirates."[3]

A mere six days after the *Amistad* had been towed ashore in New London, Connecticut, a drama troupe performed a play about its story of mutiny and piracy at New York's Bowery Theatre. Commercial artists drew images of the leader of the rebellion, a man called Cinqué, reproduced them quickly and cheaply, and had them hawked by boys about the streets of eastern cities. Artist Amasa Hewins painted a 135-foot panorama depicting the *Amistad* Africans as they surrounded and killed Captain Ramón Ferrer and seized their freedom by force of arms. Another artist, Sidney Moulthrop, created twenty-nine life-size wax figures of the Africans and the *Amistad* crew, which he cast and arranged to dramatize the shipboard insurrection. Both artists would tour with their creations, charging admission to see a visual reenactment of the uprising. The wax figures appeared in Peale's Museum and Portrait Gallery in New York, Armory Hall in Boston, and finally in Phineas T. Barnum's American Museum. Meantime, thousands of people lined up daily to pay admission and walk through the jails of New Haven and Hartford to get a glimpse of the *Amistad* prisoners. When legal proceedings began, citizens jammed the courtrooms to capacity and beyond, refusing to leave their seats during breaks for fear of losing them. Popular fascination with the case was unprecedented. Slave resistance became a commercial entertainment, a commodity to be consumed in the ever-growing American marketplace.[4]

Within the excellent scholarship on the *Amistad* rebellion, most notably by Arthur Abraham, Howard Jones, and Iyunolu Folayan Osagie,[5] remains a puzzle: how did this bloody slave revolt—in which forty-nine African men, armed with cane knives, rose up, killed the white captain of the vessel and another member of the crew, and seized their freedom by force[6]—manage to become a popular cause in a slave society, where, in 1839, two and a half million people were held in bondage? The last time anything like this had happened in the United States was 1831, when Nat Turner's Rebellion in Southampton, Virginia, convulsed the nation. Slave revolts had long caused panic throughout white American society, not least among white middle-class abolitionists, many of whom were frankly terrified of them. Why would the *Amistad* rebellion prove different? To make matters more curious, the *Amistad* rebels would achieve popularity while cooperating with abolitionists, themselves despised as extremists by many. Another odd twist is that abolitionists committed to nonviolent principles flocked to the campaign as something heaven sent to advance their cause.[7]

The outpouring of interest, most of it sympathetic, depended on the peculiar facts of the case. The *Amistad* affair centered on the slave trade, against which abolitionists on both sides of the Atlantic had already won major victories, establishing a limited but real popular consensus about its horrors. Moreover, it mattered that the slave owners, the villains of the story, were Spaniards, not Americans, and the self-emancipated heroes were Africans, who had never been American slaves. The *Amistad* rebellion did not, therefore, directly challenge *American* slavery as Nat Turner's insurrection had done. The tactics, strategy, strength, and will of the abolitionist movement also helped to generate interest in, and favorable coverage of, the case. Indeed, victory in the *Amistad* case would be one of the movement's greatest and most popular achievements.

Yet these facts cannot fully unravel the knot of contradiction: Nat Turner had become infamous, the very nightmare of many white people north and south, but Cinqué became a celebrity in the modern sense of the word. Indeed he was the first person of African descent to claim such status in the history of the United States. How can we explain this extraordinary difference in the popular images of the two best-known leaders of slave revolts in American history?[8]

An unexplored part of the answer lies in how the *Amistad* rebellion originally appeared to the American public as a pirate story. Tales of "black pirates," told in various ways in and through an increasingly commercialized mass culture, excited intense interest everywhere, rapidly making what happened on the *Amistad* a national issue of concern "among all classes of the community," including, crucially, urban workers. Less than a week after the first report, the clamor had grown so loud that the *Amistad* was now called the "famous piratical vessel."

Four case studies in the early representation of the revolt follow: the play performed at the Bowery Theatre; the images of Cinqué produced for mass circulation; a recently discovered pamphlet of 1839: *A True History of the African Chief Jingua and His Comrades*; and the legal and popular debate about piracy and its specific application to the case. Drama, art, journalism, and law shaped the popular perception of the *Amistad* rebels and ultimately the outcome of the case.[9]

Militant collective action taken by a small group of West African warriors on the deck of a small vessel off the north coast of Cuba would reverberate around the world, mobilizing an army of playwrights, actors, theater-goers, artists, correspondents, writers, readers, lawyers, judges, politicians, activists, and citizens, who would produce and consume images of the rebels and their actions. By representing the *Amistad* Africans as "black pirates," the creators of popular culture shaped the popular perception of the case. The history of slavery and the history of piracy thus intersected in complex and ambiguous ways, with profound results, for the *Amistad* case and the struggle against Atlantic slavery. The international movement against bondage would take an unexpected popular form, which would in turn help to expand, strengthen, and radicalize the anti-slavery movement and its accompanying public.[10]

The History of Piracy

The early nineteenth century witnessed the rise of sea literature in America, within which lay a special fascination with the pirate. James Fenimore Cooper wrote *The Pilot* (1823) and *Red Rover* (1828). The two greatest American writers about things maritime themselves went to sea at this time: Richard Henry Dana (from 1834 to 1836) and Herman Melville (from 1839 to 1844). Beginning with Lord Byron's influential epic poem *The Corsair* (1814) and continuing with Sir Walter Scott's novel *The Pirate* (1821) and Frederick Marryat's novel of the same title in 1836, sea robbers strengthened their grip on the literary and popular imagination. In 1837 an enthusiastic seventeen-year-old named Friedrich Engels wrote a short story called "The Pirate." By 1839, articles, stories, poems, and books about the lore and legends of piracy poured from the presses of newspapers and publishers, including, for example, the "Lives of Anne Bonny and Mary Read," the women pirates (1833), and *Blackbeard*, a novel (1835). The worldwide Romantic movement expanded popular interest in things maritime in the United States and around the Atlantic, establishing a broad predisposition to view the *Amistad* rebellion as a sea story and the rebels themselves as pirates.[11]

Newspaper writers and their readers also had specific historical reasons to see the *Amistad* rebels as "black pirates." Because the North Atlantic had long been an important theater in the history of robbery by sea, pirates themselves were deeply embedded in popular consciousness and memory, as both "enemies of all mankind" and folk heroes. During the "Golden Age of Piracy," 1650–1730, pirate crews captained by Blackbeard, Samuel Bellamy, and many others had haunted the colonial coast, producing fear, excitement, and robust popular writing on pirates, especially when a gang of them was captured, taken ashore, tried, and hanged, as happened on numerous occasions. Cotton Mather, who delivered thunderous sermons at several pirate hangings, wondered in exasperation why so many regarded these criminals as heroes.[12]

The motley pirate crews that plagued the North American coast included many Africans and African Americans, beginning in the seventeenth century, when buccaneers marauded on the Spanish Main and people of color ran away from Caribbean plantations to join them, and continuing through the 1710s and 1720s, when, for example, Blackbeard's crew of one hundred had sixty black members, Oliver La Bouche's men were "half French, half negro," and William Lewis had "40 able negro sailors." In 1723 the *Boston News-Letter* reported that an all-mulatto crew of pirates were taking ships in the Caribbean and eating the hearts of white captives. Such fantasies were rekindled in the images of the rebels aboard the *Amistad* more than a century later.[13]

There was, moreover, a recent history of piracy that would have been on the minds of many Americans in 1839. The pirates of the North African Barbary Coast had long attacked European and American shipping in the Mediterranean, prompting Britain, France, and even the fledgling navy of the United States to take measures to subdue them, which they managed finally to do with the French occupation of Algiers in 1830. The US involvement in the Tripolitan War (1801–1805) and the Algerine War (1815) had high public visibility and long-lasting consequences. At roughly the same time the Spanish American Wars of Independence (1808–1829) had produced a new explosion of piracy closer to home. Multiethnic crews, including many of African descent, attacked merchant ships around the Caribbean. The infamous privateers of Cartagena led the way.[14]

The hanging of the pirates of the ship *Panda* on June 11, 1835, in Boston vividly framed the *Amistad* case. These were the last executions of pirates ever to take place in the United States. Colombian captain Pedro Gilbert and crew had marauded in the northern Caribbean, plundering the American-owned brig *Mexican* in 1832 of $20,000 in silver off the coast of Florida before locking the crew inside the vessel, setting it afire, and sailing away. The sailors of the *Mexican* managed to break out, douse the flames, and eventually return to their home port of Salem, Massachusetts. The *Panda* was finally captured by a British cruiser off the coast of West Africa, and Gilbert and his crew were then extradited to the United States for trial. The resulting legal drama generated wide newspaper coverage, as well as several pamphlets and books.[15]

In the late 1830s, "Mitchell the Pirate," a privateer-turned-pirate who operated out of New Orleans in the Gulf of Mexico, became "notorious" for his robberies by sea. The *Connecticut Courant* announced that he and his "long, low, black schooner" had "frightened the whole country." Mitchell was captured in Mobile, Alabama, in 1838, after taking part in a port-city riot. He broke out of jail, was retaken, bound, and sent back toward confinement but "managed to loose himself" and escaped again, only to be shot by one of the guards. He soon died of the wound. He went on to become a legendary figure after his death as rumors swirled about treasure he had buried on Cat Island in the Bahamas. When the US revenue cutter *Jefferson* was retired from service, it was proudly noted that she had "brought up the '*long, low, black schooner*,' Mitchell the pirate." The story of Mitchell entered the realm of fiction in January 1839, in a pirate yarn called "The Chase" written by "Ben Bobstay."[16]

Enterprising writers used the publicity surrounding pirates to launch new books. *The Lives and Bloody Exploits of the Most Noted Pirates, their Trials and Executions, including correct accounts of the Late Piracies, committed in the West Indies, and the Expedition of Commodore Porter; also those committed on the Brig Mexican, who were Executed at Boston, in 1835* was published in 1836 by Ezra Strong in Hartford, Connecticut, where the hearings on the *Amistad* rebels would take place three years later. The following year Charles Ellms, based in Boston, published *The Pirates' Own Book; or, Authentic Narratives of the Lives, Exploits, and*

Executions of the Most Celebrated Sea Robbers, with Historical Sketches of the Joassamee, Spanish, Ladrone, West India, Malay, and Algerine Pirates, which would prove popular among sailors and indeed help to inspire future acts of resistance.[17]

The connection between the history of piracy and the *Amistad* rebellion was made explicit in a third volume of the era, Henry K. Brooke's *Book of Pirates, containing Narratives of the Most Remarkable Piracies and Murders, committed on the High Sea: Together with an Account of the Capture of the Amistad,* which was published in Philadelphia and New York in 1841. In both subtitle and text, Brooke played up the story of the "black pirates," placing their seafaring adventure alongside those of Blackbeard, Anne Bonny, Mary Read, and the most successful freebooter of them all, Bartholomew Roberts. In his preface, Brooke mentioned Scott's *The Pirate* and quoted Byron's *The Corsair* at length. After the Supreme Court ruled that the rebels were "free men," they entered the popular pirate canon as social bandits: "Pirates, robbers, and murderers, from the days of Robin Hood (1160) to the present time, have been *heroes* in the imaginations of old and young, rich and poor, the learned and the illiterate."[18]

These books placed the recent piracies of the *Panda,* the Barbary Coast, and the *Amistad* alongside the pirate narratives of the "Golden Age," reprinting large parts of the classic account by Captain Charles Johnson, *A General History of the Pyrates,* originally published in two volumes, in 1724 and 1728. The books featured fantastic stories of money and mayhem that would dominate the popular image of pirates ever after—tales of buried treasure, walking the plank, and hand-to-hand combat on deck. Another theme in all three books, repeated from Johnson, was that piracy represented a "life of liberty," an escape from the slavish conditions common sailors faced aboard the vessels under the arbitrary and dictatorial power of their captains. The success of the books was reflected in their publishing history: taken together, the three were republished twenty times before 1860. In the first sentence of his preface Charles Ellms wrote that "there are few subjects that interest and excite the curiosity of mankind" more than pirates.[19]

The "black pirates" of the *Amistad* proved the point. When reports of their activities appeared in the popular press between August 24 and September 4, 1839, readers up and down the coast and all around the country had a framework in place for viewing the case. The dramatic seizure of a ship at sea and the organization of a new social order, based on liberty, were already widely familiar and deeply popular themes.

The Long, Low, Black Schooner

On September 2, 1839, New York's Bowery Theatre began its run of *The Black Schooner, or the Pirate Slaver Armistead*—or *The Long, Low, Black Schooner*, as it was more commonly called. An advertisement announced "an entire new and deeply interesting Nautical Melo-Drama, in 2 acts, written expressly for this Theatre, by a popular author," almost certainly Jonas B. Phillips, who was the "house playwright" during the 1830s.[20] Based on "the late extraordinary Piracy! Mutiny! & Murder!" aboard the *Amistad* and the sensational newspaper reports of "black pirates," the play demonstrated how quickly the news of the rebellion spread, and with what cultural resonance. The title of the play drew on the title of the *New York Sun* article about the *Amistad* rebellion published on August 31, 1839, which in turn had drawn on the recent descriptions of Mitchell's pirate ship. The line from piracy to slave revolt was direct.[21]

In 1839 the Bowery Theatre was notorious for its rowdy, raucous working-class audiences: youthful "Bowery b'hoys and g'hals" and dandies, as well as sailors, soldiers, journeymen, laborers, apprentices, street urchins, and gang members. Prostitutes plied their trade in the theater's third tier. The audience cheered, hissed, drank, fought, cracked peanuts, threw eggs, and squirted tobacco juice everywhere. During an especially popular performance, the overflow crowd might sit on the stage amid the actors and props, or they might simply invade it and become part of the performance. The owner and manager of the theater, Thomas Hamblin, employed a pack of constables to prevent riots, which on several occasions exploded anyway. That the Bowery Theatre was associated with a big, violent anti-abolitionist riot in 1834 makes its staging of *The Long, Low, Black Schooner* all the more remarkable.[22]

The play attracted "multitudes" to the nation's largest theater. If performed every other day for two weeks (it may have been longer), at only two-thirds capacity of the theater's 3,500 seats, it would have been seen by roughly 15,000 people, about one in twenty of the city's population. Another way of estimating the number in attendance is to divide the production's estimated gross earnings of $5,250 ($131,834 in 2014 dollars) by prevailing ticket prices (most were 25 cents, some were 50 and 75 cents), which also suggests roughly 15,000 viewers. The play therefore played a major role not only in interpreting the *Amistad* rebellion, but in spreading the news of it.[23]

A detailed playbill for *The Long, Low, Black Schooner* provides a "Synopsis of Scenery, Incidents, &c." Set on the main deck of the *Amistad,* the play featured as characters the actual people who were involved in the uprising. The leading character was "Zemba Cinques, an African, Chief of the Mutineers," based on Cinqué and played by Joseph Proctor, a "young American tragedian," perhaps in burnt-cork blackface, as was common at the Bowery.[24] The "Captain of the Schooner, and owner of the Slaves" was Pedro Montes, the actual owner of four of the enslaved who sailed the vessel after the rebellion. The supercargo was Juan Ruez, based on José Ruiz, owner of forty-nine slaves on board. Cudjo, "a deformed Dumb Negro," who resembles the "savage and deformed slave" Caliban in Shakespeare's play *The Tempest,* was apparently based on the "savage" Konoma, who was ridiculed for his tusklike teeth and decried as a cannibal in the early reports of the *Amistad* Africans. Lazarillo, the "overseer of the slaves," probably drew on the slave-sailor Celestino. Other characters included Cabrero the mate, sailors, and the wholly invented damsel-soon-to-be-in-distress Inez, the daughter of Montes and the wife of Ruez.[25]

Act I begins as the vessel sets sail from Havana, passing Moro Castle and heading out to sea. The history of Zemba Cinques, the hero of the story, is recounted as a prelude to entry into the "hold of the schooner," where lay the "wretched slaves!" The bondsmen plot and soon take an "Oath of vengeance," which they (and pirates) actually did. In a rising storm, also noted in the accounts of the rebellion, "The Slaves, led by Zemba Cin[q]ues" force open the hatchway, which results in "MUTINY and MURDER!" The rebels seize the vessel and reset its course, heading eastward across the Atlantic to their native Sierra Leone. "Prospects of liberation" are at hand.[26]

Act II shifts to the captain's cabin, now occupied, after the rebellion, by Zemba Cinques, while Montes and Ruez sit as prisoners in the dark hold of the vessel (as they actually did). The world has been turned upside down: those who were below are now above and vice versa. The reversal poses great danger to Inez, who apparently has fallen into the clutches of Cudjo and now faces "terrible doom." Someone, probably Zemba Cinques, rescues her, forcing Cudjo to "surrender his intended victim." Did the audience see a black hero rescue a white woman from the hands of a black villain? This is a theme of no small significance given prevailing popular fears of racial "amalgamation," which had ignited recent anti-abolition riots.

Zemba Cinques then sees a vessel (the US brig *Washington*) sailing toward them and holds a council among his fellow mutineers to decide what to do. They choose death over slavery, a sentiment repeatedly ascribed to Cinqué in the popular press, and decide to "Blow up the Schooner!" (The *Amistad* rebels made no such decision, as many of them were ashore on Long Island when the sailors of the *Washington* captured their vessel, but pirates frequently threatened to "blow up rather than be taken," and some actually did). Alas, it is too late as the "Gallant Tars" of the *Washington* drop into the cabin from its skylight, taking control of the *Amistad*.

The end of the play is left uncertain, much like the fate of the *Amistad* captives, who sat in the New Haven jail awaiting trial on charges of piracy and murder as the play was being performed. The playbill states: "Denoument—Fate of Cingues!" What indeed will be his fate? Did the play enact his execution, an ending that many, including Cinqué himself, expected? Or did it dramatize his liberation along with all of his comrades?[27]

The Long, Low, Black Schooner was not an unusual play for its time. Slave revolt and piracy were common themes in early American theater. Rebellious slaves appeared in *Obi; or Three-Finger'd Jack*, a play about a Jamaican runaway slave-turned-bandit, which was a staple after its American premiere in 1801, and in *The Slave*, an opera by Thomas Morton about a revolt in Suriname acted first in 1817 and many times thereafter, into the 1840s. *The Gladiator* dramatized the famous slave revolt led by Spartacus in ancient Greece. It premiered in 1831, starred working-class hero Edwin Forrest, and may have been the most popular play of the decade. Pirates headlined popular nautical melodramas of the 1830s, such as *Captain Kyd, or the Wizard of the Sea*, performed first in 1830 and numerous times thereafter, then published as a novel by J. H. Ingraham in 1839. John Glover Drew adapted Byron's *The Corsair* for performance at Brook Farm in the early 1840s. The great African American actor Ira Aldridge would soon act the lead in *The Bold Buccaneer*. Slave rebels and pirates sometimes appeared in the same plays, as they did in *The Long, Low, Black Schooner:* "Three-Finger'd Jack" was something of a pirate on land, and indeed had been called "that daring freebooter." Pirates also played a significant role in *The Gladiator*.[28]

Like other melodramas of the times, *The Long, Low, Black Schooner* featured virtuous common people, usually laborers, battling villainous aristocrats—in this case, enslaved Africans striking back against the Spanish slave owners Montes and Ruez. "Low" characters like Zemba Cinques performed heroic action and spoke poetic lines and were thus were routinely celebrated for their honorable resistance, encouraging some degree of popular identification with the outlaw who dared to strike for freedom. As Peter Reed has noted, audiences "could both applaud and fear low revolts, both mourn and celebrate their defeats."[29]

The theater not only spread the news of the *Amistad* rebellion; it shaped it. Cinqué's poised and dramatic personal bearing during the legal proceedings earned him comparison to Shakespeare's Othello.[30] He was also likened to "a colored dandy in Broadway." He clearly had the "outlaw charisma" so common to the "Rogue Performances" of the era. Having captured the attention of the theater world and the public at large, it was fitting that *The Long, Low, Black Schooner* should be followed, in December 1839, by a production of *Jack Sheppard, or the Life of a Robber!*, also written by Jonas B. Phillips. Like Sheppard, whose jailbreaks became "the common discourse of the whole nation" in Britain in the 1720s and to whom the public flocked, paying admission to see his him his cell, the "black pirates" of the *Amistad* were winning in their own bid to take the good ship *Popular Imagination*. A "Nautical Melo-Drama," based on real people and dramatic current events, was playing out in American society as a whole.[31]

Cinqué as Heroic Pirate

One of the most arresting images of the *Amistad* rebellion, *Joseph Cinquez, Leader of the Gang of Negroes*, appeared around the same time as *The Long, Low, Black Schooner*, perhaps a day or two earlier. Cinqué is featured on the deck of the *Amistad*, dressed in a red sailor's frock (what is today called a buccaneer's shirt) and a pair of white duck pantaloons. (He was actually wearing similar clothes at the moment of capture; he took them from the ship's cargo en route to Puerto Príncipe.) He strikes a gallant pose, with his cane knife at the ready. Here is the consummate image of the conquering, swashbuckling hero. A man who was, at the time the image was published, soon to stand trial for piracy and murder is depicted, at the scene of the crime, with the deadly weapon in his hand, as transcendently good and noble in his cause. Indeed he appears as an executioner of justice, a slayer of tyrants. His history of resistance is simultaneously celebrated and commodified in the form of an image to be bought and sold.[32]

The original image for this color print was "Drawn from Life by J. Sketchley, Aug. 30, 1839" in New London. Sketchley had probably gone aboard the US brig *Washington* and observed the legal hearing held there soon after the vessels came to port. Below the image is a caption: "Joseph Cinquez, Leader of the Piratical Gang of Negroes, who killed Captain Ramon Ferris and the Cook, on board the Spanish Schooner Amistad, taken by Lieut. Gedney, commanding the US Brig Washington at Culloden Point, Long Island, 24th Augt 1839." Beneath the caption was a speech delivered by Cinqué in which he exhorted his mates to fight back against slavery. The leader of the pirates resembles a Roman hero.[33]

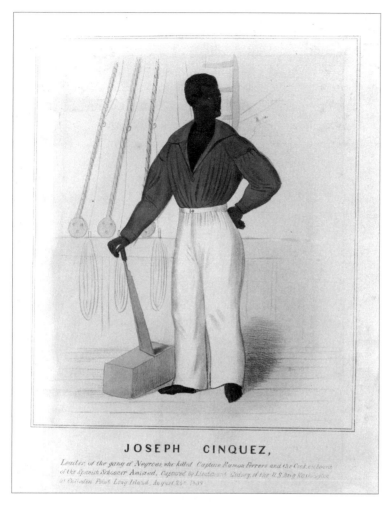

JOSEPH CINQUEZ,

Leader of the gang of Negroes who killed Captain Ramon Ferrers and the Cook on board of the Spanish Schooner Amistad, Captured by Lieutenant Gedney of the U.S Brig Washington at Culloden Point Long Island August 26th 1839

"Joseph Cinquez, Leader of the Gang of Negroes" (Stanley Whitman House)

A related image, *Joseph Cinquez, the Brave Congolese Chief,* drawn by a New London artist named Sheffield, appeared as a broadside the following day, August 31, 1839, again during the first week after the *Amistad* had come ashore. It contained another sympathetic image of Cinqué, dressed in the same frock, but this time with more explicit antislavery commentary: "JOSEPH CINQUEZ, the brave Congolese Chief, who prefers death to Slavery, and who now lies in Jail in Irons in New Haven Conn. awaiting his trial for daring for freedom." Below the caption appeared another stirring speech Cinqué gave to his comrades. The image and text, in broadside form, were hawked in the streets of the cities, spreading the association of piracy and slave revolt and the sensational news of the rebellion itself.[34]

These glorifications of armed struggle were not, as they might appear, the work of an underground group of militant abolitionists.

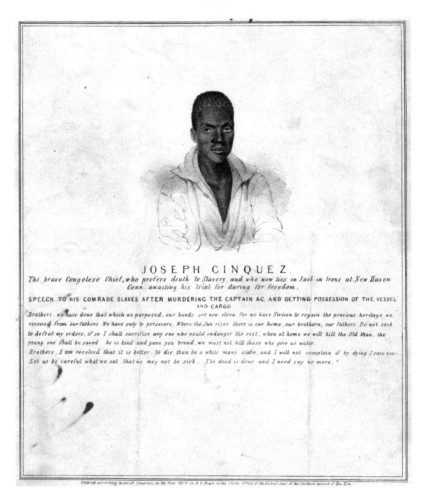

"Joseph Cinquez, the Brave Congolese Chief" (Library of Congress)

They were, rather, commissioned by, advertised in, and distributed by the penny paper the *New York Sun*. Moses Yale Beach, editor of the *Sun*, used the trope of piracy to frame the *Amistad* rebellion, to sensationalize the case, and to appeal to the popular appetite for heroic sea robbers, thereby to sell newspapers and prints to a mass public. He succeeded beyond his wildest dreams. He and the other editors of the *Sun* were shocked by the popularity of the images. Having published portraits of Cinqué on Saturday, August 31, 1839, they noted the following Monday that the supply of prints had been exhausted immediately and that they had been unable to meet the clamor for more. They announced to their readers that they would, "by an early hour this morning, have another and a very large edition printed, and shall be prepared, on the opening of our office, to supply demands for any number." They explained that they had printed enough on Saturday to satisfy "any *ordinary* demand" but encountered a "tremendous run for them" for which they were not ready. This "was as unexpected to us as it was astonishing in itself." They printed the image on "thick, fine paper, in a style of excellence," which presumably made it suitable for saving and even framing. They also noted that the print had been republished in the Sunday editions of other newspapers. They were clearly proud of what they had done. Their use of pirate imagery had worked.[35]

James Gordon Bennett and his colleagues at the proslavery *New York Morning Herald* felt otherwise. They howled in protest against the sympathetic depictions of Cinqué the pirate and declared the *Sun* to be "the New York penny nigger paper." During a time of polarization on the issue of slavery, the correspondents for the *New York Morning Herald* drew a different picture. Against the "preposterous twaddle" of other publications, these writers angrily sought "to destroy the romance which has been thrown around [Cinqué's] character." They denied that he "is dignified and graceful with the bearing of Othello." Rather, he was a "blubber-lipped, sullen looking negro, not half as intelligent or striking in appearance as every third black you meet on the docks of New York." The entire lot of the *Amistad* Africans represented nothing so much as "hopeless stupidity and beastly degradation"—they were likened to baboons. Back in Africa, they had been "slothful and thievish," and were "sunk in a state of ignorance, debasement and barbarism, of which no adequate conception can be formed." They were in no way "fit to associate on terms of equality with the whites." They were "a distinct and totally different race, and the God of nature never intended that they should live together in any other relation than that of master and slave." The depictions of Cinqué the pirate by the *New York Sun* were, it seems, egalitarian and subversive.[36]

Cinqué as Barbary Corsair

A True History of the African Chief Jingua and His Comrades was anonymously written by someone who hoped to capitalize on, and contribute to, the swell of popular interest in the rebels and their now widely known leader. It was published in October 1839 and based to a large extent on early newspaper coverage of the rebellion and its aftermath.[37] The title page indicates that it was published simultaneously in Hartford, Boston, and New York, but this may have expressed a hope for sales rather than a fact of publication. It was most likely published in Hartford after the *Amistad* captives had appeared in court there September 19–23, 1839, and in anticipation of a return visit for a second round of legal hearings scheduled for November (continued in January 1840, in New Haven). Both Hartford events drew throngs of people to the city from as far away as New York and Boston. "All inquiries" around Hartford involved the question "where is the jail?" The author of the pamphlet fleshed out the newspaper reports in the twenty-eight-page account with a variety of plagiarized sources, in large part narratives of travelers to Africa. Most of them had not been to Sierra Leone, nor the Gallinas coast, least of all to the inland areas where the *Amistad* Africans had lived before they were enslaved.[38]

The pamphlet was based, in its central assumption, on a misunderstanding. And a revealing one it was. The author wrote *A True History* in September 1839, when the ability of lawyers, judges, abolitionists, and correspondents to communicate with the *Amistad* Africans was limited by the problem of language comprehension. The mostly Mende-speaking rebels had been separated from the Afro-Cuban cabin boy Antonio, who had managed to translate between them and the two Spaniards from the time of the rebellion to their capture by the United States Coast Guard. Only one of the rebels, Burna, spoke English, and that but poorly. The time had not yet come when the Mende sailor James Covey would be found on the docks of New York to translate for the captives.

The misunderstanding occurred when people asked the *Amistad* Africans who they were and whence they came. Most of them replied that they were "Mende." But the Americans asking the questions had never heard of the Mende, who were not located on any maps of the period and not described in any of the travel literature about Africa. They therefore interpreted "Mende" to be "Manding"—a group of Senegambians (now better known as the Mandinka) who had been in contact with European and American traders for centuries and of whom they had heard.[39] This is why the anonymous author of the pamphlet includes "a Description of the Kingdom of Mandingo, and of the Manners and Customs of the Inhabitants." Because so many Mandinka had converted to Islam, the author assumed, wrongly, that the *Amistad* captives were Muslims.[40]

Pirates played a crucial role in this piece of popular writing. The author not only plagiarized from the text of the recently published *The Pirates Own Book*, by Charles Ellms, he ended the essay by referring to the recently hanged pirates of the *Panda*.[41] He concluded by calling Cuba a "receptacle of the buccaneers" and slave traders, who were also deemed pirates. Since Cuba was like the "piratical state of Barbary," the United States should take possession of it and bring it to heel as Britain, France, and the United States had recently done with Algiers.[42]

The Muslim pirates of the Mediterranean thus influenced an Orientalist engraving of Cinqué that appeared in *A True History*. The leader of the rebellion appears as a Barbary corsair, with a *keffiyah* (headdress), a *shemagh* (a traditional Muslim scarf), and a *kaif* (a curved Arabian sword), facing a rising sun with a spyglass in his hand.

*African Chief Jingua (Beinecke Rare Book and
Manuscript Library, Yale University)*

The *Amistad*'s rigging, a block, and a mast are in the background.
Another engraving featured "The Sugar Knife, with which the Captain of the Amistad was killed," thereby dramatizing the rebellion itself. A global discourse on piracy clearly shaped the perception of the
writer and illustrator of *A True History of the African Chief Jingua and His
Comrades*, and thereby their readers too.[43]

The Legal Battle over Piracy

The issue of piracy was central to the legal debate about the fate of the *Amistad* captives. The grand jury charged to look into the allegations of piracy and murder found that the Africans, "not having fear of God before their eyes, but being moved and seduced by the instigation of the devil," did, "with force and arms, upon the high seas, about ten leagues from the island of Cuba aforesaid within the Admiralty and maritime jurisdiction of the United States, and without the jurisdiction of any particular state," kill Ramón Ferrer and his slave Celestino, using "certain machetes, or cane knives," whereafter they turned pirate.[44]

The formal charges would be argued and decided by middle- and upper-class judges, attorneys, and government officials, whose attitudes to piracy were rather different from those reflected in the romantic popular accounts of the day. To these important people, piracy represented not a heroic quest for ready money and liberty; it was, first and foremost, a crime against property. The pirate was *hostes humani generis*, the "enemy of all mankind." Still, the debate about piracy kept the issue alive and before the public.

The piracy issue to be adjudicated by the courts emerged from Pinckney's Treaty of 1795, in which the United States and Spain agreed to mutual assistance for ships in distress. Article 8 stipulated that if a ship "be forced through stress of weather, pursuit of pirates or enemies, or any other urgent necessity" to seek shelter, it "shall be received and treated with all humanity" and properly assisted. Article 9 added that all ships "rescued out of the hands of any pirates or robbers on the high seas, shall be brought into some port" and restored to its original owners. The Spanish slave owners Montes and Ruiz made claims based on these articles of the treaty, as did the government of Spain through its ambassador, Angel Calderón de la Barca. If the *Amistad* Africans were pirates, they, the vessel, and the cargo would be turned over to Spain. They would be returned to Cuba and probably hanged, a proper fate for the "enemies of all mankind."[45]

Abolitionist attorneys argued that the *Amistad* rebels were *not* pirates, were *not* slaves, and that the United States government must not turn them over to Montes, Ruiz, Cuba, Spain, or anyone else for that matter. They should instead go free. Against a backdrop of the newspaper articles and images described above, and amid calls from proslavery newspapers that the US government return the African pirates to face their just punishments, a series of anonymously authored articles of learned legal opinion were published in early September, ten days to two weeks after the *Amistad* came ashore. These articles parsed the definitions of piracy and concluded that the *Amistad* rebels did not, indeed could not, fit any of them. They had no goal of enrichment in seizing the vessel and they attacked no other ships. They were merely seeking liberty and exercising their right to self-defense.[46]

Yet the abolitionists shrewdly noticed—and took advantage of—a new addition to the law of piracy since the "golden age" of freebooting in the late seventeenth and early eighteenth centuries. A US federal law of 1820, sponsored by Virginia Federalist Charles Fenton Mercer and supported by abolitionists to attack illegal slave trading that went on after formal abolition in 1808, stated that any citizen of the United States who engaged in the slave trade "shall be adjudged a pirate" and if convicted "shall suffer death." (This actually happened only once: Captain Nathaniel Gordon was hanged in New York for slave trading in 1862.) Spain's treaties with Great Britain agreeing to end the trade in human beings by May 30, 1820, strengthened the association of slave trading and piracy.[47]

Who, asked the abolitionists, are the pirates here? Not the *Amistad* rebels but rather the slave traders, in this case, Montes and Ruiz, and by implication the deceased Captain Ramón Ferrer. Even though the law technically applied to American, not Spanish, citizens, it nonetheless allowed the abolitionists to turn the tables: the Spaniards who held the *Amistad* Africans illegally in bondage were the real pirates. The main attorney of the *Amistad* captives, Roger Baldwin, stated that his clients "were not pirates, nor in any sense hostes humani generis." Their objective "was—not piracy or robbery—but . . . deliverance . . . from unlawful bondage." They were in fact themselves the "helpless victims of piracy." The idiom of piracy had become a primary means of fighting the legal battle as well as the cultural one.[48]

The abolitionists won a first victory in this battle on September 23, 1839, when Judge Smith Thompson, noting that "the feelings of the community were deeply involved" in the case, ruled that the United States Circuit Court did not have the jurisdiction to try the *Amistad* rebels as pirates and murderers. Judge Andrew Judson ruled on January 13, 1840, that the District Court did have jurisdiction and that the defendants were illegally enslaved Africans, which superseded the allegation of piracy and made it irrelevant.[49]

Yet the legal issue of piracy remained alive because the United States government challenged Judson's ruling and appealed the case to the Supreme Court. Beginning February 23, 1841, Attorney General Henry D. Gilpin argued anew that the *Amistad* Africans were pirates. They had committed a crime against property by seizing themselves. John Quincy Adams then had some fun with the contradictions of the argument. Both the American and Spanish governments had insisted on treating the *Amistad* Africans as both "merchandise," as passive property, that is to say, as slaves, and at the same time as "pirates and robbers," who were active, aggressive human agents. Referring to the Treaty of 1795, Adams remarked before the Supreme Court, "my clients are claimed under the treaty as merchandise, rescued from pirates and robbers." But who were the merchandise and who were the robbers? "According to the construction of the Spanish minister, the merchandise were the robbers, and the robbers were the merchandise. The merchandise was rescued out of its own hands, and the robbers were rescued out of the hands of the robbers." Adams then turned to the Justices and asked, no doubt with a glint of mischief in his eyes: "Is this the meaning of the treaty?" Roger Baldwin added, dryly, "It is believed that such a construction of the words of the treaty is not in accordance with the rules of interpretation which ought to govern our courts." The Supreme Court justices agreed with Adams. Judge Joseph Story, writing for the 7–1 majority, ruled on March 9, 1841, that the defendants had been "kidnapped" in Africa and that "there is no pretense to say that they are pirates or robbers." The *Amistad* rebels were neither property nor pirates. They were now officially free people.[50]

Slave, Pirate, Commodity

When the rebels on the ghost ship appeared off the coast of Long Island and then came ashore in New London in late August 1839, how could Americans of all classes have seen them, understood them, conceived of their activities? The options were limited. They could have seen them simply as the latest in a long line of Africans who rose up in rebellion aboard the slave ships. These acts of resistance had been chronicled by American newspapers for more than a century and were well known. But those stories almost always ended badly: the rebels were killed in battle or tortured in the aftermath, often executed to terrorize the survivors. The individual voyage and the larger slave trade, legal or illegal, went on as before. There were few examples of successful slave revolts at sea to make this way of understanding the *Amistad* rebels salient.[51]

A related option would have been to see the *Amistad* Africans more broadly as slave rebels, fighting an entire Atlantic institution of bondage. This was a timely image in the 1830s, after African American radical David Walker had made his appeal to the "Colored Citizens of the World" to rise up and follow the example of the Haitian Revolution. Some seemed to have taken him up on the proposition: Nat Turner in Virginia, 1831; Sam Sharpe and his "Baptist War" in Jamaica, 1831–1832; and enslaved Muslims in the Malê Revolt, Bahia, Brazil, in January 1835. Add to the mix the upheaval of British slave emancipation in 1834 and 1838, and suddenly slaveholders all around the Atlantic had plenty to be nervous about. Fear of revenge and retribution was of course undergirded by guilt, as everyone knew that slavery was based fundamentally on violence and terror. When an autonomous, armed group of black men who also happened to be in control of a tall ship, one of the most sophisticated technologies of its day, was spotted off American coasts in late August 1839, it was a fearsome thing.[52]

These fears operated in the early reports, which claimed that the rebels had murdered all the white people aboard the *Amistad*. In truth they had killed, first and foremost, an enslaved Afro-Puerto-Rican sailor and cook, who had threatened to kill them, and Captain Ferrer, in self-defense, because he had killed one or two of them.[53] None of the other four whites aboard were killed. Two sailors jumped over the side with a canoe and returned to Cuba; Montes and Ruiz came safely to Connecticut. The fantasized race massacre had never happened.

The main alternative in the early phase of the *Amistad* affair was to see the rebels as "black pirates." The image of the pirate, which was no less rebellious in its way, projected something completely different—dreams of golden doubloons and liberty, a combination of wealth and freedom aggressively seized by poor men on the high seas, beyond the control of family, religion, and state, the main institutions of social discipline. These autonomous, armed men, many of them black, inspired a different reaction: not fear, but hope.[54]

The pirate fantasy also operated in the early newspaper reports, in which the *Amistad* rebels were said to be wearing belts of gold and to have in the hold of their vessel tons of money and jewels. As it happened, the trunks thought to contain gold were actually filled with metal parts for plantation machinery, which, with human labor, were meant to produce gold in a different way. A thorough search of the *Amistad* later revealed that "not one dollar of gold or silver has been found among her goods."[55]

Did the appellation "black pirates" ultimately make a difference in the *Amistad* case? It certainly increased the level of popular interest in, and awareness of, the freedom struggle, which was truly extraordinary by the standards of the day. The newspaper coverage, the play, the prints, the engravings, the paintings, the wax figures, the pamphlets, the long lines leading to the doors of the jail and the courtroom, even the legal treatises—all depended to some extent on the image of the pirate and its place in popular culture. Taken together, these created an unusual atmosphere, which may have influenced the judges in the District, Circuit, and Supreme Courts, all of whom made rather surprising decisions favorable to the *Amistad* Africans and their claims of freedom. Circuit Court judge Andrew Judson was known to be hostile to people of color, and a majority of the Supreme Court justices were Southerners. The judges themselves were not likely swayed by the pirate image but by the popular mobilization it helped to create. Indeed, all ruling judges acknowledged in their written opinions the extraordinary degree of popular interest on the case.

By folding the nightmarish image of the violent, rebellious slave into the ambivalent and, to many, attractive image of the violent, rebellious pirate, the purveyors of popular culture helped to create a more favorable context for the liberation of the *Amistad* Africans. As they transformed resistance into a commodity using the pirate motif, they made the entire case safer for popular consumption and support. Literary and visual evidence—Zemba Cinques the mutineer, Cinquez the leader of a "Piratical Gang of Negroes," and Jingua the Barbary corsair—demonstrate the powerful process at work. This was critical to the celebration and eventual liberation of insurrectionists who had killed a white figure of authority during a rebellious time when fears of revolt were soaring.

This strange and contradictory process did not go unnoticed, or uncriticized, at the time. A writer for the *Herald of Freedom*, Nathaniel Rogers of the New Hampshire Anti-Slavery Society, observed the aggressive entry of the market into the *Amistad* case and remarked, "Our shameless people have made merchandise of the likeness of Cinque" and his "countrymen." He resented the "wood-cut representation of the royal fellow," even though he thought it a good likeness. He considered it "effrontery" that artists had studied the "lion-like" face of the "African hero" to draw the image that was now for sale. He detested the intrusion of money and profits into the realm of high principle, but he may have underestimated how much "making merchandise" of resistance helped his cause.[56]

Abolition from Below

A successful rebellion aboard a small Cuban slaving schooner, depicted as piracy, echoed around the Atlantic, not least because it was part of a larger cycle of rebellion that tore through slave societies in the 1830s. The drama cried out for representation—on the stage, on the printed page, and in the courtroom. One of the most remarkable things about the many and varied piratical portrayals of the revolt was their antislavery content. The popular depictions of the *Amistad* rebellion reflected, and in turn advanced, the growing power of a worldwide antislavery movement.[57]

The Long, Low, Black Schooner made Cinqué the mutineer its hero, including an account of his personal history early in the drama in order to create sympathetic identification among the audience. The play also highlighted the horrific Middle Passage, already made infamous by the abolitionist movement, by going below decks to the hidden space where the "wretched slaves" lay jumbled together and where they would begin their conspiracy. The appearance of the play alongside *Three-Finger'd Jack, The Slave,* and *The Gladiator,* proves theater historian Bruce McConachie's point that the "political anxieties" of the era were enacted on the stage, even if obliquely at times. The play about the *Amistad* confronted slave revolt directly because, as everyone knew, it concerned not bondsmen and rebellion in a distant time and place, but living, breathing, acting rebels, who sat in jail not far from the Bowery Theatre.[58]

The pirate-shaped images produced by the *New York Sun* likewise played up the drama of the rebellion, gave voice to its leader, conveyed strong antislavery messages, and actively sought to enlist public sympathy for the rebels and their cause. Echoing the American revolutionary leader Patrick Henry—and the African American revolutionary leader Gabriel, who planned an uprising in Richmond, Virginia, in 1800—the text that accompanied the images of Cinqué repeatedly expressed his insistence on "Death or Liberty." Here was a bold, swashbuckling hero who "dared for freedom" and justice. Significantly, the antislavery images and text produced by the *Sun* appeared, like *The Long, Low, Black Schooner,* within a week of the arrival of the *Amistad* Africans in New London, *before* Tappan, Baldwin, and other abolitionists had worked out the legal strategy to represent them as freedom fighters. Perhaps the elite abolitionists learned from the penny press, which in turn had learned from the emergent romantic literature on pirates, and from the rebels themselves.[59]

The pamphlet *A True History of the African Chief Jingua and His Com-*

rades, which pictured Cinqué as a Barbary corsair, also expressed antislavery ideas. Its title page proclaims:

Liberty is Heaven born,
'Twas man that made the slave.

The author refers to the "unfortunate victims" of the slave trade as Mandingoes, who are "cheerful, inquisitive and humane," with "moral virtues . . . strongly developed." A sympathetic (if largely invented) biography of Cinqué follows, emphasizing his "great intelligence, industry, and courage." Special emphasis is given to the enslavement of the hero, his march to the coast, and his placement, with five hundred others, including pregnant women and infants, "between the decks of a vessel with hardly room to set up right, and to undergo all the horrors of the '*middle passage.*'" In a similar vein, *The Book of Pirates,* edited by Henry K. Steele, offered a sympathetic portrait of the *Amistad* Africans, using abolitionist sources, arguments, and sentiments. Steele also noted the horrors of the Middle Passage aboard the slave ship *Teçora* (where the Africans "suffered terribly"), and he too sought to give voice to the rebels, drawing heavily in his text on the testimony of two of the rebels, Grabeau and Bau.[60]

The antislavery movement in 1839 consisted of a rebellious and sometimes insurrectionary wing of enslaved rebels, a reform wing of various, often quarreling, mostly white middle-class abolitionists, and a growing antislavery public. The *Amistad* rebellion and its popular representation as piracy helped to connect the first two and to expand the third by circulating antislavery images and ideas into new social domains—into the streets, where stories of the revolt would circulate to free and enslaved urban laborers alike; onto the waterfront, where Vigilance Committees in New York and Philadelphia were already undertaking direct action in the struggle against slavery; and into factories, where workers contributed to the defense campaign.[61]

The popular images of the *Amistad* rebels as pirates stood in sharp contrast not only to the racist anti-abolitionist images of the day, but to long-standing paternalist depictions by abolitionists that suggested either grateful deference among supplicant slaves—"Am I not a Man and a Brother?"—or their status as sentimentalized victims of atrocity. Sarah Grimké wrote that these images expressed the "speech-less agony of the fettered slave." By contrast, the black pirates of the *Amistad* appear as powerful, independent actors, not as those who are acted upon by others. They inspired admiration, not condescension, benevolence, or pity. They were not "helpless victims"—of piracy or anything else.[62]

The popular freebooting images may help to account for another curious aspect of the *Amistad* case. In a decade notorious for urban riots against African Americans and abolitionists—one of which, in 1834, resulted in an attack that moved from the Bowery Theatre to the home of Lewis Tappan—there was a signal lack of violence, or even the threat thereof, directed against the rebels or their support-ers. Certainly the opportunities for such violence were many, whether in jail as the thousands filed through, or on the New Haven Green, where the *Amistad* Africans routinely went for exercise and fresh air. An even more likely moment was in May 1841 when a group of the recently freed prisoners went on a highly publicized East Coast fund-raising tour to raise funds for their repatriation to Sierra Leone. They held public events in places where anti-abolitionist mobs had been most violent—New York and Philadelphia, among others. It is of course hard to be sure why something did *not* happen, but it may be that the positive images and the wider publicity surrounding the case, much of it based on the idiom of piracy, protected the *Amistad* rebels and their supporters against the racist violence frequently used in this period by rampaging white mobs.[63] A New York woman commented on the change: "some years ago," she explained to the British aboli-tionist Joseph Sturge, large public meetings like those featuring the *Amistad* Africans "would have excited the malignant passions of the multitude, and probably caused a popular outbreak." Now the gath-erings caused "a display of benevolent interest among all classes."[64]

A final, longer-term significance of the *Amistad* rebellion and its representations as piracy lay in the strengthening of what has been variously called "militant," "aggressive," "radical," or "physical force" abolitionism. As Stanley Harrold has written, "The slave revolts aboard the *Amistad* in 1839 and the *Creole* in 1841 were central to the sense of crisis among abolitionists," to the growth of a more militant and confrontational approach, especially among African American activists, and to abolitionist "Addresses to the Slaves," which now acknowledged the significance of resistance from below. The advance of this tendency from the time of the *Amistad* to the Civil War can be followed through the growing power and popularity of a phrase that originated with Lord Byron in *Childe Harold's Pilgrimage* (Canto II, Stanza 76):

> Hereditary Bondsmen! know ye not,
> Who would be free themselves must strike the first blow?

The street-fighting, direct-action abolitionist David Ruggles used the phrase in 1841 in an open letter announcing a black antislavery convention. Henry Highland Garnet would repeat it as he remembered the *Amistad* rebellion and called for mass resistance at a national black convention in Buffalo in 1843: American slaves who would be free "themselves must strike the first blow!" The phrase would reach its classic expression when John Brown and his fellow insurrectionists decided to "strike the first blow" in Harpers Ferry in 1859 and Frederick Douglass used it to encourage African Americans to join the Union Army in 1863. "Joseph Cinquez" had been pictured on the deck of the *Amistad* having struck a first blow as a pirate wielding a cane knife. He linked the antislavery movement from below to white middle-class abolitionism in a strategic and growing alliance. He symbolized a revolutionary future.[65]

The *Amistad* affair had a special meaning for black Americans. This was clearly expressed by the weekly newspaper the *Colored American*, published in New York by African American editors Samuel Cornish, Phillip Bell, and Charles Bennett Ray, who sounded a distinctive, often revolutionary message about the case from the beginning, comparing Cinqué to the great liberators George Washington and Toussaint Louverture and demanding that the African prisoners be emancipated immediately. When, after gaining their freedom, the *Amistad* Africans toured the eastern United States to raise money for their repatriation to Sierra Leone, the African American community turned out in huge numbers, especially when events were held in their churches, such as the African Methodist Episcopal Zion Church on Church Street in New York. At one gathering there, the reporter for the *Colored American* noted, "We do not recollect of ever having seen a larger assemblage of our people upon any occasion." During the meeting itself the community gave the *Amistad* Africans a loud and passionate embrace. The feeling was acknowledged and returned by the *Amistad* African Kinna, who said to his African American supporters, "You are my brethren, the same color as myself." The *Amistad* case helped draw many African Americans into what had been mostly a white, middle-class abolitionist movement and helped to move many black leaders, including Henry Highland Garnett, to more militant stands against slavery.[66]

The "Bloody Flag" of Piracy

On August 24, 1839, when newspapers were aflame with speculation about the black pirates, Captain Henry Bullinger and his crew encountered the *Amistad* at sea, as he noted in his logbook:

> "We asked if they wanted a pilot, and receiving no answer we hailed again and inquired if they wanted to go to New York. They said in broken English no; but that they were going to some other country, pointing to the N. E. They asked for water, but would not come for it. We then hoisted the American flag, and hailed them the third time and told them to follow us—that we were going to take them to New York."

Upon this attempt to capture the schooner, the men on the *Amistad* "rushed to the quarter deck and armed themselves with muskets and cutlasses and hoisted the bloody flag at the peak." The red or "bloody" flag, like the black flag, was commonly used by eighteenth-century pirates to signal defiance: they would accept no quarter and they would grant none. They would fight to the death. Cinqué, after all, preferred death to slavery, as the penny press had made clear. Perhaps the *Amistad* Africans really were pirates after all.[67]

Epilogue

I conclude with words written by the West Indian novelist Jamaica Kincaid:

> In the Antigua that I knew, we lived on a street named after an English maritime criminal, Horatio Nelson, and all the other streets around us were named after some other English maritime criminals. There was Rodney Street, there was Hood Street, and there was Drake Street.[1]

Note that phrase: *English maritime criminals*. To many in the English-speaking world, these words will sound heretical if not downright treasonous. I am sure the author meant them to be. In any case, they express an important truth that has been central to his book: those historical figures some see as heroes, others see as criminals. And the reverse is true: those historical figures some see as criminals, others see as heroes. This is often the way of the outlaw. Lord Nelson, hero to many, is a criminal to Jamaica Kincaid. Conversely, pirates, criminals to many, and certainly to Nelson, were heroes, in their own day as in ours, to many. It is all a question of perspective—more specifically, a question of who has power to impose perspective in the interpretation of history, as in the naming of streets, the building of museums, and the writing of books.

The old history will not do anymore—the exclusive focus on the Nelsons, Rodneys, Hoods, and Drakes, the great and the powerful of the world's navies and merchant shipping industries; the well born and the well heeled; the admirals, the commodores, the captains; the merchants, the businessmen, the entrepreneurs; on their battles by sea and their transoceanic imperial adventures; on the national glories heaped upon them; and on the national mythologies made of and through them. Perhaps the best-known writer of the old maritime history in America was Samuel Eliot Morison, the Boston patrician, patriotic admiral, and Harvard historian who wrote about the Christopher Columbuses and the John Paul Joneses of the world. This kind of history looks from the top down—history, in my view, seen from the wrong end of the spyglass.[2]

Like many other books written over the past generation, this chronicle has looked from below, shifting focus from the admirals and other elites to workers black and white, male and female, of many nations, races, and ethnicities. We have followed motley crews into crowded grogshops with scraping fiddles and wild brawls; into cold, damp jails; and onto ships with their rolling decks, billowing sails, whispered conspiracies, stowaways, and liberation. As Jesse Lemisch remarked in 1968, as history "from the bottom up" began to challenge the old history from above, this broader, more inclusive approach to the past is much more in keeping with democratic and egalitarian ideals than is the top-down variety. We now know to ask about the Afro-Caribbean woman whose nursing saved Nelson's life in 1780, and the mutineers flogged and executed by the likes of Rodney, Hood, and Drake.[3]

We have seen how seafaring people influenced people up above—how their yarns gave ideas to playwrights, novelists, poets, and philosophers. We have seen how the actions of the motley crew in Boston in 1747 gave a young Sam Adams the idea that all people were "by Nature on a Level; born with an equal Share of Freedom, and endow'd with Capacities nearly alike." This radical idea would be reactivated by a motley crew of sailors and slaves a generation later and enshrined by Thomas Jefferson in the Declaration of Independence.

We have seen how runaway seamen and enslaved Africans congregated, cooperated, and together imagined and sometimes actually built subversive alternatives to capitalism—pirate crews, maroon communities, and underground revolutionary movements of various sorts. Outlaws created independent organizations and autonomous zones that offered freedoms simply not available to the laboring many in the societies they left behind. The lords of the Atlantic struggled mightily to destroy these subversive alternatives as part of their own drive to dominance, fearing that freer ways of life might inspire others with similar grievances. Sometimes the authorities won the battle but lost the war: they obliterated the counterculture of pirates, hanging hundreds on gibbets around the Atlantic, but the swashbucklers came back around as folk heroes, more popular today than ever.

We now look back on the motley crews of the past with greater understanding than ever before, not least because contemporary globalization makes it easier to understand the importance of the original transnational worker, the deep-sea sailor, and the centrality of the seas in human endeavor as a place where important historical processes such as the genesis of ideas and class formation have taken place. Long derided as marginal and liminal, quaint and exotic, the seaman at long last emerges as a preeminent worker of the world, a cosmopolitan in the truest sense, who shaped the history of our planet in profound and lasting ways.

I close with the story of one of my favorite historical figures, who embodied many of the themes of this book. I refer to an enslaved man known to us by the name of Caesar. He first appears in the historical record in 1759, in an act of resistance against slavery near Philadelphia: he ran away from his master, who in response ran an advertisement in the *Pennsylvania Gazette* in an effort to recover his wayward property. In the ad we learn that Caesar had the kind of job that put him close to freedom: he had worked as "a Ferry man at Chester Town . . . for many years." His master believed he escaped by sea as the "Cook of a Vessel, as he has been much used on board of Ships."

Somehow, Caesar was caught and reenslaved, we know not how, but he shows up again ten years later, in 1769, having escaped another master, this time in Boston. He was now supposed to be "strolling about the country."[4]

What distinguished Caesar from the many thousands of men and women who emancipated themselves by running away by sea to become outlaws on the great Atlantic was his unusually fierce determination. For according to his second master, Caesar was "noted in town by having no legs." His first master had written that Caesar "has both his legs cut off, and walks on his Knees." Whether he lost his legs in punishment for previous acts of running away is unknown. In any case, it was, as the old saying goes, no easy walk to freedom. But a walk, and a sail, to freedom it certainly was, in the way of the outlaw.

Acknowledgments

Thinking back over the thirty-odd years of scholarship surveyed and synthesized in this book, I could name and thank a cast of thousands for their contributions. Since that is impossible I have chosen to single out five historian-activists who blazed the trail of history from below, showing me and many others the way. Their names appear on the dedication page.

Chapter 1 was conceived for a conference on "The Eighteenth Century Cosmopolis: Global Cities and Citizens in the Age of Sail," but not completed because of illness. It was finished and delivered as a keynote four years later at another conference, "Community at Sea in the Age of Sail," at Aalborg University in May 2012. Thanks to Kathleen Wilson, Johan Heinson, and Torben Neilsen.

Chapter 2 was written for, and presented at, the annual meeting of the Organization of American Historians in St. Louis, in 1986. Thanks to my fellow panelists—two gifted historians—Daniel Vickers and Philip D. Morgan.

Chapter 3 was delivered as the keynote address at a conference on "Escape," held in Strachan, Tasmania, Australia, in 2006. Thanks to Cassandra Pybus, Hamish Maxwell-Stewart, and Lucy Frost.

Chapter 4 originally appeared as "'Under the Banner of King

Death': The Social World of Anglo-American Pirates, 1716–1726" in the *William and Mary Quarterly* in 1981 (3rd series, vol. 38, pp. 203–227). It is supplemented by material subsequently presented in my book *Villains of All Nations: Atlantic Pirates in the Golden Age* (Beacon Press, 2004). I owe much to the late Michael McGiffert for the former, and to my editor at Beacon, past and happily present, Gayatri Patnaik.

Chapter 5 is a revised and rewritten version of Chapter 5 of *The Many-Headed Hydra: Sailors, Slaves, Commoners, and the Hidden History of the Revolutionary Atlantic*, which I coauthored with Peter Linebaugh (Beacon Press, 2000). Thanks to our editor, Deb Chasman, and to Peter for allowing me to include our joint essay in this collection.

Chapter 6 is a revised and rewritten version of Chapter 8 of my book *The Slave Ship: A Human History* (Viking Penguin, 2007). Thanks to Wendy Wolf and Ellen Garrison for their smart, skilled work on the book.

Chapter 7 is largely new but does draw on my book *The Amistad Rebellion: An Atlantic Odyssey of Slavery and Freedom* (Viking Penguin, 2012). Thanks again to the superb Wendy Wolf.

Portions of the Epilogue come from a keynote lecture delivered at the international congress "Outlaws in the Caribbean, Past and Present," University of Vienna, May 2010. Thanks to Christian Cwik and Michael Zeuske.

I have made only modest revisions to the three already published essays, preferring to let them stand with the scholarship with which they were engaged at their moment of publication. They are, in their own ways, historical documents, and I have sought to preserve that part of their identity.

I shout out thanks to the motley crew known as the Department of History at the University of Pittsburgh, especially to my always steady shipmate, Rob Ruck. I also wish to acknowledge and thank those whose creative work in a variety of fields has been an inspiration to me in recent years: Bill Bollendorf, the late Dennis Brutus, Tony Buba, Alessandro Camon, Anna Colin, Martín Espada, Alex Farquharson, Dave Kovics, Carmit Levité, Manuel Monestel, Karen Somerville, the late Barry Unsworth, Naomi Wallace, Nigel Williams, and Frantz Zéphirin (whose art is on the book cover). I owe special gratitude to N. John Cooper, my dean at the University of Pittsburgh, who made it possible for me to work with many of these gifted people. Thanks to my family—Wendy, Zeke, and Eva—for everything, over many years.

Warm thanks to my stellar editor at Beacon Press, Gayatri Patnaik, with whom I have been happy and privileged to work again. Her assistant, Rachael Marks, has done all kinds of useful things in helping this book make its way to print. Thanks too to my extraordinary agent, Sandy Dijkstra, who found this project the perfect home, and to my assistant Eileen Weiner, who read the entire manuscript with care and insight.

This book has something of a sound track. It began long ago and recently concluded with the poetry and music of Linton Kwesi Johnson and Dennis "Blackbeard" Bovell in my ears, and no less in my mind and heart. As LKJ wrote in "Di Great Insohreckshan," about the Brixton uprising of 1981,

> evry rebel jussa revel in dem story
> dem a taak bout di powah an di glory.

Notes

Preface

1. T.J. Stiles, *Jesse James: Last Rebel of the Civil War* (New York: Vintage, 2003).

2. These are themes in the classic works by Eric Hobsbawm: *Primitive Rebels: Studies in Archaic Forms of Social Movement in the 19th and 20th Centuries* (New York: Praeger, 1959); *Bandits* (New York: Delacorte Press, 1969).

3. Marcus Rediker, *Between the Devil and the Deep Blue Sea: Merchant Seamen, Pirates, and the Anglo-American Maritime World, 1700–1750* (New York: Cambridge University Press, 1987); Rediker, *Villains of All Nations: Atlantic Pirates in the Golden Age* (Boston: Beacon Press, 2004); Peter Linebaugh and Marcus Rediker, *The Many-Headed Hydra: Sailors, Slaves, Commoners, and the Hidden History of the Revolutionary Atlantic* (Boston: Beacon Press, 2000); Rediker, *The Slave Ship: A Human History* (New York: Viking Penguin, 2007); Rediker, *The Amistad Rebellion: An Atlantic Odyssey of Slavery and Freedom* (New York: Viking Penguin, 2012).

Prologue

1. Emma Christopher, Cassandra Pybus, and Marcus Rediker, eds., *Many Middle Passages: Forced Migration and the Making of the Modern World* (Berkeley: University of California Press, 2007). Highlights of

183

the new maritime history include Daniel Vickers, *Young Men and the Sea: Yankee Seafarers in the Age of Sail* (New Haven: Yale University Press, 2007); Paul Gilje, *Liberty on the Waterfront: American Maritime Culture in the Age of Revolution* (Philadelphia: University of Pennsylvania Press, 2007); and Peter Earle, *Sailors: English Merchant Seamen 1650–1775* (London: Methuen, 2007).

2. See Jerry Bentley, Renate Bridenthal, and Kären E. Wigen, eds., *Seascapes: Maritime Histories, Littoral Cultures, and Transoceanic Exchanges* (Honolulu: University of Hawaii Press, 2007).

3. Marcus Rediker, "Toward a People's History of the Sea," in David Killingray, Margarette Lincoln, and Nigel Rigby, eds., *Maritime Empires: The Operation and Impact of Nineteenth-Century British Imperial Trade* (Suffolk, England: Boydell and Brewer, 2004), 198; Margaret Cohen, *The Novel and the Sea* (Princeton, NJ: Princeton University Press, 2010), 106–32. Cohen uses the term "hydrophasia" to describe the disregard of the sea (14). See also Allan Sekula's brilliant *Fish Story* (Düsseldorf: Richter Verlag, 1995), 48.

4. Joseph Conrad, *Nigger of the Narcissus* (Garden City, NY: Doubleday, 1914), 45; Michel Foucault, "Of Other Spaces," *Diacritics* 16 (1986): 22–27. An important step forward in the study of maritime space was a conference organized by Bernhard Klein and Gesa Mackenthun called "Sea Changes: Historicizing the Ocean, c. 1500–c. 1900," held in Greifswald, Germany, in July 2000, on ships, port cities, and the seas, "transnational contact zones." See the collection of essays edited by Klein and Mackenthun entitled *Sea Changes: Historicizing the Ocean* (New York: Routledge, 2004).

5. Derek Walcott, *Poems, 1965–1980* (London: Jonathan Cape, 1992), 237.

6. Carlo Cipolla, *Guns, Sails, and Empires: Technological Innovation and the Early Phases of European Expansion, 1400–1700* (New York: Pantheon Books, 1965).

7. Quoted in Marcus Rediker, *The Slave Ship: A Human History* (New York: Viking Penguin, 2007), 42.

8. Marcus Rediker, *Between the Devil and the Deep Blue Sea: Merchant Seamen, Pirates, and the Anglo-American Maritime World, 1700–1750* (New York: Cambridge University Press, 1987), chap. 2.

9. Eric Hobsbawm, "The General Crisis of the European Economy in the 17th Century," 5 (1954), 40; Sir William Petty, *Political Arithmetick or a Discourse Concerning, the Extent and Value of Lands, People, Buildings:*

Husbandry, Manufacture, Commerce, Fishery, Artizans, Seamen, Soldiers; Publick Revenues, Interest, Taxes, Superlucration, Registries, Banks, Valuation of Men, Increasing of Seamen, of Militia's, Harbours, Situation, Shipping, Power at Sea (London: Robert Clavel, 1690).

10. Rediker, *Slave Ship,* chap. 10.

11. C. L. R. James, Grace C. Lee, and Pierre Chalieu, *Facing Reality* (Detroit: Bewick Editions, 1974), 115.

Chapter One

1. Captain Charles Johnson, *A General History of the Pyrates,* ed. Manuel Schonhorn (1724, 1728; repr. Columbia, SC: University of South Carolina Press, 1972), 7. It was long believed that this book was written by Daniel Defoe, but the claim has been challenged in recent years. See David Cordingly, *Under the Black Flag: The Romance and the Reality of Life Among the Pirates* (New York: Random House, 1997), xix–xx. My own view is that the book had multiple authors and that Defoe was one of them.

2. Bernhard Klein and Gesa Mackenthun, eds., *Sea Changes: Historicizing the Ocean* (London: Routledge, 2004).

3. Walter Benjamin, "The Storyteller," in *Illuminations: Essays and Reflections* (New York: Schocken, 1969). This and the following four paragraphs quote from this work.

4. Friedrich Engels, *The Condition of the Working Class in England* (1845; repr. New York: Oxford University Press, 2009), 123.

5. Herman Melville, *Moby-Dick* (1851; repr. New York: Norton, 1967), 470.

6. Marcus Rediker, *Between the Devil and the Deep Blue Sea: Merchant Seamen, Pirates, and the Anglo-American Maritime World, 1700–1750* (New York: Cambridge University Press, 1987), chap. 4.

7. Definitions of "strike" from the *Oxford English Dictionary* and William Falconer, *Dictionary of the Marine* (London, 1769).

8. Samuel Robinson, *A Sailor Boy's Experience Aboard a Slave Ship in the Beginning of the Present Century* (1867; repr. Wigtown, Scotland: G.C. Book Publishers, 1996), 6.

9. Marcus Rediker, *Villains of All Nations: Atlantic Pirates in the Golden Age* (Boston: Beacon Press, 2004), 38–42.

10. Rediker, *Devil and the Deep Blue Sea,* 93, 157, 185–86, 249.

11. William Dampier, *A New Voyage Round the World* (1697; repr. New York: Dover, 1968), 303. See also Martin Green, *Dreams of Adventure, Deeds of*

Empire (New York: Basic Books, 1979), 71; Margaret Cohen, *The Novel and the Sea* (Princeton, NJ: Princeton University Press, 2010), 45; Gary C. Williams, "William Dampier: Pre-Linnean Explorer, Naturalist, Buccaneer," *Proceedings of the California Academy of Sciences* 55 (2004): 146–66.

12. Dampier, *New Voyage*, 507.

13. Edward Ward, *The Wooden World Dissected: In the Character of a Ship of War: as also, the Characters of all the Officers, from the Captain to the Common Sailor* . . . (London, 1697),71.

14. Rediker, *Devil and the Deep Blue Sea*, 12; Jane Caplan, ed., *Written on the Body: The Tattoo in European and American History* (Princeton, NJ: Princeton University Press, 2000); Ira Dye, "The Tattoos of Early American Seafarers, 1796–1818," *Proceedings of the American Philosophical Society* 133 (1989): 520–54; Simon P. Newman, "Reading the Bodies of Early American Seafarers," *William and Mary Quarterly*, 3rd ser., 55 (1998): 59–82.

15. Michel Foucault, "Of Other Spaces," *Diacritics* 16 (1986): 22–27.

16. John Cremer, *Ramblin' Jack: The Journal of Captain John Cremer, 1700–1774*, ed. Richard Reynall Bellamy (London: Jonathan Cape, 1936), 90.

17. George Barrington, *A Voyage to Botany Bay* (1795), available through Project Gutenberg at http://gutenberg.net.au/ebooks06/0607421h .html.

18. *Spooner's Vermont Journal*, Nov. 29, 1785; *Columbian Magazine, or Monthly Miscellany*, Sept. 1786; Andrew Swinton, *Travels in Norway, Denmark, Russia, in the Years 1788, 1789, 1790 and 1791* (Dublin, 1792), 2–5; "Natural History of that Most Extraordinary Sea-Animal, called the Kraken," *The New Wonderful Magazine, and Marvellous Chronicle* (London, 1794), 313–15.

19. Rediker, *Devil and the Deep Blue Sea*, 157.

20. Information of Philip Brand, July 1729, High Court of Admiralty Papers 1/56, ff.32–33, National Archives of Great Britain, Kew Gardens.

21. Philip Edwards, *The Story of the Voyage: Sea-Narratives in Eighteenth-Century England* (Cambridge, UK: Cambridge University Press, 2004), 2.

22. Dampier, *New Voyage*, 4.

23. William Brandon, *New Worlds for Old: Reports From the New World and Their Effect on the Development of Social Thought in Europe 1500–1800* (Athens: Ohio University Press, 1986).

24. Cohen, *Novel and the Sea*, 107–12.

25. Green, *Dreams of Empire*, 71–72.

26. Cohen, *Novel and the Sea,* 7, 93. See also David Fausett, *The Strange Surprising Sources of Robinson Crusoe* (Amsterdam: Editions Rodopi B.V., 1994).

27. Williams, "William Dampier," 163; Green, *Dreams of Empire,* 90.

28. Jeremy Lewis, *Tobias Smollett* (London: Jonathan Cape, 2003), chap. 2; Green, *Dreams of Adventure,* 374; Nathan Comfort Starr, "Smollett's Sailors," *American Neptune* 32 (1972): 81–99. The quotation appears in *Roderick Random* (1748, repr. Athens: University of Georgia Press, 2012), 135.

29. Wayne Franklin, *James Fenimore Cooper: The Early Years* (New Haven, CT: Yale University Press, 2007), chap. 2; quotations at 90, 100. Cooper also served subsequently in the United States Navy but had little direct experience of life at sea. On Cooper's Atlantic influence, see Cohen, *Novel and the Sea,* chap. 4.

30. See Rediker, *Slave Ship,* chap. 10.

31. Julius Sherrard Scott III, "The Common Wind: Currents of Afro-American Communication in the Era of the Haitian Revolution," PhD diss., Duke University, 1986. For a spin-off article, see Julius Scott, "Afro-American Sailors and the International Communication Network: The Case of Newport Bowers," in *Jack Tar in History: Essays in the History of Maritime Life and Labour,* ed. Colin Howell and Richard J. Twomey (Fredericton, New Brunswick: Acadiensis Press, 1991).

32. Niklas Frykman, "The Wooden World Turned Upside Down: Naval Mutinies in the Age of Atlantic Revolution," PhD diss., University of Pittsburgh, 2010. See also Niklas Frykman, Clare Anderson, Lex Heerma van Voss, and Marcus Rediker, eds., *Mutiny and Maritime Radicalism in the Age of Revolution: A Global Survey* (Cambridge, UK: Cambridge University Press, 2013.

Chapter Two

1. The work has been published as *Barlow's Journal of His Life at Sea in King's Ships, East & West Indiamen, & Other Merchant Men from 1659 to 1703,* ed. Basil Lubbock (London, 1934) (hereafter cited as *BJ*). All subsequent references are to the published version. The quotations in this paragraph are on pages 29 and 228.

2. Ralph Davis, *The Rise of the English Merchant Shipping Industry in the Seventeenth and Eighteen Centuries* (London: Newton Abbot, 1962), 14–21. The *Royal Sovereign,* which Barlow declared to be "the best ship in

England," held 102 cannon and as many as one thousand men. See *BJ*, 124; A. G. Course, *Seventeenth Century Mariner* (London: F. Muller, 1965), Appendix I, 241–42.

3. Robert Muchembled, *Popular Culture and Elite Culture in France, 1400–1750*, trans. Lydia Cochrane (Baton Rouge: Louisiana State University Press, 1985), 3–4.

4. *BJ*, 21, 11, 15.

5. Ibid., 15, 17, 19, 20, 23, 28, 29; Course, *Seventeenth Century Mariner*, 17.

6. *BJ*, 31.

7. Ibid., 31–32, 28, 34, 213, 153.

8. Ibid., 33, 162, 226, 61.

9. Ibid., 19, 60, 32, 41, 21, 426.

10. Ibid., 90, 115. Barlow explained, "He that is bound must obey," 47.

11. Ibid., 128, 339, 90, 61. This passage goes on to say, "I had always a mind to see strange countries and fashions, which made me bear the extremities with the more patience."

12. Ibid., 61, 68; Charles A. Le Guin, "Sea Life in Seventeenth-Century England," *American Nepture* 27 (1967): 116.

13. Ibid., 204, 61, 28, 162, 204, 252, 263, 544. See Keith Wrightson, *English Society, 1580–1680* (New Brunswick: Rutgers University Press, 1982), 228, 223. It should also be noted that by the 1690s, when the economic situation improved, Barlow was beginning to make better money as a mate, and this made him less likely to leave the sea.

14. Ibid., 21.

15. Ibid., 162, 214, 161, 69; Le Guin, "Sea Life," 113, 115.

16. *BJ*, 54, 162. For other comments on pursers, see 51, 127–28, 151–52, 159.

17. Ibid., 548, 123, 164, 358, 462.

18. Ibid., 83, 358, 540, 365, 219, 528, 374, 506–7.

19. Ibid., 135, 165, 119, 107, 61.

20. Ibid., 95–96, 146.

21. Ibid., 351, 280, 308, 162–63, 242, 19.

22. Ibid., 16, 107, 162–63, 174–75.

23. Ibid., 507, 436, 305, 529. See also E. P. Thompson, "The Moral Economy of the English Crowd in the Eighteenth Century," *Past and Present* 50 (1971): 76–136.

24. *BJ*, 553, but see 310, 424, 540.

25. Ibid., 42, 44, 47.

26. Ibid., 341, 350, 365.

27. Ibid., 57, 153, 314, 318, 458, 405.

28. Ibid., 166, 90.

29. Ibid., 339, 60, 146, 175.

30. Christopher Hill, "Pottage for Free-Born Englishmen: Attitudes to Wage Labour," in *Change and Continuity in Seventeenth-Century England* (Cambridge, MA: Harvard University Press, 1975), 234–38.

31. See Peter Linebaugh's treatment of this problem in "All the Atlantic Mountains Shook," *Labour/Le Travail* 10 (1982): 99.

Chapter Three

1. Henry Pitman, *A Relation of the Great Sufferings and Strange Adventures of Henry Pitman, Chyrurgion to the Late Duke of Monmouth* (London: Andrew Sowle, 1689). The pamphlet is reprinted in *Stuart Tracts, 1603– 1693*, ed. C. H. Firth (New York: Cooper Square, 1964), 431–76.

2. N. A. T. Hall, "Maritime Maroons: *Grand Marronage* from the Danish West Indies," *William and Mary Quarterly*, 3rd ser., 42 (1985): 491–92.

3. For more on the early history of Barbados, see Richard S. Dunn, *Sugar and Slaves: The Rise of the Planter Class in the English West Indies, 1624–1713* (Chapel Hill: University of North Carolina Press, 1972); and Hilary McD. Beckles, *White Servitude and Black Slavery in Barbados, 1627–1715* (Knoxville: University of Tennessee Press, 1989).

4. Hilary McD. Beckles, "English Parliamentary Debate on 'White Slavery' in 1659," *Journal of the Barbados Museum and Historical Society* 36 (1988): 344–53.

5. Marcus Rediker, "Good Hands, Fast Feet, and Stout Heart: The History and Culture of Working People in Early America," *Labour/Le Travail* 19 (1982): 123–44.

6. P. K. Kemp and Christopher Lloyd, *Brethren of the Coast: Buccaneers of the South Seas* (New York: St. Martin's Press, 1961).

7. On maroons, see Richard Price, ed., *Maroon Societies: Rebel Slave Communities in the Americas* (Garden City, NY: Anchor Press, 1973).

8. Kemp and Lloyd, *Brethren of the Coast*, 70.

9. On the subsequent history of the Bahamas, see Hilary McD. Beckles, *A History of Barbados: From Amerindian Settlement to Caribbean Single Market* (Cambridge, UK: Cambridge University Press, 2007).

10. Peter Linebaugh and Marcus Rediker, *The Many-Headed Hydra: Sailors, Slaves, Commoners, and the Hidden History of the Revolutionary Atlantic* (Boston: Beacon Press, 2000), 200–201.

11. John Cordy Jeaffreson, ed., *A Young Squire of the Seventeenth Century*

from the Papers (A.D. 1676–1686) of Christopher Jeaffreson (London: Hurst and Blackett, 1879), 2:61.

12. Linebaugh and Rediker, *Many-Headed Hydra*, chap. 1.

13. Peter Linebaugh, *Magna Carta Manifesto: Liberty and Commons for All* (Berkeley: University of California Press, 2008).

14. Tim Severin, *In Search of Robinson Crusoe* (New York: Basic Books, 2002).

15. Karl Marx, "Production, Consumption, Distribution, Exchange," in *A Contribution to the Critique of Political Economy,* available online at http://www.marxists.org/archive/marx/works/1859/critique-pol -economy/appx1.htm.

Chapter Four

1. Alexander Spotswood to the Board of Trade, June 16, 1724, Colonial Office Papers (hereafter CO) 5/1319, National Archives of the UK.

2. Charles Johnson, *A General History of the Pyrates,* ed. Manuel Schonhorn (1724, 1728; repr. Columbia, SC: University of South Carolina Press, 1972).

3. S. Charles Hill, "Episodes of Piracy in Eastern Waters," *Indian Antiquary* 49 (1920): 37; Arthur L. Hayward, ed., *Lives of the Most Remarkable Criminals . . .* (London, 1735; repr. New York: Dodd, Mead, 1927), 37. I have, over the years, constructed a database of 778 pirates (774 men and 4 women) from documents of all varieties (as found in these endnotes). I recorded individual pirates by name, dates of activity, age, former occupation, class, family background, and miscellaneous details. Biographical data indicate that 173 of the 178 for whom a labor background is known came from one of these employments; at least 161 had been in the merchant service, and some had served in more than one of these seafaring occupations.

4. Carter Hughson, *The Carolina Pirates and Colonial Commerce, 1670– 1740,* Johns Hopkins University Studies in Historical and Political Science, vol. 12 (Baltimore, 1894), 59; Patrick Pringle, *Jolly Roger* (New York: Norton, 1953), 181, and in High Court of Admiralty Papers (hereafter HCA) 1/54 (1717), f. 113, National Archives of the UK; Johnson, *History of the Pyrates,* 132, 615; W. Noel Sainsbury et al., eds., *Calendar of State Papers, Colonial Series, America and the West Indies* (London, 1860) (hereafter *Cal. St. Papers*), 31:10; Abel Boyer, ed., *The Political State of Great Britain . . .* (London, 1711–40), 21:659. Quotation

from "Representation from Several Merchants Trading to Virginia to Board of Trade," Apr. 15, 1717, CO 5/1318. Estimates of the sizes of crews are available for thirty-seven pirate ships: The mean is 79.5. I have found reference to seventy-nine crews through mention of the ship or captain. Totals were obtained by arranging ships according to periods of activity and multiplying by the mean crew size. If this mean holds, the total population would have been 6,281. Yet this figure counts some pirates more than once. For example, many who sailed with both Howell Davis and Bartholomew Roberts are counted twice. It seems that, in all, some five thousand men were involved.

5. Deposition of John Vickers, 1716, CO 5/1317; Spotswood, Council of Trade and Plantations (hereafter CTP), May 31, 1717, CO 5/1364; Johnson, *History of the Pyrates*, 31–34; Leo Francis Stock, ed., *Proceedings and Debates of the British Parliaments Respecting North America* (Washington, DC: Carnegie Institution, 1930), 3:399; Deposition of Adam Baldridge in *Privateering and Piracy in the Colonial Period: Illustrative Documents*, ed. John Franklin Jameson (New York: Macmillan, 1923), 180–87; R. A. Brock, ed., *The Official Letters of Alexander Spotswood* . . . (Virginia Historical Society, *Collections*, N.S., II [Richmond, Va., 1882]), 168, 351; William Snelgrave, *A New Account of Some Parts of Guinea and the Slave Trade* (London, 1734), 197; Abbe Rochon, "A Voyage to Madagascar and the East Indies," in *A General Collection of the Best and Most Interesting Voyages and Travels* . . . (London, 1814), 16:767–71; William Smith, *A New Voyage to Guinea* . . . (London, 1744), 12, 42. On Johnson's credibility, see Schonhorn's introduction to Johnson, *History of the Pyrates*, xxvii–xl; Philip Gosse, *The History of Piracy* (New York: Longmans, 1932), 182; and Hugh F. Rankin, *The Golden Age of Piracy* (New York: Holt, Rinehart, and Winston, 1969), 161.

6. James Boswell, *The Life of Samuel Johnson* . . . (London, 1791), 86.

7. Probably fewer than 5 percent of pirates originated as mutineers. See Johnson, *History of the Pyrates*, 116, 196, 215–16; Snelgrave, *New Account*, 203; Deposition of Richard Simes, *Cal. St. Papers*, 32:319; Jesse Lemisch, "Jack Tar in the Streets: Merchant Seamen in the Politics of Revolutionary America," *William and Mary Quarterly*, 3rd ser., 25 (1968): 379, 375–76, 406; Richard B. Morris, *Government and Labor in Early America* (New York: Columbia University Press, 1946), 246–47, 257, 262–68; Johnson, *History of the Pyrates*, 244, 359; A. G. Course, *The Merchant Navy: A Social History* (London: Frederick Muller, 1963), 61;

Samuel Cox to CTP, Aug. 23, 1721, *Cal. St. Papers*, 32:393; Ralph Davis, *The Rise of the English Shipping Industry in the Seventeenth and Eighteenth Centuries* (London: Macmillan, 1962), 144, 154–55; *The Voyages and Travels of Captain Nathaniel Uring*, ed. Alfred Dewar (1726; repr. London, 1928), xxviii, 176–78; Arthur Pierce Middleton, *Tobacco Coast: A Maritime History of Chesapeake Bay in the Colonial Era* (Newport News, VA: Mariners' Museum, 1953), 8, 13, 15, 18, 271, 281; Christopher Lloyd, *The British Seaman, 1200–1860: A Social Survey* (Rutherford, NJ: Associated University Presses, 1970), 249, 264; John Atkins, *A Voyage to Guinea, Brasil, and the West-Indies . . .* (London, 1735), 261; G. T. Crook, ed., *The Complete Newgate Calendar . . .* (London, 1926), 3:57–58; S. Charles Hill, "Notes on Piracy in Eastern Waters," *Indian Antiquary* 46 (1927): 130; Hayward, *Remarkable Criminals*, 126.

8. Gov. Lowther to CTP, October 23, 1718, *Cal. St. Papers*, 29:350; Morris, *Government and Labor*, 247; Lemisch, "Jack Tar," 379; Davis, *English Shipping Industry*, 133–37; R. D. Merriman, ed., *Queen Anne's Navy: Documents Concerning the Administration of the Navy of Queen Anne, 1702–1714* (London: Navy Records Society, 1961), 170–72, 174, 221–22, 250; Lloyd, *British Seaman*, 44–46, 124–49; Peter Kemp, *The British Sailor: A Social History of the Lower Deck* (London: J. M. Dent, 1970), chaps. 4, 5; Arthur N. Gilbert, "Buggery and the British Navy, 1700–1861," *Journal of Social History* 10 (1976–77): 72–98.

9. Atkins, *Voyage to Guinea*, 139, 187; Captain's logbook, "At Jamaica, 1720–1721," Rawlinson Manuscripts A-299, Bodleian Library, Oxford; *The Historical Register, Containing an Impartial Relation of All Transactions . . .* (London, 1722), 7:344.

10. Merriman, *Queen Anne's Navy*, 171.

11. Course, *Merchant Navy*, 84; Lloyd, *British Seaman*, 57; Edward Cooke, *A Voyage to the South Sea* (London, 1712), v–vi, 14–16; Woodes Rogers, *A Cruising Voyage Round the World*, ed. G. E. Manwaring (1712; repr. New York: Longmans, 1928), xiv, xxv; George Shelvocke, *A Voyage Round the World* (London, 1726), 34–36, 38, 46, 157, 214, 217; William Betagh, *A Voyage Round the World* (London, 1728), 4.

12. Rogers, *Cruising Voyage*, 205. See also Shelvocke, *Voyage*, 43, 221–25.

13. Col. Benjamin Bennet to CTP, May 31, 1718, and July 30, 1717, CO 37/10, f. 18; Johnson, *History of the Pyrates*, 228.

14. See note 7 above.

15. Only twenty-six in the sample of 778 are known to have been married. In pirate confessions, regrets were often expressed to parents, seldom

to wives or children. See Cotton Mather, *Useful Remarks; An Essay upon Remarkables in the Way of Wicked Men: A Sermon on the Tragical End, unto which the Way of Twenty-Six Pirates Brought Them; At New Port on Rhode-Island, July 19, 1723* . . . (New London, CT, 1723), 38–42; and *Trials of Eight Persons Indited for Piracy* . . . (Boston, 1718), 24, 25. Quotation from John Barnard, *Ashton's Memorial: An History of the Strange Adventures, and Signal Deliverances of Mr. Philip Ashton* . . . (Boston, 1725), 3.

16. Peter Haywood to CTP, Dec. 3, 1716, CO 137/12; Lemisch, "Jack Tar," 377; Davis, *English Shipping Industry*, 114. Biographical data show that seventy-one of seventy-five pirates came from working-class backgrounds.

17. Betagh, *Voyage*, 148.

18. Johnson, *History of the Pyrates*, 167, 211–13, 298, 307–8, 321; Hayward, *Remarkable Criminals*, 37; Information of Alexander Thompson, HCA 1/55 (1723), f. 23; Snelgrave, *New Account*, 220; Jameson, *Privateering and Piracy*, 337; Rankin, *Golden Age*, 31.

19. Clement Downing, *A Compendious History of the Indian Wars* . . . (1737; repr. London: Oxford University Press, 1924), 99; Johnson, *History of the Pyrates*, 121, 139, 167–68, 195, 208, 214, 340, 352; Snelgrave, *New Account*, 199; *Trials of Eight Persons*, 24; Boyer, *Political State*, 28:152; George Roberts (believed by some to have been Defoe), *The Four Years Voyages* . . . (London, 1726), 39.

20. "Proceedings of the Court Held on the Coast of Africa upon Trying of 100 Pirates Taken by his Ma[jes]ties Ship *Swallow*," HCA 1/99 (1722), f. 59; Snelgrave, *New Account*, 217; Johnson, *History of the Pyrates*, 213–14.

21. Johnson, *History of the Pyrates*, 139; Hayward, *Remarkable Criminals*, 37; Boyer, *Political State*, 28:153; B. R. Burg, "Legitimacy and Authority: A Case Study of Pirate Commanders in the Seventeenth and Eighteenth Centuries," *American Neptune* 37 (1977): 40–49.

22. Jameson, *Privateering and Piracy*, 294; Johnson, *History of the Pyrates*, 139, 67; George Francis Dow and John Henry Edmonds, *The Pirates of the New England Coast, 1630–1730* (Salem, MA: Argosy-Antiquarian, 1923), 217; *Trials of Eight Persons*, 23; Richard B. Morris, "The Ghost of Captain Kidd," *New York History* 19 (1938): 282.

23. Snelgrave, *New Account*, 199; Burg, "Legitimacy and Authority," 44–48.

24. Hayward, *Remarkable Criminals*, 37; Johnson, *History of the Pyrates*, 42, 296, 337.

25. Johnson, *History of the Pyrates*, 423; Lloyd Haynes Williams, *Pirates of Colonial Virginia* (Richmond, VA: Dietz Press, 1937), 19.

26. Roberts, *Four Years Voyages*, 37, 80; *The Tryals of Major Stede Bonnet and Other Pirates* . . . (London, 1719), 37; Snelgrave, *New Account*, 199–200, 238–39; Boyer, *Political State*, 28:153; Johnson, *History of the Pyrates*, 213–25; *Trials of Eight Persons*, 24, 25; *Tryals of Thirty-Six Persons for Piracy* . . . (Boston, 1723), 9; *Boston News-Letter*, July 15–22, 1717; quotations from Johnson, *History of the Pyrates*, 213; Downing, *Compendious History*, 99.

27. Boyer, *Political State*, 28:151; Snelgrave, *New Account*, 272; Johnson, *History of the Pyrates*, 138–39, 312.

28. Johnson, *History of the Pyrates*, 88–89, 117, 145, 167, 222–25, 292, 595; *Trials of Eight Persons*, 24; Downing, *Compendious History*, 44, 103; Hill, "Episodes of Piracy," 41–42, 59; Roberts, *Four Years Voyages*, 55, 86; Boyer, *Political State*, 28:153. Quotation from Betagh, *Voyage*, 148.

29. Johnson, *History of the Pyrates*, 211–12, 307–8, 342–43; Dow and Edmonds, *Pirates of the New England Coast*, 146–47; Hayward, *Remarkable Criminals*, 37; *Tryals of Major Stede Bonnet*, 22; Morris, "Ghost of Captain Kidd," 283.

30. See note 20, this chapter; Gosse, *History of Piracy*, 103; John Biddulph, *The Pirates of Malabar; and, An Englishwoman* . . . *in India* . . . (London, 1907), x, 155; "A Narrative of the Singular Sufferings of John Fillmore and Others on Board the Noted Pirate Vessel Commanded by Captain Phillips," Buffalo Historical Society, *Publications* 10 (1907), 32.

31. Johnson, *History of the Pyrates*, 212, 308, 343; Dow and Edmonds, *Pirates of the New England Coast*, 147; pirate Jeremiah Huggins, quoted in Morris, "Ghost of Captain Kidd," 292; Hill, "Episodes of Piracy," 57.

32. Johnson, *History of the Pyrates*, 307, 212, 157–58, 339; see note 4, this chapter.

33. *Tryals of Major Stede Bonnet*, 30; Johnson, *History of the Pyrates*, 211, 212, 343; Biddulph, *Pirates of Malabar*, 163–64; Rankin, *Golden Age*, 37.

34. Johnson, *History of the Pyrates*, 212, 343; Snelgrave, *New Account*, 256; *American Weekly Mercury* (Philadelphia), May 30–June 6, 1723.

35. Jameson, *Privateering and Piracy*, 304; *Trials of Eight Persons*, 19, 21; Brock, *Letters of Alexander Spotswood*, 249; Johnson, *History of the Pyrates*, 260. Some men, usually those with important skills, were occasionally pressed; see *Cal. St. Papers*, 33:365.

36. *Trials of Eight Persons*, 21; deposition of Samuel Cooper, CO 37/10 (1718), f. 35; Johnson, *History of the Pyrates*, 116, 196, 216, 228; Boyer, *Political State*, 28:148; governor of Bermuda quoted in Pringle, *Jolly*

Roger, 181; deposition of Richard Symes, CO 152/14 (1721), f. 33; *American Weekly Mercury*, Mar. 17, 1720; *New-England Courant* (Boston), June 25–July 2, 1722.

37. Dow and Edmonds, *Pirates of the New England Coast*, 278; Johnson, *History of the Pyrates*, 225, 313; Lt. Gov. Bennett to Mr. Popple, Mar. 31, 1720, *Cal. St. Papers*, 32:19.

38. Hayward, *Remarkable Criminals*, 37; Johnson, *History of the Pyrates*, 226, 342.

39. The total of 3,600 is reached by multiplying the number of ship captains shown in the figure by the average crew size of 79.5. See Johnson, *History of the Pyrates*, 41–42, 72, 121, 137, 138, 174, 210, 225, 277, 281, 296, 312, 352, 355, 671; *New-England Courant*, June 11–18, 1722; *American Weekly Mercury*, July 6–13, 1721, Jan. 5–12 and Sept. 16–23, 1725; Pringle, *Jolly Roger*, 181, 190, 244; Biddulph, *Pirates of Malabar*, 135, 187; Snelgrave, *New Account*, 196–97, 199, 272, 280; Hughson, *Carolina Pirates*, 70; *Boston News-Letter*, Aug. 12–19, 1717, Oct. 13–20 and Nov. 10–17, 1718, Feb. 4–11, 1725, June 30–July 7, 1726; Downing, *Compendious History*, 51, 101; Morris, "Ghost of Captain Kidd," 282, 283, 296; *Tryals of Bonnet*, iii, 44–45; Dow and Edmonds, *Pirates of the New England Coast*, 117, 135, 201, 283, 287; *Trials of Eight Persons*, 23; Jameson, *Privateering and Piracy*, 304, 341; Boyer, *Political State*, 25:198–99; Hill, "Notes on Piracy," 148, 150; Capt. Matthew Musson to CTP, July 5, 1717, *Cal. St. Papers*, 29:338; ibid., 31:21, 118; ibid., 33:274; John F. Watson, *Annals of Philadelphia and Pennsylvania . . .* (Philadelphia, 1844), 2:27; *Boston Gazette*, Apr. 27–May 4, 1724; British Library, Add. Mss. 40806, 40812, 40813.

40. Testimony of Thomas Checkley (1717) in Jameson, *Privateering and Piracy*, 304; *Trials of Eight Persons*, 11.

41. E. J. Hobsbawm, *Primitive Rebels: Studies in Archaic Forms of Social Movements in the 19th and 20th Centuries* (New York: Norton, 1959), 5, 17, 18, 27, 28; see also his *Bandits* (New York: Delacorte Press, 1969), 24–29.

42. *The Tryals of Sixteen Persons for Piracy . . .* (Boston, 1726), 5; *Tryals of Major Stede Bonnet*, iii, iv; Crook, *Complete Newgate Calendar*, 61; Hughson, *Carolina Pirates*, 121; Rankin, *Golden Age*, 28; Johnson, *History of the Pyrates*, 116, 342; Downing, *Compendious History*, 98. An analysis of the names of forty-four pirate ships reveals the following patterns: eight (18.2 percent) made reference to revenge; seven (15.9 percent) were named *Ranger* or *Rover*, suggesting mobility and perhaps a watchful-

ness over the way captains treated their sailors; five (11.4 percent) referred to royalty. It is noteworthy that only two names referred to wealth. Other names indicated that places (*Lancaster*), unidentifiable people (*Mary Anne*), and animals (*Black Robin*) constituted less significant themes. Two names, *Batchelor's Delight* and *Batchelor's Adventure*, tend to support the probability (see note 15, this chapter) that most pirates were unmarried; see Johnson, *History of the Pyrates*, 220, 313; William P. Palmer, ed., *Calendar of Virginia State Papers* . . . (Richmond, VA, 1875), 1:194; and *Cal. St. Papers*, 30:263.

43. Betagh, *Voyage*, 41.

44. Petition of Randolph, Cane, and Halladay (1722) in Palmer, *Virginia State Papers*, 202.

45. "Proceedings of the Court held on the Coast of Africa," HCA 1/99 (1722), f. 101; Johnson, *History of the Pyrates*, 338, 582; Snelgrave, *New Account*, 212, 225; Dow and Edmonds, *Pirates of the New England Coast*, 301; *Voyages and Travels of Captain Nathaniel Uring*, xxviii.

46. Hawkins in Boyer, *Political State*, 28:149–50; Johnson, *History of the Pyrates*, 352–53; Dow and Edmonds, *Pirates of the New England Coast*, 278; Betagh, *Voyage*, 26.

47. Crook, *Newgate Calendar*, 59; Boyer, *Political State*, 32:272; *Boston Gazette*, Oct. 24–31, 1720; Rankin, *Golden Age*, 35, 135, 148; Cotton Mather, *The Vial Poured Out upon the Sea: A Remarkable Relation of Certain Pirates* . . . (Boston, 1726), 21; Watson, *Annals of Philadelphia*, 227; quotation from *Boston Gazette*, Mar. 21–28, 1726. It should be stressed that Lyne's bloodletting was exceptional.

48. *Boston News-Letter*, Nov. 14–21, 1720.

49. Snelgrave, *New Account*, 196, 199.

50. Ibid., 202–8.

51. Ibid., 212, 225.

52. Snelgrave, *New Account*, 241. For other examples of giving cargo to ship captains and treating them "civilly," see deposition of Robert Dunn, CO 152/13 (1720), f. 26; deposition of Richard Symes, CO 152/14 (1721), f. 33; Biddulph, *Pirates of Malabar*, 139; Brock, *Letters of Alexander Spotswood*, 339–43; *Boston Gazette*, Aug. 21, 1721; Hill, "Episodes of Piracy," 57; Morris, "Ghost of Captain Kidd," 283; Elizabeth Donnan, ed., *Documents Illustrative of the History of the Slave-Trade to America* (Washington, DC, 1935), 4:96; *Tryals of Major Stede Bonnet*, 13; Boyer, *Political State*, 27:616; deposition of Henry Bostock, *Cal. St.*

Papers, 30:150–51; *Boston News-Letter*, Nov. 14–21, 1720; and Spotswood to Craggs: "It is a common practice with those Rovers upon the pillageing of a Ship to make presents of other Commodity's to such Masters as they take a fancy to in Lieu of that they have plundered them of," May 20, 1720, CO 5/1319.

53. Snelgrave, *New Account*, 241, 242, 243.

54. Ibid., 275, 276, 284.

55. Johnson, *History of the Pyrates*, 351; Jameson, *Privateering and Piracy*, 341.

56. Mather, *Vial Poured Out*, 21, 48; Boyer, *Political State*, 32:272; Benjamin Colman, *It is a Fearful Thing to Fall into the Hands of the Living God . . .* (Boston, 1726), 39.

57. *Tryals of Major Stede Bonnet*, 2, 4, 3, 34. See also Hughson, *Carolina Pirates*, 5; Johnson, *History of the Pyrates*, 264, 377–79; Dow and Edmonds, *Pirates of the New England Coast*, 297; Brock, *Letters of Alexander Spotswood*, 339.

58. Boyer, *Political State*, 14:295, 21:662, 24:194; Johnson, *History of the Pyrates*, 79; Hill, "Episodes of Piracy," 39; *American Weekly Mercury*, July 13–20, 1721.

59. *American Weekly Mercury*, Mar. 17, 1720; Brock, *Letters of Alexander Spotswood*, 338. For other cases of hanging in chains, see Brock, *Letters of Alexander Spotswood*, 342; Jameson, *Privateering and Piracy*, 344; *Tryals of Sixteen Persons*, 19; Johnson, *History of the Pyrates*, 151; *Boston Gazette*, Aug. 27–Sept. 3, 1722; Boyer, *Political State*, 24:201; Gov. Hart to CTP, *Cal. St. Papers*, 33:275.

60. Deposition of Henry Bostock, CO 152/12 (1717); Snelgrave, *New Account*, 253; Johnson, *History of the Pyrates*, 217; Spotswood to Board of Trade, May 31, 1717, CO 5/1318; Jameson, *Privateering and Piracy*, 315.

61. Deposition of Edward North, CO 37/10 (1718).

62. *Tryals of Major Stede Bonnet*, 8.

63. Snelgrave, *New Account*, 199; Johnson, *History of the Pyrates*, 138, 174; Morris, "Ghost of Captain Kidd," 282.

64. James Craggs to CTP, *Cal. St. Papers*, 31:10; Board of Trade to J. Methuen, Sept. 3, 1716, CO 23/12; Johnson, *History of the Pyrates*, 315, 582; Downing, *Compendious History*, 98, 104–5; *Voyages and Travels of Captain Nathaniel Uring*, 241; Shelvocke, *Voyage*, 242; H. R. McIlwaine, *Executive Journals of the Council of Colonial Virginia* (Richmond, VA, 1928), 3:612; Dow and Edmonds, *Pirates of the New England Coast*, 341;

deposition of R. Lazenby in Hill, "Episodes of Piracy," 60; "Voyage to Guinea, Antego, Bay of Campeachy, Cuba, Barbadoes, &c, 1714–1723," British Library, Add. Ms. 39946.

65. *Boston News-Letter*, Aug. 15–22, 1720; *American Weekly Mercury*, Sept. 6–13, 1722.

66. Trial of Thomas Davis (1717) in Jameson, *Privateering and Piracy*, 308; *Boston News-Letter*, Nov. 4–11, 1717.

67. *Tryals of Major Stede Bonnet*, 45.

68. Lt. Gov. Benjamin Bennet to CTP, *Cal. St. Papers*, 30:263; *Tryals of Major Stede Bonnet*, 29, 50; Johnson, *History of the Pyrates*, 195.

69. Gov. Walter Hamilton to CTP, *Cal. St. Papers*, 32:165; *American Weekly Mercury*, Oct. 27, 1720; *Boston Gazette*, Oct. 24–31, 1720.

70. Spotswood to CTP, *Cal. St. Papers*, 32:328.

71. Council Meeting of May 3, 1721, in McIlwaine, *Executive Journals*, 542; abstract of Spotswood to Board of Trade, June 11, 1722, CO 5/1370; Spotswood to Board of Trade, May 31, 1721, CO 5/1319.

72. Dow and Edmonds, *Pirates of the New England Coast*, 281–82; Johnson, *History of the Pyrates*, 355; *American Weekly Mercury*, May 21–28, 1724.

73. Hope to CTP, Jan. 14, 1724, CO 37/11, f. 37. See also Treasury Warrant to Capt. Knott, T52/32 (Aug. 10, 1722), National Archives of the UK. Captain Luke Knott, after turning over eight pirates to authorities, requested compensation for "his being obliged to quit the Merchant Service, the Pirates threatning to Torture him to death if ever he should fall into their hands." Robert Walpole personally awarded Knott 230 pounds for the loss of his career.

74. Barnard, *Ashton's Memorial*, 2, 4; emphasis added.

75. Smith, *New Voyage*, 42–43. See also Morris, "Ghost of Captain Kidd," 286.

76. Anthropologist Raymond Firth argues that flags function as instruments of both power and sentiment, creating solidarity and symbolizing unity. See his *Symbols: Public and Private* (Ithaca, NY: Allen and Unwin, 1973), 328, 339; Hill, "Notes on Piracy," 147. For particular pirate crews known to have sailed under the Jolly Roger, see *Boston Gazette*, Nov. 29–Dec. 6, 1725 (Lyne); *Boston News-Letter*, Sept. 10–17, 1716 (Jennings? Leslie?), Aug. 12–19, 1717 (Napin, Nichols), Mar. 2–9, 1719 (Thompson), May 28–June 4, 1724 (Phillips), June 5–8, 1721 (Rackam?); Jameson, *Privateering and Piracy*, 317 (Roberts); *Tryals of Sixteen Persons*, 5 (Fly); Snelgrave, *New Account*, 199 (Cocklyn,

LaBouche, Davis); *Trials of Eight Persons*, 24 (Bellamy); Hughson, *Carolina Pirates*, 113 (Moody); *Tryals of Major Stede Bonnet*, 44–45 (Bonnet, Teach, Richards); Dow and Edmonds, *Pirates of the New England Coast*, 208 (Harris), 213 (Low); Boyer, *Political State*, 28:152 (Spriggs); Biddulph, *Pirates of Malabar*, 135 (Taylor); Donnan, *Documents of the Slave Trade*, 96 (England); Johnson, *History of the Pyrates*, 240–41 (Skyrm), 67–68 (Martel), 144 (Vane), 371 (captain unknown), 628 (Macarty, Bunce), 299 (Worley). Royal officials affirmed and attempted to reroute the power of this symbolism by raising the Jolly Roger on the gallows when hanging pirates. See Johnson, *History of the Pyrates*, 658; *New-England Courant*, July 22, 1723; and *Boston News-Letter*, May 28–June 4, 1724. The symbols were commonly used in the gravestone art of this period and did not originate with piracy. The argument here is that new meanings, derived from maritime experience, were attached to them.

77. Boyer, *Political State*, 28:152. Pirates also occasionally used red or "bloody" flags.

78. Ibid.

79. Hill, "Episodes of Piracy," 37.

80. Ibid.; Snelgrave, *New Account*, 236.

81. See note 42, this chapter.

82. Johnson, *History of the Pyrates*, 28, 43, 244, 159, 285, 628, 656, 660; Hayward, *Remarkable Criminals*, 39; Rankin, *Golden Age*, 155; Mather, *Vial Poured Out*, 47; Jameson, *Privateering and Piracy*, 341; Lt. Gen. Mathew to Gov. Hamilton, Sept. 29, 1720, *Cal. St. Papers*, 32:167; Bartholomew Roberts (pirate) to Lt. Gen. Mathew, ibid., 169.

83. Gov. Hamilton to CTP, Oct. 3, 1720, *Cal. St. Papers*, 32:165.

84. Boyer, *Political State*, 28:153. For similar vows and actual attempts, see *Tryals of Major Stede Bonnet*, 18; Johnson, *History of the Pyrates*, 143, 241, 245, 298, 317; Dow and Edmonds, *Pirates of the New England Coast*, 239, 292; Watson, *Annals of Philadelphia*, 227; Hayward, *Remarkable Criminals*, 296–97; Atkins, *Voyage*, 12; Jameson, *Privateering and Piracy*, 315; Arthur L. Cooke, "British Newspaper Accounts of Blackbeard's Death," *Virginia Magazine of History and Biography* 56 (1953): 305–6; *American Weekly Mercury*, June 16–23, 1720; *Tryals of Thirty-Six*, 9; Spotswood to Board of Trade, Dec. 22, 1718, CO 5/1318.

85. Cotton Mather, *Instructions to the Living, From the Condition of the Dead: A Brief Relation of Remarkables in the Shipwreck of above One Hundred Pi-*

rates . . . (Boston, 1717), 4; meeting of Apr. 1, 1717, in *Journal of the Commissioners for Trade and Plantations* . . . , ed. H.C. Maxwell Lyte (London, 1924), 3:359.

86. Johnson, *History of the Pyrates*, 7.

87. Virginia Merchants to Admiralty, CO 389/42 (1713).

88. Lloyd, *British Seaman*, 287, table 3.

89. Jameson, *Privateering and Piracy*, 291; Pringle, *Jolly Roger*, 95; James G. Lydon, *Pirates, Privateers, and Profits* (Upper Saddle River, NJ: Gregg Press, 1970), 17–20; Rankin, *Golden Age*, 23; Nellis M. Crouse, *The French Struggle for the West Indies* (New York: Columbia University Press, 1943), 310.

90. Davis, *English Shipping Industry*, 136–37.

91. Ibid., 27.

92. Ibid., 154.

93. Lloyd, *British Seaman*, 287, table 3; Davis, *English Shipping Industry*, 27, 31.

94. Davis, *English Shipping Industry*, 136–37;

95. Pringle, *Jolly Roger*, 266–67; Violet Barbour, "Privateers and Pirates of the West Indies," *American Historical Review* 16 (1910–11): 566; Boyer, *Political State*, 28:152; Hayward, *Remarkable Criminals*, 37; "A Scheme for Stationing Men of War in the West Indies for better Securing the Trade there from Pirates," CO 323/8 (1723); *Boston News-Letter*, July 7–14, 1726. Gary M. Walton, "Sources of Productivity Change in American Colonial Shipping, 1675–1775," *Economic History Review* 20 (1967): 77. Walton notes that the economic uncertainty occasioned by piracy declined after 1725.

96. See "An Act for the more effectual Suppressing of Piracy" (8 George I, c. 24, 1721), in Sir Thomas Parker, *The Laws of Shipping and Insurance, with a Digest of Adjudged Cases* (London, 1775), republished in *British Maritime Cases* (Abingdon, Oxfordshire, 1978), 24: 94–95. If the population range discussed previously is accurate, about one pirate in ten died on the gallows, which would have represented a vastly higher ratio than in any other period of piracy.

97. E.P. Thompson, "The Moral Economy of the English Crowd in the Eighteenth Century," *Past & Present* 50 (1971): 76–136.

98. Hayward, *Remarkable Criminals*, 37. See also Christopher Hill, *The World Turned Upside Down: Radical Ideas in the English Revolution* (New York: Viking, 1972).

99. William McFee, *The Law of the Sea* (Philadelphia, Lippincott, 1951), 50, 54, 59, 72.

100. Barnaby Slush, *The Navy Royal: Or a Sea-Cook Turn'd Projector* (London, 1709), viii.

Chapter Five

1. Henry Laurens to J.B., Esq., Oct. 26, 1765; Laurens to John Lewis Gervais, Jan. 29, 1766; Laurens to James Grant, Jan. 31, 1766; all in *The Papers of Henry Laurens*, ed. George C. Rogers Jr., David R. Chesnutt, and Peggy J. Clark (Columbia: University of South Carolina Press, 1968), vol. 5 (1765–68), 38–40, 53–54, 60; Bull quoted in Pauline Maier, "The Charleston Mob and the Evolution of Popular Politics in Revolutionary South Carolina, 1765–1784," *Perspectives in American History* 4 (1970): 176.

2. Peter Linebaugh and Marcus Rediker, *The Many-Headed Hydra: Sailors, Slaves, Commoners, and the Hidden History of the Revolutionary Atlantic* (Boston: Beacon Press, 2000), chaps. 5–6.

3. Jesse Lemisch, "Jack Tar in the Streets: Merchant Seamen in the Politics of Revolutionary America," *William and Mary Quarterly*, 3rd ser., 25 (1968): 371–407; Marcus Rediker, *Between the Devil and the Deep Blue Sea: Merchant Seamen, Pirates, and the Anglo-American Maritime World, 1700–1750* (Cambridge, UK: Cambridge University Press, 1987), chap. 5.

4. Dora Mae Clark, "The Impressment of Seamen in the American Colonies," *Essays in Colonial History Presented to Charles McLean Andrews by his Students* (New Haven, CT: Yale University Press, 1931), 217; Richard Pares, "The Manning of the Navy in the West Indies, 1702–1763," *Transactions of the Royal Historical Society* 20 (1937): 48–49; Daniel Baugh, *British Naval Administration in the Age of Walpole* (Princeton, NJ: Princeton University Press, 1965), 162.

5. Peter Warren to the Duke of Newcastle, June 18, 1745, in *The Royal Navy and North America: The Warren Papers, 1736–1752*, ed. Julian Gwyn (London: Navy Records Society, 1973), 126.

6. Charles Knowles to ?, Oct. 15, 1744, Admiralty Papers (hereafter ADM) 1/2007, f. 135, National Archives of the UK; "The Memorial of Captain Charles Knowles" (1743), ADM 1/2006; Peter Warren to Thomas Corbett, June 2, 1746, in *Warren Papers*, 262.

7. Thomas Hutchinson, *The History of the Colony and Province of Massachusetts-Bay*, ed. Lawrence Shaw Mayo (Cambridge, MA: Harvard

University Press, 1936, republished, 1970), 2:330–31; William Shirley to Lords of Trade, Dec. 1, 1747; Shirley to Duke of Newcastle, Dec. 31, 1747; Shirley to Josiah Willard, Nov. 19, 1747; all in Charles Henry Lincoln, ed., *Correspondence of William Shirley, Governor of Massachusetts and Military Commander of America, 1731–1760* (New York: Macmillan, 1912), 1:415, 416, 417, 418, 421, 422; John Lax and William Pencak, "The Knowles Riot and the Crisis of the 1740s in Massachusetts," *Perspectives in American History* 19 (1976): 182, 186 (Knowles quoted, my emphasis), 205, 214; Douglass Adair and John A. Schutz, eds., *Peter Oliver's Origin and Progress of the American Rebellion: A Tory View* (Stanford, CA: Stanford University Press, 1961), 41, 39; William Roughead, ed., *Trial of Captain Porteous* (Toronto: Canada Law Book Co., 1909), 103.

8. Lax and Pencak, "Knowles Riot," 199; John C. Miller, *Sam Adams: Pioneer in Propaganda* (Stanford, CA: Stanford University Press, 1936), 15–16.

9. *Independent Advertiser*, Jan. 4, 1748; Shirley to Lords of Trade, *Correspondence of William Shirley*, 1:412; Resolution of the Boston Town Meeting, Nov. 20, 1747, and Resolution of the Massachusetts House of Representatives, Nov. 19, 1747, both in the Boston weekly *Post-Boy*, Dec. 21, 1747; Hutchinson, *History of the Colony*, 2:332; William Douglass, *A Summary, Historical and Political, of the First Planting, Progressive Improvements, and Present State of the British Settlements in North America* (Boston, 1749), 254–55; *Independent Advertiser*, Aug. 28, 1749; Amicus Patriae, *An Address to the Inhabitants of the Province of Massachusetts-Bay in New-England; More Especially, To the Inhabitants of New England; Occasioned by the late Illegal and Unwarrantable Attack upon their Liberties* (Boston, 1747), 4.

10. *Independent Advertiser*, Feb. 8, 1748; Mar. 6, 1749; Apr. 18, 1748; Jan. 25, 1748; Mar. 14, 1748; Jan. 11, 1748.

11. Jonathan Mayhew, *A Discourse on Unlimited Submission* (Boston, 1750), reprinted in Bernard Bailyn, ed., *Pamphlets of the American Revolution: 1750–1776*, vol. 1, *1750–1765* (Cambridge, MA: Belknap Press of Harvard University Press, 1965), 213–47; Charles W. Akers, *Called Unto Liberty: A Life of Jonathan Mayhew, 1720–1766* (Cambridge, MA: Harvard University Press, 1964), 53, 67, 84.

12. Lord Colvill to Philip Stephens, Sept. 9, 1764, and Nov. 30, 1764, ADM 1/482, ff. 386, 417–19; Neil R. Stout, "Manning the Royal Navy in North America, 1763–1775," *American Neptune* 23 (1963): 175.

13. Rear Admiral Colvill to Mr. Stephens, July 26, 1764, in *Records of the*

Colony of Rhode Island and Providence Plantations in New England, ed.
John Russell Bartlett (Providence: Knowles, Anthony & Co., 1861),
6: 428–29; Thomas Hill, "Remarks on board His Maj[esty]'s Schooner St. John in Newport Harbour Rhode Island," ADM 1/482, f. 372;
Thomas Langhorne to Lord Colvill, Aug. 11, 1764, ADM 1/482, f.
377. See also *Newport Mercury,* July 23, 1764; Colvill to Stephens, Jan.
12, 1765, ADM 1/482, f. 432.

14. Governor Samuel Ward to Captain Charles Antrobus, July 12, 1765,
in *Records of the Colony of Rhode Island and Providence Plantations in New
England,* ed. John Russell Bartlett (Providence: Knowles, Anthony &
Co., 1861), 6:447; Lords of Admiralty to Mr. Secretary Conway, Mar.
20, 1766, in *Calendar of Home Office Papers of the Reign of George III,
1766–1768,* ed. Joseph Redington (London, 1879), 2:26; Hutchinson, *History of the Colony,* 3:138; Donna J. Spindel, "Law and Disorder: The North Carolina Stamp Act Crisis," *North Carolina Historical
Review* 57 (1980): 10–11; *Pennsylvania Journal,* Dec. 26, 1765; Adair
and Schutz, *Peter Oliver's Origin,* 69; Lemisch, "Jack Tar in the Streets,"
392; David S. Lovejoy, *Rhode Island Politics and the American Revolution,
1760–1776* (Providence: Brown University Press, 1958), 157; Paul A.
Gilje, *The Road to Mobocracy: Popular Disorder in New York City, 1763–
1834* (Chapel Hill: University of North Carolina Press, 1987), 63.

15. *Oxford English Dictionary,* s.v., "strike"; C. R. Dobson, *Masters and Journeymen: A Prehistory of Industrial Relations, 1717–1800* (London: Croom
Helm, 1980), 154–70; Oliver M. Dickerson, *The Navigation Acts and the
American Revolution* (Philadelphia: University of Pennsylvania Press,
1951), 218–19.

16. J. Cunningham, *An Essay on Trade and Commerce* (London, 1770), 52,
58. On Wilkes, see Pauline Maier, *From Resistance to Revolution: Colonial
Radicals and the Development of American Opposition to Britain, 1765–
1776* (New York: Vintage Books, 1972), 162–69; George Rudé, *Wilkes
and Liberty: A Social Study of 1763–1774* (Oxford: Clarendon Press,
1962).

17. Nauticus, *The Rights of the Sailors Vindicated, In Answer to a Letter of Ju-
nius, on the 5th of October, wherein he asserts The Necessity and Legality
of pressing men into the Service of the Navy* (London, 1772); Nicholas
Rogers, "Liberty Road: Opposition to Impressment in Britain during
the War of American Independence," in *Jack Tar in History: Essays in
the History of Maritime Life and Labour,* ed. Colin Howell and Richard

Twomey (Fredericton, New Brunswick: Acadiensis Press, 1991), 53–75.

18. Prince Hoare, *Memoirs of Granville Sharp* (1820); Edward Lascelles, *Granville Sharp and the Freedom of Slaves in England* (London: Oxford University Press, 1928); John Fielding, *Penal Laws* (London, 1768).

19. R. Barrie Rose, "A Liverpool Sailors' Strike in the Eighteenth Century," *Transactions of the Lancashire and Cheshire Antiquarian Society* 68 (1958): 85–92; "Extract of a Letter from Liverpool, Sept. 1, 1775," *Morning Chronicle and London Advertiser*, Sept. 5, 1775, republished in Richard Brooke, *Liverpool as it was during the Last Quarter of the Eighteenth century, 1775 to 1800* (Liverpool, 1853), 332.

20. *A Letter To the Right Honourable The Earl of T-----e: or, the Case of J--- W-----s, Esquire* (London, 1768), 22, 39; Maier, *From Resistance to Revolution,* 161; Adair and Schutz, *Peter Oliver's Origin,* 56; *The Trial at Large of James Hill . . . , Commonly known by the Name of John the Painter . . .* 2nd edition (London, 1777).

21. Edward Long, *The History of Jamaica, or General Survey of the Antient and Modern State of that Island; Reflections on its Situation, Settlements, Inhabitants, Climate, Products, Commerce, Laws, and Government* (London, 1774), 2:462; Mervyn Alleyne, *Roots of Jamaican Culture* (London, 1988), chap. 4.

22. Douglas Hall, ed., *In Miserable Slavery: Thomas Thistlewood in Jamaica, 1750–1786* (London: Macmillan, 1989), 106; Michael Craton, *Testing the Chains: Resistance to Slavery in the British West Indies* (Ithaca, NY: Cornell University Press, 1982), 125–39.

23. Long, *History of Jamaica,* 2:460; Hall, *In Miserable Slavery,* 98.

24. J. Philmore, *Two Dialogues on the Man-Trade* (London, 1760), 9, 7, 8, 10, 14; David Brion Davis, *The Problem of Slavery in the Age of Revolution, 1770–1823* (Ithaca, NY: Cornell University Press, 1975); Davis, "New Sidelights on Early Antislavery Radicalism," *William and Mary Quarterly,* 3rd ser., 28 (1971): 585–94.

25. Philmore, *Two Dialogues,* 45, 51, 54; Anthony Benezet, *A Short Account of that Part of Africa Inhabited by the Negroes . . .* (Philadelphia, 1762); Benezet, *Some Historical Account of Guinea* (Philadelphia, 1771); Davis, *Problem of Slavery,* 332.

26. James Otis, *The Rights of the British Colonies Asserted and Proved* (Boston, 1764), republished in Bailyn, *Pamphlets of the American Revolution,* 419–82; *Boston News-Letter,* June 19, July 10, Sept. 18, and Oct. 30, 1760; Feb. 2, 1761.

27. Charles Francis Adams, ed., *The Works of John Adams* (Boston: Little, Brown, 1856), 10:247, 272, 314–16; Adair and Schutz, *Peter Oliver's Origin*, 35.

28. Craton, *Testing the Chains*, 138, 139, 140; O. Nigel Bolland, *The Formation of a Colonial Society: Belize, from Conquest to Crown Colony* (Baltimore: Johns Hopkins University Press, 1977), 73.

29. See Peter Wood, "'Taking Care of Business' in Revolutionary South Carolina: Republicanism and the Slave Society," in *The Southern Experience in the American Revolution*, ed. Jeffrey J. Crow and Larry E. Tise (Chapel Hill: University of North Carolina Press, 1978), 276, and "'The Dream Deferred': Black Freedom Struggles on the Eve of White Independence," in *In Resistance: Studies in African, Caribbean, and Afro-American History*, ed. Gary Y. Okihiro (Amherst, MA: University of Massachusetts Press, 1986), 170, 172–73, 174–75; Jeffrey J. Crow, "Slave Rebelliousness and Social Conflict in North Carolina, 1775 to 1802," *William and Mary Quarterly*, 3rd ser., 37 (1980): 85–86; Herbert Aptheker, *American Negro Slave Revolts* (New York: Columbia University Press, 1943), 87, 200–202; Benjamin Quarles, *The Negro in the American Revolution* (Chapel Hill: University of North Carolina Press, 1961), 14.

30. Sylvia R. Frey, *Water from the Rock: Black Resistance in a Revolutionary Age* (Princeton, NJ: Princeton University Press, 1991), 38, 61–62, 202.

31. Gary B. Nash, *Forging Freedom: The Formation of Philadelphia's Black Community, 1720–1840* (Cambridge, MA: Harvard University Press, 1988), 72; Quarles, *Negro in the American Revolution*, 84; Lemisch, "Jack Tar in the Streets," 375; Shane White, "'We Dwell in Safety and Pursue Our Honest Callings': Free Blacks in New York City, 1783–1810," *Journal of American History* 75 (1988): 453–54; Ira Dye, "Early American Merchant Seafarers," *Proceedings of the American Philosophical Society* 120 (1976): 358; Philip D. Morgan, "Black Life in Eighteenth-Century Charleston," *Perspectives in American History*, New ser., 1 (1984): 200; Wood, "Taking Care of Business," 276; Crow, "Slave Rebelliousness," 85; Henry Laurens to John Laurens, June 18, 1775, and June 23,1775, in Rogers, Chesnutt, and Clark, *Papers of Henry Laurens*, 10:184, 191.

32. F. Nwabueze Okoye, "Chattel Slavery as the Nightmare of the American Revolutionaries," *William and Mary Quarterly* 3rd ser., 37 (1980): 12; Anthony Benezet to Granville Sharp, Mar. 29, 1773, in *Am I Not a Man and a Brother: The Antislavery Crusade of Revolutionary America,*

1688–1788, ed. Roger Bruns (New York: Chelsea House Publishers, 1977), 263.

33. John M. Bumsted and Charles E. Clark, "New England's Tom Paine: John Allen and the Spirit of Liberty," *William and Mary Quarterly* 3rd ser., 21 (1964): 570; Bruns, *Am I Not a Man,* 257–62; Thomas Paine, "African Slavery in America" (1775), in *The Collected Writings of Thomas Paine,* ed. Philip S. Foner (New York: Citadel Press, 1945), 17, 19; Wood, "Dream Deferred," 168, 181.

34. Sharon Salinger, *"To Serve Well and Faithfully": Indentured Servitude in Pennsylvania, 1682–1800* (Cambridge, UK: Cambridge University Press, 1986), 101–2; Morgan, "Black Life," 206–7, 219.

35. Arthur Meier Schlesinger, "Political Mobs and the American Revolution, 1765–1776," *Proceedings of the American Philosophical Society* 99 (1955): 244–50; Lemisch, "Jack Tar in the Streets"; Pauline Maier, "Popular Uprisings and Civil Authority in Eighteenth-Century America," *William and Mary Quarterly,* 3rd ser., 27 (1970): 3–35; Dirk Hoerder, *Crowd Action in Revolutionary Massachusetts, 1765–1780* (New York: Academic Press, 1977).

36. Hutchinson, *History of the Colony,* 2:332; Carl Bridenbaugh, *Cities in Revolt: Urban Life in America, 1743–1776* (New York: Capricorn Books, 1955), 309; Jeremiah Morgan to Francis Fauquier, Sept. 11, 1767, ADM 1/2116; Miller, *Sam Adams,* 142; Lemisch, "Jack Tar in the Streets," 386, 391; Colden to General Gage, July 8, 1765, Colden Letter-Books, 1760–1765 in *Collections of the New York Historical Society* (1877), 23; Elaine Forman Crane, *A Dependent People: Newport, Rhode Island in the Revolutionary Era* (New York: Fordham University Press, 1985), 113.

37. Oliver Morton Dickerson, ed., *Boston Under Military Rule, 1768–1769, as revealed in A Journal of the Times* (Boston: Chapman and Grimes, Mount Vernon Press, 1936), entry for May 4, 1769, 94, 95, 110; Allen, *Oration on the Beauties of Liberty,* in Bruns, *Am I Not a Man,* 258, 259 (emphasis in original).

38. Gary B. Nash, *The Urban Crucible: Social Change, Political Consciousness, and the Origins of the American Revolution* (Cambridge, MA: Harvard University Press, 1979), 366; Schlesinger, "Political Mobs," 244; Edmund S. Morgan and Helen M. Morgan, *The Stamp Act Crisis: Prologue to Revolution* (Chapel Hill: University of North Carolina Press, 1953), 162, 208, 231–39; Adair and Schutz, *Peter Oliver's Origin,* 51.

39. Hutchinson quoted in Anthony Pagden, *Spanish Imperialism and the*

Political Imagination: Studies in European and Spanish-American Social and Political Theory, 1513–1830 (New Haven, CT: Yale University Press, 1990), 66; Lovejoy, *Rhode Island Politics*, 105; Redington, *Calendar of Home Office Papers*, 1:610; Morgan and Morgan, *Stamp Act Crisis*, 196; Lloyd I. Rudolph, "The Eighteenth Century Mob in America and Europe," *American Quarterly* 11 (1959): 452; Spindel, "Law and Disorder," 8; *Pennsylvania Journal*, Nov. 21, 1765, Dec. 26, 1765; Alfred F. Young, "English Plebeian Culture and Eighteenth-Century American Radicalism," in *The Origins of Anglo-American Radicalism*, ed. Margaret Jacob and James Jacob (London: George Allen and Unwin, 1984), 193–94; Gage quoted in Schlesinger, "Political Mobs," 246.

40. Lemisch, "Jack Tar in the Streets," 398; Lovejoy, *Rhode Island Politics*, 156, 159, 164.

41. Lee R. Boyer, "Lobster Backs, Liberty Boys, and Laborers in the Streets: New York's Golden Hill and Nassau Street Riots," *New York Historical Society Quarterly* 57 (1973): 289–308; Hiller B. Zobel, *The Boston Massacre* (New York: Norton, 1970); L. Kinvin Wroth and Hiller B. Zobel, eds., *Legal Papers of John Adams* (Cambridge, MA: Belknap Press of Harvard University Press, 1965), 3:266; Hoerder, *Crowd Action*, chap. 13.

42. Timothy quoted in Maier, "Charleston Mob," 181; Edward Countryman, *A People in Revolution: The American Revolution and Political Society in New York, 1760–1790* (Baltimore: Johns Hopkins University Press, 1981), 37, 45; Gage to Conway, Nov. 4, 1765, in *The Correspondence of General Thomas Gage, with the Secretaries of State, 1763–1775*, ed. Edwin Carter (New Haven, CT: Yale University Press, 1931), 1:71; Barrington quoted in Tony Hayter, *The Army and the Crowd in Mid-Georgian London* (Totowa, NJ: Rowman and Littlefield, 1978), 130; Charles G. Steffen, *The Mechanics of Baltimore: Workers and Politics in the Age of Revolution, 1763–1812* (Urbana: University of Illinois Press, 1984), 73.

43. Clarence S. Brigham, *Paul Revere's Engravings* (Worcester, MA: American Antiquarian Society, 1954), 41–57; Quarles, *Negro in the American Revolution*, 125.

44. Steffen, *Mechanics of Baltimore*, 73; Gouverneur Morris to Mr. Penn, May 20, 1774, in *American Archives*, 4th ser., ed. Peter Force (Washington, DC, 1837), 1:343; Maier, "Charleston Mob," 185; Leonard W. Labaree, ed., *The Papers of Benjamin Franklin* (New Haven, CT: Yale University Press, 1961), vol. 3 (1745–1750), 106; Adair and Schutz,

Peter Oliver's Origin, xv, 35, 51–55, 88, 107; Joseph Chalmers, *Plain Truth* (Philadelphia, 1776), 71.

45. Richard B. Morris, *Government and Labor in Early America* (New York: Harper and Row, 1946), 189; Lovejoy, *Rhode Island Politics*, 159; Leonard quoted in Esmond S. Wright, *Fabric of Freedom, 1763–1800*, rev. ed. (New York: Hill and Wang, 1978), 77–78.

46. Rush quoted in Eric Foner, *Tom Paine and Revolutionary America* (New York: Oxford University Press, 1976), 138; David S. Lovejoy, *Religious Enthusiasm in the New World: Heresy to Revolution* (Cambridge, MA: Harvard University Press, 1985), 223–24; Davis, *Problem of Slavery*, 333.

47. Don M. Wolfe, *Leveller Manifestoes of the Puritan Revolution* (New York: Thomas Nelson and Sons, 1944), 227, 300, 125, 287, 320, 405. See also Robin Blackburn, *The Overthrow of Colonial Slavery, 1776–1848* (London: Verso, 1988), chap. 1; Pauline Maier, *American Scripture: Making the Declaration of Independence* (New York: Knopf, 1997), 51 ff; Garry Wills, *Inventing America: Jefferson's Declaration of Independence* (Garden City, NY: Doubleday, 1978).

48. Maier, *From Resistance to Revolution*, 76, 97–100; Gilje, *Road to Mobocracy*, 48; Wroth and Zobel, *Legal Papers of John Adams*, 3:269; *Works of John Adams*, 2:322.

49. Carl Becker, *The Declaration of Independence: A Study in the History of Political Ideas* (New York: Harcourt Brace, 1922), 214.

50. Alyce Barry, "Thomas Paine, Privateersman," *Pennsylvania Magazine of History and Biography* 101 (1977): 459–61.

51. Maier, "Charleston Mob," 181, 186, 188, and "Popular Uprising and Civil Authority," 33–35; Hoerder, *Crowd Action*, 378–88; Gordon S. Wood, *The Creation of the American Republic, 1776–1787* (Chapel Hill: University of North Carolina Press 1969), 319–28.

52. Charles Patrick Neimeyer, *America Goes to War: A Social History of the Continental Army* (New York: New York University Press, 1996), chap. 4; Quarles, *Negro in the American Revolution*, 15–18; Frey, *Water from the Rock*, 77–80; Cassandra Pybus, *Epic Journeys of Freedom: Runaway Slaves of the American Revolution and Their Global Quest for Liberty* (Boston: Beacon Press, 2007).

53. James Madison, "Republican Distribution of Citizens," *National Gazette*, Mar. 3, 1792, republished in *The Papers of James Madison*, vol. 14 (1791–1793), 244–46; David Humphreys, Joel Barlow, John Trumbull, and Dr. Lemuel Hopkins, *The Anarchiad: A New England Poem (1786–*

1787), ed. Luther G. Riggs (Gainesville, FL: Scholars' Facsimiles & Reprints, 1967), 29, 56, 38, 69, 14, 15, 34.

54. Madison's notes and Abraham Yates's notes, June 26, 1787, in *The Records of the Federal Convention of 1787*, ed. Max Farrand (New Haven, CT: Yale University Press, 1937), 1:423, 431.

55. Staughton Lynd, "The Abolitionist Critique of the United States Constitution," in *Class Conflict, Slavery, and the United States Constitution* (Indianapolis: Bobbs-Merrill, 1967), 153–54.

56. James D. Essig, *The Bonds of Wickedness: American Evangelicals against Slavery, 1770–1808* (Philadelphia: Temple University Press, 1982), 132.

57. Barbara Jeanne Fields, "Slavery, Race, and Ideology in the United States of America," *New Left Review* 181 (1990): 101; Frey, *Water from the Rock*, 234–36. Adams quoted in Schlesinger, "Political Mobs," 250.

58. Sidney Kaplan and Emma Nogrady Kaplan, *The Black Presence in the Era of the American Revolution*, rev. ed. (Amherst: University of Massachusetts Press, 1989), 68–69; Forrest McDonald, "The Relation of the French Peasant Veterans of the American Revolution to the Fall of Feudalism in France, 1789–1792," *Agricultural History* 25 (1951): 151–61; Horst Dippel, *Germany and the American Revolution, 1770–1800: A Sociohistorical Investigation of Late Eighteenth-Century Political Thinking*, trans. Bernard A. Uhlendorf (Chapel Hill: University of North Carolina Press, 1977), 228, 236.

59. Arthur N. Gilbert, "The Nature of Mutiny in the British Navy in the Eighteenth Century," in *Naval History: The Sixth Symposium of the US Naval Academy*, ed. Daniel Masterson (Wilmington, DE: Scholarly Resources, 1987), 111–21; Richard B. Sheridan, "The Jamaican Slave Insurrection Scare of 1776 and the American Revolution," *Journal of Negro History* 61 (1976): 290–308; Julius Sherrard Scott III, "The Common Wind: Currents of Afro-American Communication in the Era of the Haitian Revolution," PhD diss., Duke University, 1986, 19, 204, 52.

60. Lord Balcarres to Commander-in-Chief, July 31, 1800, CO 137/104, quoted in Scott, "Common Wind," 33; Pybus, *Epic Journeys of Freedom*.

61. Rediker, *Slave Ship*, 321–22.

Chapter Six

1. Silas Told, *An Account of the Life, and Dealings of God with Silas Told, Late Preacher of the Gospel . . .* (London: Gilbert and Plummer, 1785), 22–24. For the voyage of the *Loyal George* see David Eltis, Stephen D. Behrendt,

David Richardson, and Herbert S. Klein, *The Transatlantic Slave-Trade Data Base* (www.slavevoyages.org), no. 16490 (hereafter *TSTD*).

2. William D. Piersen, "White Cannibals, Black Martyrs: Fear, Depression, and Religious Faith as Causes of Suicide Among New Slaves," *Journal of Negro History* 62 (1977): 147–59.

3. Sidney W. Mintz and Richard Price, *The Birth of African-American Culture: An Anthropological Perspective* (1976; repr. Boston: Beacon Press, 1992); Michael A. Gomez, *Exchanging Our Country Marks: The Transformation of African Identities in the Colonial and Antebellum South* (Chapel Hill: University of North Carolina Press, 1998); Stephanie E. Smallwood, *Saltwater Slavery: A Middle Passage from Africa to American Diaspora* (Cambridge, MA: Harvard University Press, 2006).

4. Antonio T. Bly, "Crossing the Lake of Fire: Slave Resistance during the Middle Passage, 1720–1842," *Journal of Negro History* 83 (1998): 178–86; Richard Rathbone, "Resistance to Enslavement in West Africa," in *De la traite à l'esclavage: Actes du colloque international sur la traite des noirs*, ed. Serge Daget (Nantes, 1988), 173–84.

5. John Riland, *Memoirs of a West-India Planter* (London, 1827), 52; Testimony of James Morley, 1790, in *House of Commons Sessional Papers of the Eighteenth Century*, ed. Sheila Lambert (Wilmington, DE: Scholarly Resources, 1975) (hereafter *HCSP*), 73:160–61.

6. Testimony of Isaac Parker, 1790, *HCSP*, 73:124–25, 130; *TSTD*, no. 91135.

7. *Edward Fentiman v. James Kettle* (1730), HCA 24/136; *TSTD*, no. 76618; Testimony of James Towne, 1791, *HCSP*, 82:21; "The Deposition of John Dawson, Mate of the Snow *Rainbow*," 1758, in *Documents Illustrative of the History of the Slave Trade to America*, ed. Elizabeth Donnan, vol. 4, *The Border Colonies and Southern Colonies* (Washington, DC: Carnegie Institution of Washington, 1935), 371–72.

8. T. Aubrey, *The Sea-Surgeon, or the Guinea Man's Vade Mecum* (London, 1729), 128. For another judgment that violence did not work against the will of the enslaved, see "Information of Janverin" in *Substance of the Evidence of Sundry Persons on the Slave Trade . . .* , ed. Thomas Clarkson (London, 1789), 249.

9. William Snelgrave, *A New Account of Some Parts of Guinea and the Slave Trade* (London, 1734), 190; "Anecdote IX" (author unnamed), in Clarkson, *Substance of the Evidence*, 315–16; *Jones v. Small*, Law Report, *Times* (UK), July 1, 1785.

10. "Voyage to Guinea," Add. Ms. 39946, f. 8 (*TSTD*, no. 75489); *Mem-*

oirs of the Late Captain Hugh Crow of Liverpool . . . (London: Longman, Rees, Orme, Brown, and Green, 1830), 44; James Hogg to Humphrey Morice, Mar. 6, 1732, Humphrey Morice Papers, Bank of England Archives, London.

11. *Connecticut Journal*, Feb. 2, 1786; Testimony of Falconbridge, 1790, *HCSP*, 72: 307–8; "Extract from a Letter on Board the Prince of Orange," Apr. 7, 1737, *Boston News-Letter*, Sept. 15, 1737.

12. Testimony of Isaac Wilson, 1790, *HCSP*, 72: 281; Testimony of Claxton, *HCSP*, 82:35–36; *Pennsylvania Gazette*, May 21, 1788. Clarkson retold his story in a letter to Mirabeau, Dec. 9, 1789, Papers of Clarkson, Huntington Library, San Marino, CA. On the *Zong*, see Granville Sharp to the Lord Commissioners of the Admiralty, London, July 2, 1783, "Documents Related to the Case of the *Zong* of 1783," Manuscripts Department, National Maritime Museum, REC/19, fo. 96.

13. Testimony of Wilson and Falconbridge, both in *HCSP*, 72: 279, 300; log of the brig *Ranger*, Captain John Corran, Master, 1789–1790, 387 MD 56, Liverpool Record Office; [John Wells], "Journal of a Voyage to the Coast of Guinea, 1802," Add. Ms. 3,871, f. 15, Cambridge University Library; Testimony of Mr. Thompson, *Substance of the Evidence*, 207.

14. Extract of a letter to Mr. Thomas Gatherer, in Lombard Street; dated Fort-James, River Gambia, Apr. 12, 1773, *Newport Mercury*, Dec. 27, 1773; *Independent Journal*, Apr. 29, 1786; *Newport Mercury*, Mar. 3, 1792; *Newport Mercury*, Nov. 25, 1765; *Connecticut Journal*, Jan. 1, 1768; "The Log of the *Unity*, 1769–1771," Earle Family Papers, Merseyside Maritime Museum, Liverpool, D/EARLE/1/4; *Providence Gazette and Country Journal*, Sept. 10, 1791.

15. "Extracts of such Journals of the Surgeons employed in Ships trading to the Coast of Africa, since the first of August 1788, as have been transmitted to the Custom House in London, and which relate to the State of the Slaves during the Time they were on Board the Ships," Slave Trade Papers, May 3, 1792, HL/PO/JO/10/7/920; "Log-books, etc. of slave ships, 1791–7," Main Papers, June 17–19, 1799, HL/PO/JO/10/7/1104; "Certificates of Slaves Taken Aboard Ships," 1794, HL/PO/JO/10/7/982, all in the House of Lords Record Office, Westminster. It should be noted that not all surgeons listed causes of death; therefore these archives contain more than the eighty-six journals analyzed here. Some of these journals formed the empirical base of a study by Richard H. Steckel and Richard A. Jensen, "New

Evidence on the Causes of Slave and Crew Mortality in the Atlantic Slave Trade," *Journal of Economic History* 46 (1986): 57–77.

16. For the legal ruling, see *Jones v. Small,* Law Report, *Times* (UK), July 1, 1785. Like other forms of resistance, "reports of the action of jumping overboard circulated from the Atlantic back to the metropolis, where various writers immortalized the decision of death before dishonorable slavery in poetry. A well-known abolitionist poem, "The Negroe's Complaint," jointly but anonymously written by Liverpool patricians William Roscoe and Dr. James Currie, said of African protagonist Maratan: "Tomorrow the white-man in vain / Shall proudly account me his slave! / My shackles, I plunge in the main—/ And rush to the realms of the brave." See Dr. James Currie to Admiral Sir Graham Moore, Mar. 16, 1788, 920 CUR 106, Papers of Dr. James Currie, Liverpool Record Office. The poem was originally published in the *World* and was later republished in the United States. See the *Federal Gazette, and Philadelphia Evening Post,* Apr. 8, 1790. The same conceit appears in Roscoe's *The Wrongs of Africa* (London, 1788). See James G. Basker's magnificent compilation, *Amazing Grace: An Anthology of Poems about Slavery, 1660–1810* (New Haven, CT: Yale University Press, 2002).

17. Testimony of Ellison, *HCSP*, 73:374.

18. Testimony of Arnold, *HCSP*, 69:130.

19. *Times,* July 1, 1785; "Log of the *Unity*," Earle Family Papers, D/EARLE/1/4; *Connecticut Journal,* Feb. 2, 1786; Testimony of Robert Hume, 1799, in *House of Lords Sessional Papers,* ed. F. William Torrington (Dobbs Ferry, NY: Oceana Publications, 1974), 3:110; Testimony of Trotter, *HCSP*, 73:87; John Atkins, *A Voyage to Guinea, Brasil, and the West Indies* (London, 1735), 72–73. For boys, see extract of a letter to Mr. Thomas Gatherer, Apr. 12, 1773, *The Newport Mercury,* Dec. 27, 1773.

20. William Butterworth, *Three Years Adventures of a Minor, in England, Africa, the West Indies, South Carolina and Georgia* (Leeds, 1822), 96; Snelgrave, *A New Account,* 77; Testimony of Fountain, *HCSP*, 68:273; John Thornton, *Warfare in Atlantic Africa, 1500-1800* (New York: Routledge, 1999), 140.

21. *Pennsylvania Gazette,* May 16, 1754; Lieutenant Governor Thomas Handasyd to the Board of Trade and Plantations, from Jamaica, Oct. 5, 1703, in Donnan, *Documents Illustrative of the History,* 2:4; *Boston News-Letter,* May 6, 1731 (also *Boston Gazette,* Apr. 26, 1731); *Bath Jour-*

nal, Dec. 18, 1749; *Boston Gazette*, Oct. 4, 1756; *Pennsylvania Gazette*, May 31, 1764; *New London Gazette*, Dec. 18, 1772; *Newport Mercury*, Dec. 27, 1773; William Fairfield to Rebecca Fairfield, Cayenne, Apr. 23, 1789, in Donnan, *Documents Illustrative of the History*, 3:83; *Providence Gazette and Country Journal*, Sept. 10, 1791; *Massachusetts Spy: Or, the Worcester Gazette*, Apr. 4, 1798; *Federal Gazette & Baltimore Daily Advertiser*, July 30, 1800; *Newburyport Herald*, Mar. 22, 1808.

22. William Smith, *A New Voyage to Guinea* (London, 1744), 28. On the Coromantee, see Thomas Trotter, *Observations on the Scurvy* (London, 1785), 23; Alexander Falconbridge, *An Account of the Slave Trade on the Coast of Africa* (London, 1788), 70. See also Snelgrave, *New Account*, 168–69, 177–78.

23. *Felix Farley's Bristol Journal*, Mar. 24, 1753.

24. Stephanie Smallwood, *Saltwater Slavery: A Middle Passage from Africa to African Diaspora* (Cambridge, MA: Harvard University Press, 2009), 123.

25. *Newburyport Herald*, Dec. 4, 1801.

26. *Boston Post Boy*, Aug. 13, 1750.

27. *Pennsylvania Gazette*, Nov. 9, 1732; Atkins, *Voyage to Guinea*, 175–76; see also Butterworth, *Three Years Adventures*, 103.

28. *Boston News-Letter*, Sept. 18, 1729; *TSTD*, no. 77058; *Bath Journal*, Dec. 18, 1749; *TSTD*, no. 90233.

29. *American Mercury*, Jan. 31, 1785.

30. Testimony of Ellison, *HCSP*, 73:375; Snelgrave, *New Account*, 167, 173; "Anecdote I" (author unnamed), in Clarkson, *Substance of the Evidence*, 311; Testimony of Arnold, *HCSP*, 69:134.

31. Testimony of Towne, 1791, *HCSP*, 82:21; David Richardson, "Shipboard Revolts, African Authority, and the Atlantic Slave Trade," *William and Mary Quarterly*, 3rd ser., 58 (2001): 82–90.

32. *Boston News-Letter* Sept. 9, 1731; Richardson, "Shipboard Revolts," 74–75.

33. Thomas Clarkson, *An Essay on the Slavery and Commerce of the Human Species, particularly The African, translated from a Latin Dissertation*, . . . (London, 1786; repr., Miami, FL: Mnemosyne Publishing, 1969), 88–89.

34. *Newburyport Herald*, Dec. 4, 1801; Clarkson to Mirabeau, Dec. 9, 1789, ff. 1–2, Papers of Clarkson, Huntington Library.

35. Piersen, "White Cannibals, Black Martyrs," 147–59.

36. "Anonymous Account," Add. Ms. 59777B, ff. 40–41, British Library;

Testimony of John Douglas, 1791, *HCSP*, 82:125: Michael Mullin, *Africa in America: Slave Acculturation and Resistance in the American South and British Caribbean, 1736–1831* (Urbana: University of Illinois Press, 1992), 66–69; Smallwood, *Saltwater Slavery*, 147.

37. "Voyage to Guinea," Add. Ms. 39946, ff. 9–10; Testimony of Millar, *HCSP*, 73:394; Hawkins, *A History of a Voyage to the Coast of Africa*, 108; Clarkson, *Essay on the Slavery*, 143–44. For other references to the belief, see *Times*, Feb. 2, 1790; Atkins, *Voyage to Guinea*, 175–76.

38. "Anonymous Account," Add. Ms. 59777B, ff. 40–41.

39. Testimony of Claxton, 1791, *HCSP*, 82:35; Snelgrave, *New Account*, 183–84; *Memoirs of the Late Captain*, 26.

40. Clarkson to Mirabeau, Dec. 9, 1789, f. 1, Papers of Clarkson, Huntington Library.

41. John Thornton, *Africa and Africans in the Making of the Atlantic World, 1400–1800* (New York: Cambridge University Press, 1992), 195.

42. Butterworth, *Three Years Adventures*, 80–82; Testimony of William James, *HCSP*, 69:49; Testimony of Wilson, *HCSP*, 72:281–82; Testimony of Arnold, *HCSP*, 69:50, 137–38; Testimony of Trotter, *HCSP*, 73:97, 99–100.

43. John Matthews, *A Voyage to the River Sierra Leone, on the Coast of Africa* (London, 1788), 153; Information of Bowen, Clarkson, *Substance of the Evidence*, 230.

44. Thomas Winterbottom, *An Account of the Native Africans in the Neighbourhood of Sierra Leone* (London, 1803), 1:212; Butterworth, *Three Years Adventures*, 126.

45. Testimony of Falconbridge, *HCSP*, 72:308; Testimony of Ellison, *HCSP*, 73:381.

46. Testimony of Trotter, *HCSP*, 73:88; Information of Bowen, *Substance of the Evidence*, 230; "Extract of a letter from Charleston to the Editor of the Repertory, dated March 8th," *Massachusetts Spy, or Worcester Gazette*, Apr. 4, 1804.

47. Testimony of Thomas King, 1789, *HCSP*, 68:333; Testimony of Arnold, *HCSP*, 69:50.

Chapter Seven

1. *New York Morning Herald*, Aug. 24, 1839. All quotations in this and the following paragraph appear in this article.

2. *New York Morning Herald*, Aug. 26, 1839; *New York Journal of Commerce*,

Aug. 28, 1839; *New York Morning Herald*, Sept. 2, 1839; *New Orleans Bee*, Sept. 4, 1839.

3. *Richmond Enquirer*, Oct. 25, 1839. The "The Long Low Black Schooner" was the title of the article published in the *New York Sun*, Aug. 31, 1839, and republished in various forms by at least nine other newspapers, from Essex, Massachusetts, to Charleston, South Carolina, to New Orleans, Louisiana over the following two weeks. On the rise of the penny press, see James L. Crouthamel, *Bennett's New York Herald and the Rise of the Popular Press* (Syracuse, NY: Syracuse University Press, 1989), chap. 2. See page 22 for Bennett's founding comment about reaching "the great masses of the community."

4. *New York Commercial Advertiser*, June 16, 1840; *New York (Morning) Herald*, Oct. 3, 1847.

5. Arthur Abraham, *The Amistad Revolt: An Historical Legacy of Sierra Leone and the United States* (Washington, DC: US Department of State International Information Programs, 1998); Howard Jones, *Mutiny on the Amistad: The Saga of a Slave Revolt and Its Impact on American Abolition, Law, and Diplomacy* (New York: Oxford University Press, 1987); Iyunolu Folayan Osagie, *The Amistad Revolt: Memory, Slavery, and the Politics of Identity in the United States and Sierra Leone* (Athens: University of Georgia Press, 2000).

6. On June 28, 1839, the *Amistad* set sail from Havana to transport fifty-three enslaved Africans (forty-nine men, four children) three hundred miles eastward to Puerto Príncipe, Cuba. The Africans revolted, killing the captain and one sailor, Celestino, the ship's cook. Two white passengers, Pedro Montes and José Ruiz, were kept alive to steer the vessel back to Sierra Leone, the African homeland of the enslaved. Montes, however, sailed the vessel east by day, toward the sun, west and north by night, hoping to be captured, as indeed the vessel was, by the US brig *Washington* on August 26, 1839. Taken to New London, Connecticut, Cinqué and his comrades were charged with piracy and murder. Abolitionists rallied to the cause and organized a popular and legal defense campaign. A series of dramatic court cases resulted in a Supreme Court ruling in March 1841 freeing the *Amistad* captives, who returned to Sierra Leone in November of that year.

7. For a revealing comparison, see Stanley Harrold, "Romanticizing Slave Revolt: Madison Washington, the Creole Mutiny, and Abolition-

ist Celebration of Violent Means," in *Antislavery Violence: Sectional, Racial, and Cultural Conflict in Antebellum America*, ed. John R. McKivigan and Stanley Harrold (Knoxville: University of Tennessee Press, 1999), 89–107.

8. On celebrity in this period, see Paul Johnson, *Sam Patch, the Famous Jumper* (New York: Hill and Wang, 2004).

9. *A True History of the African Chief Jingua and his Comrades, with a Description of the Kingdom of Mandingo, and of the Manners and Customs of the Inhabitants—An Account of King Sharka, of Gallinas, A Sketch of the Slave Trade and Horrors of the Middle Passage; with the Proceedings on Board the "Long, Low, Black Schooner"* (Hartford, New York, and Boston: 1839); *Colored American*, Oct. 5, 1839.

10. *New York Morning Herald*, Aug. 29, 1839.

11. James Fenimore Cooper, *The Pilot: A Tale of the Sea* (New York, 1823); Cooper, *The Red Rover: A Tale* (Philadelphia, 1828); Richard Henry Dana, *Two Years before the Mast* (New York, 1840); Mary K. Bercaw Edwards, *Cannibal Old Me: Spoken Sources in Melville's Early Works* (Kent, OH: Kent State University Press, 2009); Lord Byron, *The Corsair* (London, 1814); Sir Walter Scott, *The Pirate* (London, 1821); Frederick Marryat, *The Pirate* (London, 1836); Frederick Engels, "The Pirate," *Collected Works of Karl Marx and Frederick Engels* (New York: International Publishers, 1975), 2: 557–71; "The Lives of Anne Bonny and Mary Read," *Waldie's Select Circulating Library* (1833); "From the New Novel—Blackbeard," *New York Mirror*, June 6, 1835.

12. Marcus Rediker, *Villains of All Nations: Atlantic Pirates in the Golden Age* (Boston: Beacon Press, 2004), 173.

13. *Boston News-Letter*, Apr. 4, 1723; Rediker, *Villains of All Nations*, 53–56. See also Kenneth J. Kinkor, "Black Men Under the Black Flag" in *Bandits at Sea: A Pirates Reader*, ed. C. R. Pennell (New York: New York University, 2001), 195–210.

14. Lawrence A. Peskin, *Captives and Countrymen: Barbary Slavery and the American Public, 1785–1816* (Baltimore: Johns Hopkins University Press, 2009); Frederick C. Leiner, *The End of Barbary Terror: America's 1815 War against the Pirates of North Africa* (Oxford, UK: Oxford University Press, 2006); Frank Lambert, *The Barbary Wars: American Independence in the Atlantic World* (New York: Hill and Wang, 2006); Hester Blum, "Barbary Captivity and Intra-Atlantic Print Culture," in her *The View from the Masthead: Maritime Imagination and Antebellum American*

Sea Narratives (Chapel Hill: University of North Carolina Press, 2008), 46–70.

15. See *A Report of the Trial of Pedro Gilbert* (Boston: Russell, Oridorne and Metcalf, 1834), which proved so popular that it went into second and third editions immediately; *Trial of the Twelve Spanish Pirates of the Schooner Panda, A Guinea Slaver . . . For Robbery and Piracy, Committed on Board the Brig Mexican, 20th Sept. 1832* (Boston: Lemuel Gulliver, 1834); and *A Supplement to the Report of the Trial of the Spanish Pirates, with the Confessions or Protests, Written by Them in Prison* (Boston: Lemuel Gulliver, 1835).

16. *Public Ledger*, June 6, 1838; *Connecticut Courant*, Jan. 9, 1841; *Army & Navy Chronicle*, Mar. 14, 1839; Ben Bobstay, "The Chase," *The Hesperian: or, Western Monthly Magazine*, Jan. 1839. See also (Baltimore) *Sun*, July 3, 1839.

17. The book published by Strong was an update of Thomas Carey, *The History of the Pirates, Containing the Lives of Those Noted Pirate Captains, Misson, Bowen, Kidd, Tew, Halsey, White, Condent, Bellamy, Fly, Howard, Lewis, Cornelius, Williams, Burgess, North, and Their Several Crews . . .* (Haverhill, MA, 1829). It was republished in Hartford in 1829, and again in 1834 and 1835. See Philip Gosse, *A Bibliography of the Works of Captain Charles Johnson* (London: Dulau and Company, 1927), 53–64. See also Blum, *View from the Masthead*, 35, 47.

18. Henry K. Brooke, comp., *Book of Pirates, Containing Narratives of the Most Remarkable Piracies and Murders, Committed on the High Sea: Together with an Account of the Capture of the Amistad, and a Full and Authentic Narrative of the Burning of the Caroline* (Philadelphia: J. B. Perry and New York: N. C. Nafis, 1841), 184–96; quotations at 185, 196, x (emphasis in original).

19. Gosse, *Bibliography*, 50–51; Charles Ellms, *The Pirates' Own Book; or, Authentic Narratives of the Lives, Exploits, and Executions of the Most Celebrated Sea Robbers, with Historical Sketches of the Joassamee, Spanish, Ladrone, West India, Malay, and Algerine Pirates*, iii. Strong's volume was republished in 1837, 1839, 1847, 1849, 1850, 1851, 1855, and 1860; Ellms's every year from 1841 to 1846 and again in 1855, 1856, and 1859; Brooke's in 1845, 1846, and 1847.

20. David Grimsted, *Melodrama Unveiled: American Theater and Culture, 1800–1850* (Chicago: University of Chicago Press, 1968), 149; Bank, *Theatre Culture*, 159.

21. The playbill is in the Harvard Theatre Collection. *New York Commercial Advertiser*, Sept. 4, 1839, *New York Sun*, Aug. 31, 1839. See Bruce A. Mc-Conachie, "'The Theatre of the Mob': Apocalyptic Melodrama and Preindustrial Riots in Antebellum New York," in *Theatre for Working-Class Audiences in the United States, 1830–1980*, ed. McConachie and Daniel Friedman (Westport, CT: Greenwood Press, 1985), 17–46; the same author's *Melodramatic Formations: American Theatre and Society, 1820–1870* (Iowa City: University of Iowa Press, 1992); and Peter Reed, *Rogue Performances: Staging the Underclasses in Early American Theatre Culture* (London: Palgrave Macmillan, 2009).

22. Christine Stansell, *City of Women: Sex and Class in New York, 1789–1860* (New York: Knopf, 1986), 89, 90, 93–95; McConachie, *Melodramatic Formations*, 122; Reed, *Rogue Performances*, 9, 11, 15; Rosemarie K. Bank, *Theatre Culture in America, 1825–1860* (Cambridge, UK: Cambridge University Press, 1997), 84; Peter George Buckley, "To the Opera House: Society and Culture in New York City, 1820–1860," PhD diss., State University of New York at Stony Brook, 1984, 181–82.

23. *Philadelphia Inquirer*, Sept. 2, 1839; *New York Mirror*, Sept. 14, 1839, which listed the play as one of the successes of the season. The estimated revenue comes from a well-researched but undocumented article by Perry Walton, "The Mysterious Case of the Long, Low, Black Schooner," *New England Quarterly* 6 (1933): 360. He also notes that the play was performed at the Park Theatre, the National Theatre, and Niblo Garden, as well as the Bowery. I have not been able to confirm the revenue or the other venues in primary sources. The last newspaper mention of the play was in the *New Orleans Bee*, Sept. 17, 1839.

24. *New York Commercial Advertiser*, Sept. 4, 1839; *New York Morning Herald*, Feb. 28, 1840; *Public Ledger*, Apr. 11, 1839; Bank, *Theatre Culture*, 72.

25. The name Zemba apparently came from a story, "Tales of the Niger: Zemba and Zorayde," published in *The Court Magazine, containing Original papers by Distinguished Writers* (London: Bull and Churton, 1833), vol. 3 (July–Dec. 1833), 71–74, republished in the *Philadelphia Inquirer* on Jan. 2, 1838.

26. The use of the hold of the schooner as a setting made the play unusual. Heather Nathans has noted that the Middle Passage "virtually disappeared" from the American stage at mid-century as the slave trade was rethought as something internal to the nation's borders.

See her *Slavery and Sentiment on the American Stage, 1787–1861: Lifting the Veil of Black* (New York: Cambridge University Press, 2009), 129–30.

27. Peter Reed writes that a staged execution was not likely and that a more common plot outcome at the time would have been a reprieve for the hero. Personal communication to the author, Dec. 14, 2010.

28. Bank, *Theatre Culture*, 96; *Supplement to the Royal Gazette*, Jan. 27, 1781–Feb. 3, 1781, 79, cited in Diana Paton, "The Afterlives of Three-Fingered Jack," in *Slavery and the Cultures of Abolition: Essays Marking the Bicentennial of the Abolition Act of 1807*, ed. Brycchan Carey and Peter J. Kitson (London: D. S. Brewer, 2007), 44; McConachie, *Melodramatic Formations*, 70–71, 142, 143; and Reed, *Rogue Performances*, 21, 37, 100, 122, 159–60.

29. Reed, *Rogue Performances*, 5, 13 (quotation), 43; McConachie, *Melodramatic Formations*, 97–100.

30. "Private Examination of Cinquez," *New York Commercial Advertiser*, Sept. 13 1839; *New York Sun*, Aug. 31, 1839.

31. Reed, *Rogue Performances*, 10, 175–85; Jonas B. Phillips, *Jack Sheppard, or the Life of a Robber! Melodrama in Three Acts founded on Ainsworth's Novel* (1839).

32. *Joseph Cinquez, Leader of the Gang of Negroes, who killed Captain Ramon Ferrers and the Cook, on board the Spanish Schooner Amistad, Captured by Lieutenant Gedney of the US Brig Washington at Culloden Point, Long Island, Aug. 24th 1839*, hand-colored lithograph, Stanley Whitman House, Farmington, Connecticut.

33. *Joseph Cinquez, Leader of the Piratical Gang of Negroes, who killed Captain Ramon Ferris and the Cook, on board the Spanish Schooner Amistad, taken by Lieut. Gedney, commanding the U.S. Brig Washington at Culloden Point, Long Island, 24th Aug. 1839, Drawn from Life by J. Sketchley, Aug. 30, 1839*, lithograph by John Childs, New Haven Colony Historical Society.

34. *Joseph Cinquez, The brave Congolese Chief, who prefers death to Slavery, and who now lies in Jail at New Haven Conn. awaiting his trial for daring for freedom*, Library of Congress. A second, smaller version of the image—perhaps a handbill—is in the Frances Manwaring Caulkins Scrapbook, reference 029.3 Scr 15, Misc. American, 1830–1850, New London County Historical Society, New London, Connecticut. The *New York Sun* of Aug. 31, 1839, identified "James

Sheffield of New London" as the artist, but it appears the main maritime artist of New London in this period was Isaac Sheffield (1798–1845). See H. W. French, *Art and Artists in Connecticut* (Boston, 1879), 60.

35. "Portrait of Cinquez" from the Monday, Sept. 2, 1839 edition, reprinted in the *New York Sun*, Sept. 7, 1839, Country Edition, Weekly—No. 147.

36. *New York Morning Herald*, Sept. 17, 1839; Oct. 9, 1839.

37. *New York Sun*, Aug. 31, 1839; *New York Journal of Commerce*, Sept. 10 1839; *New York Commercial Advertiser*, Sept. 13, 1839; *New Hampshire Sentinel*, Oct. 2, 1839; *Colored American*, Oct. 5, 1839.

38. Among the works quoted and, more commonly, plagiarized are Mungo Park, *Travels in the Interior Districts of Africa: Performed in the Years 1795, 1796, and 1797* (London, 1799); Richard Lander, *Journal of an Expedition to Explore the Course and Termination of the Niger* (London, 1832); Joseph Hawkins, *A History of a Voyage to the Coast of Africa, and Travels into the Interior of that Country* (Troy, NY, 1797); Captain J. K. Tuckey, *Narrative of an Expedition to Explore the River Zaire* (London, 1818); and Sir Thomas Fowell Buxton, *The African Slave Trade, and its Remedy* (London, 1839). On the visitors to Hartford, see *New York Commercial Advertiser*, Sept. 20, 1839.

39. *New York Commercial Advertiser*, Sept. 6, 1839.

40. The author probably drew on an article in the *New York Sun* (Sept. 10, 1839), in which Lewis Tappan incorrectly identified the captives as Mandingo.

41. The author draws on a chapter entitled "History of the Adventures, Capture, and Execution of the Spanish Pirates," in Ellms, *Pirates Own Book*.

42. The final paragraph of *A True History* is taken from the *African Repository and Colonial Journal* 8 (1832): 121 (quotation).

43. The 1820s and 1830s witnessed a popular fascination with "Moorish culture," not least because of Byron's influence.

44. "Records of the U.S. District and Circuit Courts for the District of Connecticut: Documents Relating to the Various Cases Involving the Spanish Schooner Armistad," Folder II: *U.S. v. Faqnannah et. Al*, September 1839 term, RG-21 USCC CT (United States Circuit Court, Connecticut), Frederick C. Murphy Federal Records Center, Waltham, MA.

45. Jones, *Mutiny on the Amistad*, 50–53.

46. *New York Commercial Advertiser*, Sept. 4, 1839; *New York Journal of Commerce*, Sept. 4, 1839; *New York Journal of Commerce*, Sept. 5, 1839; *Emancipator*, Sept. 14, 1839.

47. *New York Journal of Commerce*, Sept. 5, 1839. See also Jones, *Mutiny on the Amistad*, 138–44, and Douglas R. Egerton, *Charles Fenton Mercer and the Trial of National Conservatism* (Jackson: University of Mississippi Press, 1989), 179–81.

48. *New York Journal of Commerce*, Sept. 14, 1839.

49. *The African Captives: Trials of the Prisoners of the Amistad on the Writ of Habeas Corpus, before the Circuit Court of the United States, for the District of Connecticut, at Hartford, Judges Thompson and Judson, September Term, 1839* (New York, 1839), 44.

50. *New York Journal of Commerce*, Mar. 17, 1841; *Argument of John Quincy Adams Before the Supreme Court of the United States in the Case of the United States, Appellants, vs. Cinque, and others, Africans, captured in the schooner Amistad, by Lieut. Gedney, Delivered on the 24th of February and 1st of March 1841* (New York: S. W. Benedict, 1841), 23; *Argument of Roger S. Baldwin, of New Haven, before the Supreme Court of the United States, in the Case of the United States, Appellant, vs. Cinque, and Others, Africans of the Amistad* (New York: S. W. Benedict, 1841), 20. See also Jones, *Mutiny on the Amistad*, chap. 10.

51. See the wide array of newspaper articles about revolts on slave ships cited in Marcus Rediker, *The Slave Ship: A Human History* (New York: Viking Penguin, 2007).

52. David Walker, *Walker's Appeal in Four Articles; Together with a Preamble, To the Coloured Citizens of the World, but in Particular, and Very Expressly, to Those of the United States of America* (Boston, 1829); Peter Hinks, *To Awaken My Afflicted Brethren: David Walker and the Problem of Antebellum Slave Resistance* (State College: Pennsylvania State University Press, 1996); Kenneth S. Greenberg, ed., *Nat Turner: A Slave Rebellion in History and Memory* (New York: Oxford University Press, 2004); Michael Craton, *Testing the Chains: Resistance to Slavery in the British West Indies* (Ithaca, NY: Cornell University Press, 1982); João José Reis, *Slave Rebellion in Brazil: The Muslim Uprising of 1835 in Bahia* (Baltimore: Johns Hopkins University Press, 1995).

53. See Kale to John Adams, Jan. 4, 1841, reprinted in *New York Journal of Commerce*, Mar. 20, 1841.

54. The pirate image was important in the early, formative stage of *Amistad* case but would be eclipsed by abolitionist arguments over time.

55. *New York Morning Herald*, Sept. 9, 1839.

56. The article from the *Herald of Freedom* was republished in the *Colored American*, Oct. 19, 1839.

57. An important work on abolitionism from below is Merton L. Dillon, *Slavery Attacked: Southern Slaves and the Allies, 1619–1865* (Baton Rouge: Louisiana State University Press, 1990).

58. Reed, *Rogue Performances*, 11; McConachie, *Melodramatic Formations*, 97–100.

59. Douglas R. Egerton, *Gabriel's Rebellion: The Virginia Slave Conspiracies of 1800 and 1802* (Chapel Hill: University of North Carolina Press, 1993), 40, 51, 109; Egerton, *Death or Liberty: African Americans and Revolutionary America* (New York: Oxford University Press, 2009).

60. The couplet would later appear in the *Chartist Circular*, published in Glasgow, May 1, 1841, in a poem entitled "Liberty! Universal Liberty!" by "Argus." See *True History of the African Chief*, frontispiece.

61. Mary Cable, *Black Odyssey: The Case of the Slave Ship "Amistad"* (New York: Penguin, 1971), 121.

62. Phillip Lapsansky has written: "As part of their effort to defuse fears of violence, the antislavery movement did not produce representations of black violence, self-assertion, or control." See his "Graphic Discord: Abolitionists and Antiabolitionist Images," in *The Abolitionist Sisterhood: Women's Political Culture in Antebellum America*, ed. Jean Fagan Yellin and John C. Van Horne (Ithaca, NY: Cornell University Press, 1994), 218–21. See also Marcus Wood, *Blind Memory: Visual Representations of Slavery in England and America, 1780-1865* (Manchester, UK: Manchester University Press, 2000), chap. 5, and Nathans, *Slavery and Sentiment*, 129–30, 202.

63. One minor instance of violence occurred in Farmington, Connecticut, after the Supreme Court decision, when several of the *Amistad* Africans got into a fight with a gang of local toughs and apparently beat them up. See John Pitkin Norton's account of the fight in the John Pitkin Norton Papers, MS 367, Diaries, Volume III: June 29, 1840–Sept. 15, 1841, Box No. 3, Folder 18, Manuscripts and Archives, Sterling Memorial Library, Yale University, entries for Tuesday, Sept. 7, 1841, and Wednesday, Sept. 8, 1841. In *Gentlemen of Property and*

Standing: Anti-Abolition Mobs in Jacksonian America (New York: Oxford University Press, 1971), Leonard L. Richards notes the decline of anti-abolition mobs in 1838–1839 (see chap. 6). See also David Grimsted, *American Mobbing, 1828–1861: Toward Civil War* (Oxford, UK: Oxford University Press, 1998).

64. "Joseph Sturge's Visit to the United States," *Edinburgh Journal*, Apr. 1842.

65. Stanley Harrold, *The Rise of Aggressive Abolitionism: Addresses to the Slaves* (Lexington: University of Kentucky Press, 2004), 37–38, 155; Henry Highland Garnet, "An Address to the Slaves of the United States of America" (1843), republished in Harrold, *Rise of Aggressive Abolitionism*, 179–88. On Ruggles, see *Liberator*, Aug. 13, 1841, quoted in Herbert Aptheker, "Militant Abolitionism," *Journal of Negro History* 26 (1941): 438–84; and Graham Russell Gao Hodges, *David Ruggles: A Radical Black Abolitionist and the Underground Railroad in New York City* (Chapel Hill: University of North Carolina Press, 2010). See also Jane H. Pease and William H. Pease, "Black Power—The Debate in 1840," *Phylon* 29 (1968): 19–26, republished in Patrick Rael, ed., *African-American Activism before the Civil War* (New York: Routledge, 2008), 50–57.

66. Marcus Rediker, *Amistad Rebellion*, 171, 206–8.

67. *New York Morning Herald*, Aug. 26, 1839.

Epilogue

1. Jamaica Kincaid, *A Small Place* (New York: Farrar, Straus and Giroux, 1988), 24.

2. Samuel Eliot Morison, *Admiral of the Ocean Sea: A Life of Christopher Columbus* (Boston: Little, Brown, 1942); Morison, *John Paul Jones: A Sailor's Biography* (New York: Time-Life Books, 1959).

3. Jesse Lemisch, "The American Revolution Seen from the Bottom Up," in *Towards a New Past: Dissenting Essays in American History*, ed. Barton J. Bernstein (New York: Vintage, 1967), 29.

4. *Pennsylvania Gazette*, Sept. 20, 1759; *Boston Weekly News-Letter*, Aug. 24, 1769.

Index